'The garden is a place of pleasure, filled with joy, but it resounds in love, laments of poets; it is a refuge for private meditation; it is a place for feasts, entertainment for friends, a place of sexual and intellectual freedom, a setting for philosophical discussions, and a restorative for both the body and soul. It is a well ordered model of the universe, an experiment in immortality, a never-ending apparition of spring. It assumes the function of a sculpture gallery, a horticultural encyclopedia, a centre of botanical and medical research and a theatre for fantastic imitation. Finally it is a perpetual source of moral instruction.'

BATTISTI – 'NATURA ARTIFICIOSA'

the secret life of the garden

Chris Beardshaw

LONDON, NEW YORK,
MUNICH, MELBOURNE, DELHI

Editor Candida Frith-Macdonald
Designer Alison Shackleton
Illustrator Debbie Maizels

Managing Editor Anna Kruger
Managing Art Editor Alison Donovan
DTP Designer Louise Waller
Picture Research Lucy Claxton,
Mel Watson
Production Controller Mandy Innes

First published in Great Britain
in 2007 as
How Does Your Garden Grow?

This edition published in 2009 by
Dorling Kindersley Ltd
80 Strand London
WC2R 0RL

A Penguin Company

2 4 6 8 10 9 7 5 3 1

Copyright © 2007, 2009
Dorling Kindersley Limited
Text copyright © 2007, 2009
Chris Beardshaw

A CIP catalogue record for this book
is available from the British Library.

ISBN 978 1 4053 3856 1

Reproduced by
Colourscan, Singapore
Printed and bound by
Hung Hing, China

Discover more at
www.dk.com

CONTENTS

Introduction 6

INTRODUCTION

The ingenuity and versatility of plants fascinated me from the moment I started to watch them grow. The speed at which seedling stems elongated, the way they chased the light, the development of their leaves, creating canopies that relentlessly followed the sun, and then the glory and complexity of the flowers dancing in the breeze, awakened my close relationship with and curiosity about plants. Like an ephemeral carnival the garden became a dynamic and otherworldly place into which I escaped to join literally millions of unseen, unacknowledged organisms that all played a more significant part than I. Interdependence, coexistence, and endless struggles for survival are all part of everyday life in the garden and while gardeners claim the credit for the result, in truth our efforts are nothing more than a split second in the life of the plants.

I often find myself reassuring gardeners who lack confidence in their abilities that they have nothing to worry about: the species that we choose to fill our gardens, or those that invite themselves to the banquet, are perfect survivors. They all seize life and every opportunity that is to hand, and have been doing so relentlessly for about 300 million years of evolution. During this time, diversity and specialism have been celebrated and rewarded with life and we as gardeners have only had the last few thousand years to exhibit such works of art. Ask yourself what else in our technology-rich lives has such a heritage of endless design refinement as our plants. The answer is nothing, not even ourselves. There is for me an irony in the fact that as self-proclaimed complex organisms, we still fail to unravel and replicate some of the most basic functions performed by our plants, such as the efficient and non-polluting conversion of sunlight into energy, or even the passage of water from the roots of a tree to the tip of its highest leaf. And it often comes as something of a shock to gardeners to learn that plants have absolutely no desire to please or impress us; their sole focus is on employing whatever mechanism is best to ensure the furthering of their offspring among the hundreds of thousands of species we have so far encountered.

Given the diversity and complexity in the plant kingdom, it comes as no surprise that gardens and the plants they contain have long provided a source of inspiration for us. They have a unique ability to touch and influence everyone at some point in their lives, whether at the age of four, like me, or later in life as homes, families, retirements and even deaths come to play a part. It seems that no matter what our emotional, physical or spiritual state, the garden can offer us something. Even on the coldest and most inclement of days, when icy rain drips off your nose as you slavishly cultivate the ground in preparation for next season's plants, there is always a reward: a bud unfurling, a splash of sun highlighting a stem, or a cheery bird diligently standing by in anticipation of a grub for lunch. In truth the garden is as complex in its human rewards as it is in its survival tactics. Expressing this diversity is a challenge, but the passage on the opening page of this book, which I first came across as a student, is one that I feel best explains the multitude of purposes that a garden serves, and despite its sixteenth-century origins this piece of writing is as true today as when it was penned.

Such a description surely comes close to the very reason for the existence of the garden, as a worldly portrayal of paradise, a perfect space in which eternal provisions are present. And so as gardeners, armed with whatever knowledge and skills we possess, we embark on sculpting and moulding our own snapshot of paradise, a collection of all that we hold most dear. This is surely not only the starting point of any great garden, but also the origin of a garden with a great connection to its creator.

It has always amused me that in striving for paradise some gardeners can't rest until their absolute control and authority are clearly demonstrated in the garden. Plants stand to attention, the choreography in the borders perfectly rehearsed, and nature is chastised. So often these gardeners are also obsessed with an artificial concept of perfection, in which every plant is in its prime, no petal is faded, no blade of grass too long, and all that buzzes, crawls or creeps is at the very least swept to the boundary. Such concepts of perfection are flawed, as no garden remains static; the result is that the garden lacks life and the gardener is overrun by angst and frustration, constantly battling nature, never taking the opportunity to rest. Only when it dawns that there is beauty to be found in all aspects and stages of the garden does the garden itself seem to breathe deeply, prosper, and excel while the gardener rests on a seat of contentment in their paradise. Of course, it is not that everything in the garden is of equal visual merit, just that all have a potential role, and that of the gardener is to stage-manage the performance.

It is with all this in mind that this book began. My aim is to boost the confidence of all those striving to achieve their vision of paradise; to slice through the myriad overly complex and unnecessarily technical instructions offered by experts of all stature; and to provide the tips and hints that were once commonly passed over the garden gate, between allotment holders, or from one gardening generation to the next. To this I've added the science, the explanations and reasons behind these actions, to create reliable information. It seems to me that only if gardeners have transferable truths and the self confidence to act upon them will gardening really thrive.

My approach is due to two people in my life, the first being my grandmother. As a self-taught gardener, irreverent in her approach, she assiduously studied every plant in her garden, without knowing it by name. She acted not when texts dictated, but when the plants spoke. She watched and responded to their needs, enthusiastically and sensitively filling every available crevice with the most unlikely of species – and it worked. The second person is my father, whose engineering brain was never content until reason and explanations had been wrestled to the fore. I returned home after school once to find the hall strewn with blankets on which lay the fragments of a carefully dissected vacuum cleaner, laid out like a medical specimen, each part stripped, cleaned, and carefully placed in sequence. Tiptoeing

through the debris it became clear that a curious mind had dismantled the machine, not to correct a mechanical malfunction, but just to explore the processes, components, and relationships at work. Before reassembly, several additional elements were fashioned and included to aid the running of the machine, and I am pleased to report that some forty years after it was made, it is still in fine tune.

Blend these two styles and you are armed with a relentless curiosity to learn, openness of mind, and an aptitude to recognise the importance of all elements, no matter how seemingly insignificant, plus a deep passion for cultivating your plants and an ability to effortlessly and instinctively charm them to produce a wonderful performance, free of the shackles of convention.

Finally, it is perhaps worth remembering that the plants around us are far from simply ornamental appendages and superfluous elements to our lives. Their processes and interactions with countless organisms and environments are fundamental not only to our own enjoyment but also to our survival. Indeed, it could be argued that their lives are more complex than our own: they just seem to focus on what is truly important, get on with life and make little fuss about it; but then, perhaps, that is to be expected when dealing with perfection.

This book is for Lily and Georgia, for whom I hope the natural world is a constant source of inspiration, enlightenment, and entertainment.

The start of life

Throwing a few seeds onto a damp
tissue is, I believe, solely responsible
for stimulating my mind and heart,
provoking a career in horticulture and a
life long passion for both growing plants
and designing with them. All this from a
few unpromising dark capsules, smooth as
silk to touch and crunchy in texture, as
not all of them ended up being sown.
The process of transformation from pearly
spheres to a healthy crop of cress
absolutely captivated me.

STARTING FROM SEED

Sowing seed is the most rewarding of all gardening activities and instils a huge sense of responsibility, for how can the start of life not be taken seriously? Whether the plants are wildly exotic or common as cress, nothing compares to that moment when they peek from the soil. I know experienced gardeners who impatiently poke and prod, eager for signs of life. Given just half a chance, these perfect survivors fill the garden with foliage, flowers, and of course seeds.

Time capsules

The seed is essentially a mechanism for distributing populations over broad areas and also for surviving conditions that might endanger the complete plant, such as prolonged periods of drought or winter cold. While the seed can be viewed as a time capsule, storing all the genetic information of the species and sufficient food to burst into life, it is not a static phase in the plant's life. Energy is still released through respiration (*see p.83*), albeit at a reduced rate while temperatures are low and moisture is absent. For this reason, treat your seeds as living organisms, keeping them cool in a sealed environment to ensure they retain maximum potential for growth. Pay particular attention to small seeds, as they may offer less protection to the stresses of the outside world and so are more vulnerable to disease and dehydration.

Inside the seed

Dissecting the science of a seed does little to dispel the magic of germination. Technically a seed is a fertile and ripened ovule that contains the embryonic plant. This is combined, usually, with a food source, and encased in a seed coat called the testa. The basic shape, form and size of seeds varies tremendously, from the microscopic seeds produced by many tropical orchids to that of the coconut. On many large seeds it is possible to discern the component parts – on the pea, for example, you can separate the coat or testa. This tough layer is

Seaborne seed
One of the largest seeds known, the coconut can be as heavy as 10kg (22lb), but floats on ocean currents.

Pine seedlings

*The tiny seeds of the Japanese black pine
(Pinus thunbergii) come through the snowy
winters of its natural range to burst into life
with the spring thaws.*

formed from neutral cells on the outer section of the ovule after fertilization, and is also called an integument. Its function is to protect, primarily from excessive drying out but also against attack from disease. Also evident on the outside of some seeds is the hilum, a scar where the ovule was attached to the ovary. On some seeds, such as broad beans, it is even possible to see the micropyle, the point at which the pollen tube entered when fertilization took place (*see pp.102–103*), and through which water enters prior to germination.

Sorting by seeds

Botanically speaking, only the most sophisticated plants are able to produce seeds, and these are called the spermatophyta, from the Greek *sperma*, meaning seed, and *phyton*, meaning plant. This broad division contains many of the key plants within our gardens, and is subdivided into three areas: conifers, ginkgo, and flowering plants.

"Examining the seed reveals a multitude of information about the plant. Even the way that it is carried is a guide to the plant's position within the plant kingdom."

The conifers and ginkgo produce "naked" seeds, without the protection of any additional tissue such as seed pods or fruits. They are called the gymnosperms (from the Greek *gym*, meaning naked), and usually have needle-like leaves and female flowers that mature into dry cones. Flowering plants surround their seeds with protective tissues, and are called the angiosperms (from the Greek *angio*, meaning vessel). They are the largest group, with an estimated 25,000 species colonizing a diverse range of habitats from mountaintops to deserts.

Flowering plants are divided on the basis of their seed leaves or cotyledons (*see opposite*); these are easily spotted in large seeds as the tissue inside the seed coat. Monocotyledon or monocot plants have one, and tend to produce linear leaves with distinctive parallel veins, including irises, rushes, and palms. Dicotyledons or dicots have two, and produce broad leaves with branching veins, from the oak (*Quercus*) or beech (*Fagus*) to buttercups (*Ranunculus*).

The role of seed leaves

Every seed contains an embryo plant composed of the radicle that will form the first root, the plumule that develops into the shoot, and the hypocotyl or stem joining the two. These are nourished by cotyledons or seed leaves, and all seeds have either one or two cotyledons.

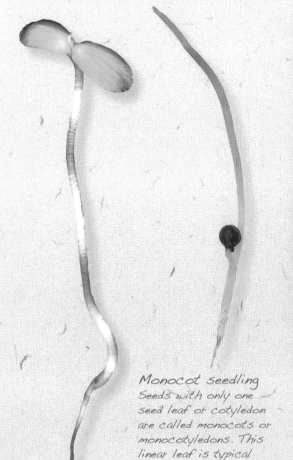

Monocot seedling
Seeds with only one seed leaf or cotyledon are called monocots or monocotyledons. This linear leaf is typical monocot form.

Emerging seed leaves and coats
Dicots tend to push their cotyledons up to use as a temporary leaf; this is called epigeal germination. Monocots tend to leave the cotyledons in the soil, which is called hypogeal germination.

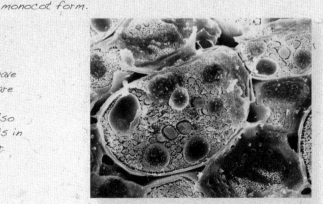

Dicot seedling
Broad-leaved plants have two seed leaves and are known as dicots or dicotyledons. They also differ from monocots in leaf shape from their first appearance.

Energy reserves
The cotyledons act as a food reserve. These large grains of starch fuel the early stages of the embryo's growth. As the food is absorbed by the embryo, the fat seed leaves thin out and become more leaflike.

Prolific poppies
Many annuals produce masses of seed that shower down around the parent. This ensures the seedlings start out where the parent has already grown successfully.

HARVEST AND STORAGE

Success starts with obtaining healthy seeds from a known source. There are plentiful suppliers of commercially available seed that is carefully harvested, packaged and stored, but like all perishable goods, look out for a sow-by date. Avoid seeds from shelves in full sun or close to radiators, where temperature fluctuations may cause harm. The most abundant and least expensive seed is of course that gathered from the garden. Some of my own earliest seed collections were made with conker championships in mind, but nature intervened before the potential prizewinners were threaded.

Inside a seed capsule
In an unripe, green capsule, the seeds are supported on the partition walls. These and the outer wall will dry as the seeds ripen and fall free.

Grow your own

Almost no plant in my garden is safe from roving hands as the seeds ripen and begin to fall towards the end of the plants' growing season. Each collection is carefully stashed in paper envelopes till sowing time, although I will happily admit to having secret stashes of seed, the origins of which have been lost in the passing seasons. So periodically I scatter miscellaneous parcels over naked areas of the garden, what follows is a pick and mix floral display. As a teenager, I often found seeds germinating in the freshly laundered pockets of various garments when I failed to retrieve them before the washing was done.

Most plants are worthy of close inspection: no matter how insignificant the bloom, any flowering plant is predisposed to produce seeds. It is, after all, the entire point of flowering. There are a few notable exceptions, as some double blooms have sacrificed reproductive parts for petals, becoming virtually sterile.

When the time is right

Patience may not come naturally, but allow seeds to ripen on the parent before harvesting them. Some plants declare their readiness, like poppies and nigella with their beautiful burnished capsules. These swollen ovaries (*see pp.102–103*) of the plant enclose the ripening seeds and act as nature's percussion section,

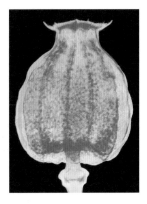

Poppy seedhead
At the point of readiness, the seeds cascade in their thousands into the base of the papery capsule.

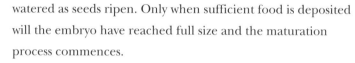

rattling as the parched stems move in a breeze. The members of the pea family or Papilionaceae carry their precious cargo in pods that split and explode as they ripen in the summer sun. And who can fail to be moved by the nodding, melancholic heads of the sunflower (*Helianthus*), marking the passing of the flower and readiness of the seed? Then there are plants with obvious fruits and berries (*see pp.104–105*) such as apples, plums, and pears, whose seeds ripen only as the succulent and swollen fruit is despatched from the parent plant.

"The moral is, don't be too eager, as the longer seeds have to ripen the more viable they will become."

Ripe and ready

Ripening involves the plant moving nutrients into the seed, just like charging a battery. This means the plant has a higher reliance particularly on minerals such as nitrogen and phosphorus (*see p.131*); plants starved of these nutrients tend to produce less viable seed, so keep your parent plants well fed and watered as seeds ripen. Only when sufficient food is deposited will the embryo have reached full size and the maturation process commences.

At this stage the plant removes moisture from the seed, essentially dehydrating it. So effective is this removal of moisture that while a parent plant might consist of up to 95 per cent water by weight, the seed typically has its water content reduced to less than 15 per cent of its weight. One reason for this is that if the seed is exposed to frost, the water expands as it freezes, which can rupture cells already full of water, so reducing moisture prevents frost damage. Reducing moisture also lowers the metabolic rate within the seed, ensuring it doesn't waste precious resources while waiting for germination. This is why seeds allowed to dry naturally on the plant will remain viable for longer than those harvested too soon or dried artificially.

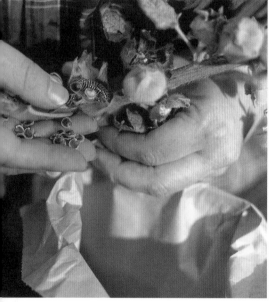

Collecting seeds
Gather seeds into a paper bag that will not trap moisture around them, removing chaff that could harbour pests or mould spores.

Cleaning up

In essence the seed is a perfectly designed parcel, with all that a plant requires to prosper bundled into, often, the smallest possible package, and all wrapped in a coat to offer protection from the hostile world. As a result, very little action is needed once the seed is collected and separated from the vessel that carried

Ingenious mechanisms
The stems of cyclamen (inset) coil to pull the seeds down to the soil, while the pods of geraniums and their relations spring open and fling their seeds from the curling sides.

Saving Seed

- Collect your seed on a dry day in the afternoon when moisture levels will be low, minimizing the chance of seeds suffering fungal problems.

- To reduce spillage, place a paper bag over the head of the faded bloom and hold securely before cutting.

- Hang bags of harvested seed heads in a warm, dry place, such as the airing cupboard, to encourage seeds to separate from the plant remains.

- A cool, dry environment is best for long-term storage – an old fridge is perfect.

it. In some cases, such as plants like the poppies and the yellow rattle (*Rhinanthus minor*) the separation process happens all too readily, and sleight of hand is required to avoid a population explosion around the parent plant.

Other seeds, especially those enclosed in fleshy tissues, should be subjected to a few minutes soaking in tepid water and light scrubbing to remove all trace of soft tissue. An easy process in theory, but cleaning more than a handful requires real determination. It is worth persevering, because decaying soft tissue promotes fungal infections, which are often responsible for compromising seed viability. As you stand and scrub minute seeds of tomatoes, fingers numb and eyes straining, just remember that cladding the seed in soft flesh is all part of the plant's distribution strategy. It is the necessary postage stamp that entices a varied fauna to carry the seed to a new home, usually in its gut after digesting the flesh (*see p.108*). It is also often rich in chemicals that actively inhibit germination until the time is right.

Safely stowed

Following cleaning, store the naked seeds in a cool and dry environment, away from heat sources that could cause excessive drying out. The seed coat may appear resilient, but by design most allow the gradual passage of moisture into the seed to facilitate germination, and if water can enter it may also leave, damaging the potential for future growth. Similarly avoid damp conditions that might lead to moisture entering the seed coat, starting the inevitable and irreversible process of germination.

To keep moisture in balance, seed houses now supply loose seed in foil packets that create relatively static conditions and help ensure good germination rates. Unless you are absolutely sure of creating the perfect conditions in which many seeds are capable of remaining viable for decades, you should avoid keeping your own seed and any opened packets of seed for longer than one season.

Storing seeds for long periods of time involves precise management of their moisture content, the humidity in storage, and temperature of storage. Some plants such as rice and peas can be stored at temperatures as low as –18°C (0°F) and remain viable for many hundreds of years, in fact some estimates suggest that peas could last as long as 1,000 years. However, the vast majority of garden plants in temperate regions should be dried at room temperature and then packed in airtight containers for storage in a domestic fridge.

Testing viability

Casting seeds in spring with the expectation that the garden will be riotous with colour or crops by summer is a leap of faith. Just how do you know if all the collection, cleaning, and storage efforts are worthwhile? Viability is the seed's potential for germination, indicating active cells within it. Most seeds last till the next growing season with proper ripening and storage, but even in perfect conditions they lose viability over time. So how do you check the viability of your seeds?

Well, my biology teacher taught several courses of action to determine if a seed was viable. The first was to slice the seed in half with a scalpel and examine the interior for signs of life. If the seed coat and embryo are intact, then the seed was probably viable – at least until it was sliced in two! Second, cast the seeds on water and see whether they float or sink after soaking overnight. Those that sink are considered viable while those that float are not, because viable seeds absorb water just before germination. Great in theory, but some seeds, such as birch (*Betula*), are equipped with a buoyancy aid for distribution while others, like lettuce, have a seed coat that by design is naturally buoyant. And of course the water absorbed may prompt germination. In truth, the only way to guarantee the viability of seeds is simply to sow them and wait, even if this results in a glut or famine. And don't feel too bad if germination is poor; the precise science of seed deterioration isn't clear. At warm temperatures fungi might be responsible, but viability also falls in low temperatures and sterile conditions, so scientists continue to seek the reasons.

Phoenix palm
Found in an archaeological dig, the 2,000 year old seed of an extinct strain of the date palm (Phoenix dactylifera) is the oldest seed known to produce a viable young plant.

Winter sedums (inset) and rosehips
Protected from the elements, many seeds remain on the plant until spring, providing emergency rations for wildlife and winter interest for the gardener.

SLUMBERING SEEDS

Even with full ripening, careful harvest, and ideal storage, some plants are awkward about germination, being reluctant to grow until they have just the right sequence of conditions: this is the essence of dormancy. Frustrating as this might be it is, at least in my eyes, excusable. Plants have evolved to survive the vagaries of the seasons, and simply cannot afford to make mistakes. Germinating at the wrong time could jeopardise the species, with either many seedlings competing against one another or the failure of an entire generation due to unfavourable conditions.

Defining dormancy

Technically dormancy is a delay between ripening and germination, and varies wildly between species. Annual weeds that complete several generations in a year are only dormant for a short period, while desert plants are able to remain dormant for decades, and a batch of Arctic lupin (*Lupinus arcticus*) are reported to have germinated after being frozen in the tundra for 10,000 years. Dormancy may be innate or induced. Innate dormancy is governed by internal factors, such as chemicals in the seed: if these factors are reduced or removed, germination can begin. Induced dormancy is controlled by outside factors, with the seed simply slumbering on until the right trigger is provided.

Sparked into life

Pehaps the most dramatic innate dormancy is in plants that need fire to break down their germination inhibitors, like banksia or protea. These originate in scrub areas where fires are a natural part of life, such as South Africa, southern Europe, and the southern United States. After torching seeds at home I found that the process is more complex than just heating; lengthy exposure to smoke from leaf litter also improved germination, particularly of proteas. Luckily for my mum, I perfected filling the house with acrid smoke after leaving home!

Protea flower
Protea and restios require both moisture and smoke to break dormancy, simulating brush fire conditions.

Simulating the physical stresses seeds experience in the soil is called scarifying, and helps to break dormancy. There are various methods, depending on the size of the seed and the thickness of the coat.

Using a knife Nicking or scraping the coats of larger seeds makes a weak spot for water to enter. Be careful not to cut too deep.

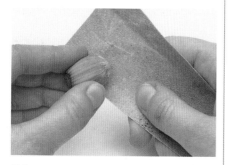

Using sandpaper Rubbing thick coats, such as the shells of nuts, with coarse sandpaper also works, as it thins and weakens the coat.

Using water Warm water is traditionally used to crack the coats of smaller seeds. Drain after, and leave the seeds on damp tissue.

Winter washing

Some seeds, such as those of the carrot family or Apiaceae, are dosed with germination-inhibiting chemicals by the parent plant as they ripen. Believed to be abscisic acids (*see p.105*), these stay in the seeds after they fall, until washed out by rains. One result of this is that seedlings tend not to appear at the base of the parent plant, where they might compete for nutrients and light. Another is that seed shed in autumn will not germinate in the harsh winter weather. When rains have removed the chemicals, they germinate in the spring: a simple but effective way of plants holding seeds back till good conditions prevail. This is why hardy annuals, such as calendula, eschscholzia, and nigella are best sown in late summer. Washed with rain, the seeds are persuaded that winter is over and germinate while the soil and air are still warm. The plants come through the winter to give early flowers the next season. Some seeds, including those of many annual weeds, seem to contain varied quantities of inhibitors. This is thought to be a natural insurance policy: a few seeds germinating over a long period will thrive better than all germinating at once.

Commercial growers flush these seeds with chemicals, usually growth hormones like gibberellic acid and ethylene (*see p.115*), but also hydrogen peroxide and cyanide. At home, the best approach is to lay "difficult" seeds on wet tissue paper, rinse twice a day for three days with water to replicate winter rains, then sow.

Seeds that chill out

Other inhibitors within the seed are broken down by heat or cold. This is a way of responding to seasonal progression. For instance, seeds of desert plants often require prolonged periods at over 40°C (104°F) to break down inhibitors and release hormones to stimulate growth; this keeps seeds dormant through summer and ensures germination coincides with autumn rains. Conversely, seeds of plants from temperate regions, especially trees such as sorbus, ash (*Fraxinus*), and hemlock (*Thuja*), require periods of cold to simulate winter, and some alpine species need prolonged periods below 4°C (40°F), followed by flushing with water to simulate thawing snows, then warm temperatures to indicate spring. Periods of cold, or stratification, can be recreated by placing cleaned seeds in a polythene bag of damp sand in the refrigerator for two to three weeks – a practice my mum got used to as I loaded her fridge with bags of stratifying seeds as a boy.

Animal assistance

A further technique employed by some seeds, particularly cotoneaster, holly (*Ilex*), hawthorn (*Crataegus*), and some sorbus, is to use the digestive tract of animals and birds, often combined with the requirement for a period of cold, to help break dormancy. This presumably allows the seed not only to know when winter has passed but also helps distribute the seed far from the parent (*see pp.108–109*). I first saw this in action when working on a farm during a Christmas break from school. I was told we were planting hedges, but we went out with no plants, only a bale of rope and several wooden posts. After knocking the posts in, we tied the rope across them and headed back to the farm for breakfast with not a hedging plant in sight. However, next spring a line of hedgerow seedlings grew under the rope, thanks to the songbirds that had gorged on the fruits of local plants and then perched on the rope to rest and relieve themselves, supplying stratified seeds in a little parcel of nutrients.

Well wrapped up

Some seeds are kept dormant by an extraordinarily thick seed coat, for example those of the pea family (Papilionaceae). The coat gives physical protection but also inhibits germination by keeping the seed dry until soil bacteria and/or the movement of soil particles erode the coat. This can be cheated by soaking the seeds in acid or cutting or breaking the coat (*see opposite*). My grandmother's technique was to put some coarse, dry sand into a jar, throw in a few seeds, screw on the lid, and then wander around the garden for half an hour or so using the jar as a percussion instrument and singing – the choice of song is, apparently, optional.

Discouraging parents
Decomposing beech (Fagus) leaf litter is thought to produce chemicals that keep beech seeds dormant, preventing excessive competition.

Tough customers
The seeds of sweet peas (Lathyrus) have very tough coats that should be broken for reliable germination.

Waiting for water and light

While innate dormancy is a part of the normal life cycle for some plants, not all play this game of horticultural hide and seek. Some are kept dormant just by external conditions, even though the seed is primed for germination inside. This is referred to as enforced or induced dormancy, and can be broken by altering the conditions to suit the seed. For instance, seeds of almost all plants remain dormant while dry, and are enticed out of this dormant state simply by adding water. This is the basis for the preferred low-humidity seed storage.

Many seeds remain in a dormant state due to an absence of light. This is thought to be because millions of years of evolutionary trial and error have shown that a deeply buried seed doesn't have enough energy reserves to grow up to the surface, and therefore it sits dormant instead until something brings it to the surface and light strikes the seed coat. Some seeds, such as lettuce, lobelia, and salvia, seem to respond to a specific wavelength, requiring red light. This is detected in the leaf by phytochrome, and it is thought that its importance lies in the way that leaves absorb light. In sunlight, lettuce germination is likely to be good, but under the canopy of other plants, it is poor. Analysis of the light under the canopy reveals that is it low in red light, which is absorbed by the overhanging leaves; the seed, deprived of red light, will not germinate because it detects competition. This strategy is typical of plants that grow in clearings and those whose seedlings are poor competitors.

Too hot, too cold, or just right

Lettuce is also a good example of a plant whose germination is inhibited by warmth; this relates to the plant's need for water. Temperatures over 25°C (77°F) imply low soil moisture, so seeds stay dormant; reduce the temperature and they germinate freely. This is one reason why early and late sowings of lettuce, spinach, and pak choi do better than those made in midsummer. Some seeds, like evening primrose (*Oenothera*), need alternating warm and cool temperatures. Seasonal variations are thought to trigger a carefully orchestrated set of chemical reactions in the seed that remove inhibitors and promote growth hormones. Like picking a safe lock, it needs the right time, at the right temperature, in the right sequence. Some seeds, such as peonies, viburnum, and lilies (*Lilium*), show epicotyl dormancy, named after the shoot above the cotyledons (*see pp.14–15*). Warmth sparks germination, but only roots develop; shoots and leaves grow after further cold, with the competitive advantage of established roots to fuel them.

Permission to cheat

While unravelling dormancy can give huge satisfaction, most of us want seeds to germinate freely, and trade in treated seeds is brisk. These are usually treated with dormancy-busting chemicals for sure germination and fungicides to protect them in storage and after sowing. Also available are pregerminated seeds in a gel, with the emergent growth clearly visible. It is reassuring to see this, but remember that these seedlings require planting immediately, usually via a syringe, to avoid stress. Treated seeds are a little more expensive, but worthwhile if you experience poor germination or don't have the right initial conditions – remember, once the crop is growing, you can claim all the credit.

Parsley and the devil

Parsley seed is notoriously difficult to germinate, being said to travel to the devil and back at least seven times before growing. Some gardeners talk of "scalding the devil" by pouring boiling water over parsley seed to speed up its germination. Leaving aside the devil, the hot water is likely to crack the tough seed coat, allowing water to enter and germination to commence. The same process can be used on many other tough-coated seeds.

SOWING AND GROWING

As a boy it seemed to me that seeds scattered with abandon in any reasonable conditions and at almost any time of year gave bountiful flowers and crops. As an adult the mind becomes polluted with fragments of knowledge that cause endless questioning and dips in confidence. Suddenly the most straightforward, natural process is embroiled in anxiety. Some gardeners religiously follow instructions, timing sowings to the day; others exercise a refreshing freedom, sowing when the mood takes them and conditions feel right.

"Don't be fooled into thinking that complex and expensive equipment is required to give your seeds the best start in life."

Choosing the right time

Plants naturally cast their seeds free once each is ripe, and then the seeds sit waiting for the right conditions to arise for germination several months later. So why then do gardeners have such a preoccupation with sowing on a prescribed day or week, long after the parent plant has deemed the seeds ripe?

The truth is that the plants growing naturally in your neighbourhood, or native to the part of the country you live in, are probably just as happy being sown at the time they are released from the parent, as they can then experience the natural climatic conditions and germinate when most appropriate. This method works well for most hardy annuals, meadow species, or native shrubs and trees.

If you wish to pamper your plants a little, use a cold frame to provide shelter from the worst of the winter wet and prevent compost from becoming waterlogged, or just place a perspex sheet over their pots. Further germination aids could include introducing a little bottom heat from a propagator in spring, as the resultant increase in metabolic rate speeds germination. The major disadvantage of sowing at the time of ripeness is that the seeds will spend all winter prone to pest and disease attack, just as they are in nature, but aside from that there is no reason to wait.

Watering seedlings
To get the best from seeds, simply give them the same temperature, moisture, and light they get in the wild.

Warming up

For more exotic and introduced plants that aren't fully hardy, timing will rely on the temperature being right for germination. These plants tend to need warmer temperatures, so are usually started in propagation units or glasshouses and on window sills. It is often difficult to find specific information on the right temperature, but unless trying to germinate something from the tropics, 18–20°C (64–68°F) is good for most.

Another consideration is that some exotic crops, such as tomatoes, chilies, and peppers, require a long growing season to fruit well, so to make the most of avilable time, gardeners tend to sow them early with heat. My great uncle used an old drawer turned upside down with a basic light fitting screwed onto the inside: after placing seed trays on top, he turned the low-wattage light bulb on to keep the pots warm, and this worked perfectly.

Room to grow

There is always a tendency to sow too thickly, resulting in a colony of seedlings jostling for position and competing for light, water, and nutrients. Sown thinly, seedlings remain more content till transplanting, and better airflow reduces disease incidence. And even for large seeds don't worry which way up they are – they will adjust themselves.

Depth of sowing is always the point at which most gardeners' confidence wanes. Just remember that a seed is packed with nutrients to drive the embryo plant to the surface, and it stands to reason that the smaller the seed the less energy it has to reach the surface; therefore if in doubt sow shallowly. A general guide is that most seeds should be sown about as deep in the soil as the seed is wide. If you get to the point of squinting as you try to estimate the width of a dust-like seed in the palm of your hand, the chances are that it requires light to germinate and should be sown on the surface. To ensure that these seeds remain moist, try covering the top of the pot with cling film to maintain high

SOWING FINE SEEDS

Seeds need plenty of space to grow well, but it can be tricky to avoid sowing fine seeds too densely, even with a steady hand.

Mix with sand A simple, effective way of sowing small seeds is to tip them into a bag with fine sand and shake until mixed.

Make a valley Tip the mix onto folder paper and tap out gently over the pot – slightly larger seeds can be sown like this without sand.

SOWING LARGER SEEDS

Spacing out Larger seeds need more space between them, like these beans, and should usually also be sown at greater depths.

humidity, or mist the compost daily. For large seeds and those that romp away quickly, or those that sulk when transplanted such as peas, beans, brassicas, beets and alliums, sow two seeds to a module pot and thin one out once germinated.

Life begins

Water and air are vital triggers for germination. First moisture from the soil enters the seed, raising its water content from as little as 10 per cent to 70 per cent. Initially water molecules are drawn into the spaces between proteins like water into a sponge, a process called imbibition. It may be tempting to encourage your seeds by soaking them, but the speed at which water enters is critical. Too fast and it can kill the seed, and submerging the seeds in water starves them of vital oxygen. Water colder than the minimum temperature at which the seeds germinate will also cause them to perish, so always use tepid water to mist seeds.

Once the seed is fully hydrated, enzymes get to work on large carbohydrates, fat, and protein molecules. These are broken down into more easily transported sugars and amino acids, which are supplied to the embryo to fuel cell growth. Air, specifically oxygen, is essential to this respiration (*see p.83*), and since air largely diffuses into the seed from the soil it is essential that seed composts are well aerated (*see p.176*).

The radicle grows away first and immediately seeks water to supply the seedling growth via osmosis (*see p.123*). The plumule then heads to the surface with the apical bud that will form the basis of the plant (*see p.70*). This is wrapped in a leaf and dragged up, with the strain of pushing taken by the arched stem. Once the shoot breaks the surface germination is complete, although for most gardeners the unfurling of the first leaves indicates success. At this point the plant switches from relying on food from seed reserves, a state called heterotrophic, to using photosynthesis (*see pp.80–83*) and becoming self-supporting, or autotrophic. In some plants you can see the spent food source, as the cotyledons may be lifted by the emerging shoot (*see p.15*).

The process of germination

Germination is the growth of seeds into seedlings. Some seeds are ready to germinate as soon as they are shed from their parent plant, but gardeners know from experience that most are more fickle, demanding just the right combination of water, oxygen, warmth, and light or darkness. Germination is a relatively straightforward affair, but once commenced the process cannot be halted, so be diligent in caring for seeds and seedlings.

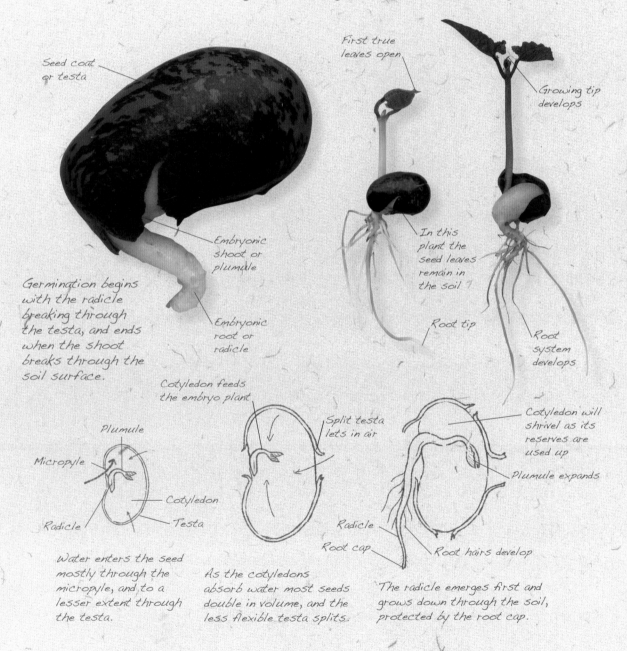

Seed coat or testa

First true leaves open

Growing tip develops

Embryonic shoot or plumule

Germination begins with the radicle breaking through the testa, and ends when the shoot breaks through the soil surface.

Embryonic root or radicle

In this plant the seed leaves remain in the soil

Root tip

Root system develops

Cotyledon feeds the embryo plant

Split testa lets in air

Cotyledon will shrivel as its reserves are used up

Plumule expands

Plumule

Micropyle

Cotyledon

Radicle

Testa

Radicle

Root cap

Root hairs develop

Water enters the seed mostly through the micropyle, and to a lesser extent through the testa.

As the cotyledons absorb water most seeds double in volume, and the less flexible testa splits.

The radicle emerges first and grows down through the soil, protected by the root cap.

Youth on age

Agaves die after their spectacular single flowering. As an insurance, young plantlets grow along the stem, a feature also seen in the flowerheads of some alliums (inset).

LIFE WITHOUT SEEDS

Not all plants rely solely on the vagaries of weather, insects, pollen, and the multitude of other factors that all play a part in successful seed production. In evolutionary terms, the ability to reproduce without the need for seeds is primitive; however some plants, even the most sophisticated, have retained the ability to reproduce asexually, without the exchange of genetic material. In a few cases this vegetative reproduction is a key method of spreading.

Natural processes

This ability often helps plants to establish in a particular niche. Growing along rivers, crack willow (*Salix fragilis*) and alder (*Alnus glutinosa*) might shed a bough in storms that washes down stream. Once this becomes embedded in moist soil further down river, a high proportion of stems or twigs will root, and new trees form. Similarly on steep mountain slopes, where unstable soils combine with winter gales, plants like the resilient houseleek (*Sempervivum*), stonecrop (*Sedum acre*), and roseroot (*Rhodiola rosea*) all doggedly cling to meagre supplies of organic matter in rock faults and fissures. For these plants life is a balancing act, and when intense weather causes rockslides their colonies can be ripped apart. Such potentially disastrous events are seized as opportunities by the plants to colonize new areas, because wherever fragments of the plants fall, a few will take root.

Seeking soil
In poor soil the specially adapted stems or stolons of Saxifraga platysepala *offer two advantages. They can produce new plants where they touch soil, and these are far enough away not to outcompete their parent.*

Perhaps more familiar to gardeners are the actions of several weed species whose dominance and persistence in the garden relies on the same approach. The irritatingly invasive couch grass, fresh green bindweed that twines its way into the heart of our herbaceous borders, and even the savagely thorned bramble all owe their survival success to vegetative reproduction. Of course it isn't that these plants don't flower, it's just that they can supplement the often protracted and costly floral process with more instantaneous methods.

Self-layering tree
This mature specimen of
Thuja plicata shows that even
trees use layering to spread.
If the central trunk dies, a
circular grove of separate
trees will continue to grow
around the stump.

How do they do it?

All of this is possible simply because every plant retains the wonderful ability to recreate itself from fragments of the original parent plant. The nucleus of a plant cell contains a complete set of genetic information specific to that plant (*see p.48–49*). Armed with this information any cell can, in theory, develop into any specialist cell within the plant, an ability described as "totipotent". Under normal conditions only some of the genetic information is used, and hormones stimulate the cells to become either stems or roots, and so on.

However once a cell, or clusters of cells, are removed from the influence of the parent plant, whether by winter floods in the case of the willow, or by my grandmother's deft hands as she tours a garden coveting another's fuchsias, this precise order is lost. The result is that cells can re-order and reorganize themselves to produce organs and appendages not usually found at that point on the plant. This is called adventitious growth and is the basis of vegetative reproduction. It may take the form of shoots produced from roots, roots from shoots, or even roots and shoots produced from a leaf as multiple cells develop and take on a new purpose.

As gardeners we exploit this ability of plants to recreate themselves from even the smallest part, as we diligently take cuttings, divide herbaceous plants, and allow bulbs to naturalize in the lawn. These techniques, called vegetative propagation, are useful for those plants that don't come true from seed, like most cultivars, or for obtaining new mature plants more quickly than we can from seed. Many of the plants we buy are the result of such processes, but armed with a sharp knife and an unswerving confidence it is possible to turn your fingers green and propagate almost anything in the garden this way.

Hormone factories

The best method and material to use is largely dictated by the presence and blend of two growth hormones, auxin and cytokinin (*see pp.112–15*). These dictate the ordering of the cells and new growth patterns – just how isn't clearly understood, but research suggests that the ratio of these hormones at the cutting point is critical to successful propagation. The two perform opposing and varied roles: auxin is required to promote root growth but if it dominates, the cells appear to produce little root. If cytokinin dominates, shoot growth is strong and root growth is weak. And if both are present in high concentrations, the cells, presumably finding themselves in something of a conflict, produce scar tissue, known as callus.

Research suggests that cytokinin is produced at the tip of the root, from where it is distributed upward throughout the plant, while auxin is manufactured in the shoot tips and moves downwards. The easiest way to remember this, as my frustrated biology teacher explained it to a less-than-attentive class many years ago, is that the hormone with more letters is heavier and sits on the ground to make leaves.

The rooting hormone powders often used by gardeners to promote growth contain synthetic blends of these hormones. They should therefore be used with care, as the artificial hormones are designed to promote either root or shoot growth depending on the type of cutting – stem or root – being taken.

As one of the principle functions of these two hormones is to stimulate growth, it will come as no surprise that the cells richest in this finely balanced cocktail are the most recent additions to the plant, basically the current

"Every plant may be propagated without seed; the key to success is to find the most successful method, with the minimum of effort and the fewest losses."

Peonies for the impatient
For many perennials, trees, and shrubs, using vegetative propagation is a shortcut to a garden bursting with blooms.

season's growth. The other places they can be found are areas where cell growth is about to take place, so particularly around the nodes – the joint between a leaf and the stem, where buds lie dormant until stimulated by the hormones. This is why most propagation material, whether it is root or shoot, is taken as cuttings from the fresh growth, and that on stems the cuts are made just below the nodal points.

Choosing your material

Spotting maturity on some plants may be easy, but inevitably it is more difficult on others. Once again, we are only just beginning to unlock the science behind what we see, but the aging process can be easily seen on some plants. One useful and clear sign that maturity has been reached on woody plants is that stems carry flowers; juvenile stems cannot do this, and this is the reason gardeners are so often told to take their cuttings from non-flowering shoots. In fact, this is not always necessary, as the maturing stems of some species, such as most fuchsia, contain sufficient hormones to root enthusiastically, but it is always best to remove the flowers from cuttings to divert energy into rooting.

Plentiful material
A long green stem of fresh growth can yield several cuttings, each ending just below one of the leaf nodes.

Clear evidence of maturity is also seen in beech (*Fagus*) species. These trees tend to retain their old foliage through the winter on their juvenile stems but discard it on mature ones, which is why regularly clipped beech hedges hold onto their foliage. Some conifers, such as juniper (*Juniperus*) have soft, downy foliage on their juvenile growth that becomes aggressive and spiny when the stems mature.

Some cuttings also adopt the habit of the stem from which they were removed. For instance, propagating the top section of the stem with the terminal bud (the one at the tip that reaches for the sky), tends to result in plants that have an upright appearance, rarely branching from low down. On the other hand, cuttings taken from side shoots tend to produce more freely branching plants, which are more aesthetically interesting from a gardener's perspective. When taking cuttings in the nursery from genera such as mahonia, berberis, and magnolia, we always opted for material the young side shoots. Cuttings from some species will even adopt a permanent juvenile state. Most notable of these is ivy (*Hedera helix*), which produces small, three-lobed leaves on lithe, eagerly ascending stems when juvenile, but with age bears large and rounded leaves and takes on a rather portly, shrub-like appearance. Try taking a cutting from these two stages of growth and watch what happens: the cuttings taken from stems with mature foliage will rapidly perform their normal transition from juvenile to maturity, while cuttings taken from juvenile stems remain in a Peter Pan state, rarely displaying the signs of aging.

Look after the parents

When I worked in a plant nursery, we retained several parent specimens of each plant, from which cuttings were annually harvested. These pruned and compact plants were provided with near-perfect growing conditions, keeping them young and vigorous, in return for their crops of cutting material. Such treatment ensures not only plentiful supplies of fresh tissue, but also holds the plant in a permanently juvenile state. This is important, because the buds at the tips of the plant govern its progress from juvenile through mature to geriatric, and only the juvenile phase propagates well. If they are allowed to grow unchecked, the shoots will naturally reach maturity, and the opportunity to propagate easily from them is lost.

Another curious way of influencing plant rooting was demonstrated to me one May Day when, out for a walk with the dog, I started chatting to an ageing gardener as he tended a parterre. After exchanging the ubiquitous comments on the weather and seasons he started burying a box (*Buxus*) and a lavender (*Lavandula*) in a dustbin by tipping sand around their base until the bottom two thirds of the plants were covered. He explained that he wanted cutting material from those shoots in spring and was guaranteed to get good rooting if they were under the ground.

This strange practice illustrates perfectly the ability of rooting hormones to congregate in different tissues in response to external conditions. Science has yet to explain the detail, but what seems to happen in the buried stems is that the absence of light causes rooting hormones to be mobilized; so when taking your cuttings, either invest in plenty of dustbins or make sure you insert at least two thirds of any cutting into the compost.

Hedera helix 'Anne Marie'
Variegated plants will not "come true" from seed, and must usually be propagated from shoots; in ivies, cuttings also guarantee the retention of juvenile foliage.

"The best cuttings come from the fresh growth of stems less than one year old, on enthusiastic plants."

NEW PLANTS FROM OLD

These propagation techniques can sound like a laboratory lesson in nodes, hormones, and buds. I however had an irreverent teacher, who could grasp a piece of plant and have it form roots before it touched the ground – at least that's how it seemed as I watched my grandmother when I was five. Plants, she said, have two chances – they live or they die. Very few of hers opted for the latter, because she responded to their personalities, be they easy-going or cussed.

Cuttings from happy-go-lucky plants

These are the plants that burst into life with enthusiasm and energy, including penstemon, pelargonium, fuchsia, abutilon, and choisya. They grow rampantly

each year and bounce back quickly from pruning. Clearly they are, like teenagers, bursting with hormones and will therefore root easily, so cuttings are taken when the plant is in leaf. They are referred to as softwood or semi-ripe cuttings, depending on whether the cutting is taken in the early part of the season when the tissue is soft, or later in the summer when it becomes stiffer. A quick test to determine the soft from the hard is to take a cutting and try inserting into a loosely filled pot of compost; if the stem buckles and bends it is definitely softwood.

The beauty of these cuttings is that with a couple of leaves retained at the tip, they have the capacity to photosynthesise in light (*see pp. 80–83*), producing sugars to fuel the development of roots. This development relies on the metabolic rate of the plant, so to increase this stand the cuttings on a source of bottom heat such as a propagator tray. Use a well-drained compost (*see p. 177*), otherwise water, which warms slowly, can linger in the pot and slow rooting. Warming the compost is much better than warming the air around the plant, because warm air will increase moisture loss through the leaf and, as the cutting has no roots to take up water, this puts it in a precarious position;

Easy does it
Packed with life and hormones, the fuchsia is among the easiest plants to propagate from cuttings.

for the same reason keep cuttings out of sunlight. Water loss from the leaf can be reduced by increasing humidity around the foliage, so place a polythene bag over the pot or a lid on the propagator. Some ventilation is needed, because during photosynthesis and respiration the leaf uses carbon dioxide and releases oxygen, so in a sealed environment the carbon dioxide reduces, potentially slowing the metabolic rate and rooting. Therefore, let fresh air in periodically by removing the cover or opening propagator lid vents.

Cuttings from tough-as-old-boots plants

These are plants like dogwoods (*Cornus*), willow (*Salix*), or evergreen *Prunus* species, which grow well and enthusiastically and are tough enough to look after themselves as cuttings. The cuttings are taken late in the growing season, after leaf fall if the plants are deciduous, and are referred to as hardwood cuttings. They are inserted either into the ground or into pots and left in a cold frame over winter. Evergreen cuttings are taken in the same way, but should be covered to retain moisture, because the leaf will place the cutting under stress from water loss.

These plants aren't rife in rooting hormones, and those without leaves have no means of manufacturing sugars, but all the stems that are sufficiently developed and sturdy will retain carbohydrates, and these are used to fuel the production of roots. Rooting takes longer than the happy-go-lucky plants, relying on the spring sunshine to warm the soil and increase metabolism, and usually the cuttings are left for several months before transplanting. Cuttings of this type are best taken at about pencil size and inserted into the rooting medium at least two thirds of their length; remove the tip of the shoot to encourage branching. If they fail, try layering instead.

Layering contrary plants

These plants are the ones that are considered difficult to root. They struggle and sulk, and so layering is used if all else fails. Layering involves selecting a stem from the lower part of the plant, wounding the bark, and burying the wounded stem in a trench, with a stone placed on the buried section to secure it. The tip of the shoot is left protruding from the ground and the other end is left attached to the parent plant while the buried section produces new roots.

SOFTWOOD CUTTINGS

Achillea, Buddleia, Begonia, Caryopteris, Chrysanthemum, Delphinium, Erigeron, Gypsophila, Hebe, Lupinus, Magnolia, Mentha, Nepeta, Penstemon, Philadelphus, Sedum, Spiraea, Thymus, Viola

SEMI-RIPE CUTTINGS

Abelia, Abutilon, Berberis, Calluna, Camellia, Ceanothus, Chaenomeles, Choisya, Cistus, Clematis, Cotinus, Cotoneaster, Cytisus, Daphne, Deutzia, Dianthus, Erica, Escallonia, Euonymus, Fatsia, Hedera, Helianthemum, Hibiscus, Ilex, Jasminum, Kolkwitzia, Lavandula, Lonicera, Osmanthus, Pieris, Potentilla, Pyracantha, Rhododendron, Rosmarinus, Syringa, Taxus, Viburnum, Vinca, Weigela

HARDWOOD CUTTINGS

Actinidia, Cornus, Forsythia, Laburnum, Ligustrum, Malus, Ribes, Rosa, Salix, Sorbus, Tilia

LAYERING

Amelanchier, Calluna, Camellia, Chaenomeles, Clematis, Cornus, Cotinus, Cotoneaster, Daphne, Dianthus, Erica, Hamamelis, Hibiscus, Ilex, Jasminium, Magnolia, Rhododendron, Wisteria

LAYERING A SHRUB

This technique works best when done in early summer. Choose a stem of the current or most recent season's growth: it may be worth cutting back low stems the previous winter to promote the fresh growth that's ideal for layering.

Prepare the shoot *Leave the foliage on about 10cm (4in) of stem at the tip, and strip off the leaves from the section below this.*

Lower and lay *Make a trench about 10–15cm (4–6in) deep. Scratch or nick the stem and lay it in the bottom, pinning with wire if necessary.*

Bury the stem *Fill the trench with soil, firm in, and keep moist. The buried stem should root in a few weeks; some take longer.*

Layering is particularly successful as the leaves on the tip of the plant produce sugars that fuel root production, the buried section allows dormant buds to break as roots, and the parent plant supplies additional water and carbohydrates from the base. It is thought that the knife cut aids by interrupting the flow of sugars from the leaf tip to the roots, concentrating them around the dormant buds. Although it may sound like a highly artificial method of propagation, it is frequently adopted naturally by roses, clematis, and several herbs and suckering shrubs.

Dividing frost shy plants

My grandmother described all the herbaceous plants that wither and retreat into the security of the ground at the first sign of frost as "frost shy". They are the traditional herbaceous species that produce a clump of foliage in summer and either a dense mat of roots or thick, fleshy, underground stems called rhizomes (*see p.42*). Division is easily carried out by lifting the plant from the ground in autumn and using bare hands, knife, or fork to rip the crown into sections, each with roots, a portion of stem on which there are dormant buds, and possibly leaves.

Division for me typifies the way gardening is made to sound complex by some gardeners. As a student, I endured a full morning's lecture on the art of textbook division. The lecturer, eager to demonstrate the precise practical application of his notes to the assembled students, lumbered into the room with a great mature crown of geranium, placing it in the middle of the laboratory desk. He jumped on the desk, with a large garden fork in each hand, and struck one then the other into the heart of the plant, so that the two stood back to back, handles leaning away from each other. Then with a running commentary he squatted astride the clump, grasped a fork in each hand and pushed their handles towards one another so that the curved prongs would lever the plant apart – perfect. Unfortunately the plant didn't yield, so with ever more breathless effort, a fractured commentary, and increasingly prominent veins on a reddening forehead, he applied more effort, crouching under the strain. We sat silent as a battle of wills raged at the front of the lab, the plant unforgiving and the lecturer determined not to be embarrassed by a geranium. After several minutes of wrestling and grunting one last monumental heave was followed by the rapid coming together of fork handles, and the two pieces of plant material were catapulted across the room. Unfortunately the speed at which the geranium surrendered took the lecturer by surprise and, not removing his head quickly enough from its position between the fork handles, he was knocked unconscious. It all went to show that plants are amazingly resilient and can recover from the most traumatic experiences (the geranium grew away very happily) but lecturers don't (he left shortly afterwards to pursue an alternative career).

Plantlets from hop-skip-and-jump plants

Few plants adopt this strategy, but when they do it works with great reliability. The plant sends out a specially adapted stem known as a stolon, along which dormant buds produce adventitious roots and small plantlets. The stolon is not a storage organ, it is slender and cannot be used in its own right as a cutting, but the young plants formed at the nodes can be harvested by gardeners, complete with roots, and grown on as for the parent.

Root cuttings for herbaceous prima donnas

These plants can be the stars of the herbaceous border, but their reduced stems preclude the possibility of taking summer cuttings from most of them. They tend to store large quantities of carbohydrate in their thick roots, and for this reason it is the roots that are harvested for cuttings. This is done during late summer or autumn, when they are fully charged with carbohydrates after a long season of growing.

Remove short sections of the most fleshy root, as long as your little finger, and critically remember which end was closest to the parent plant. This is because roots retain the ability to know which way is up (*see p.112–14*) and will therefore always produce shoots from dormant buds at the end of the root cutting originally closest to the parent. Insert the root vertically into the rooting medium, so the tip is just beneath the surface.

DIVISION

Achillea, Alchemilla, Aquilegia, Astilbe, Campanula, Coreopsis, Delphinium, Doronicum, Epimedium, Erigeron, Euphorbia, Geranium, Geum, Helleborus, Hemerocallis, Heuchera, Kniphofia, Lavatera, Liatris, Lupinus, Meconopsis, Mentha, Monarda, Nymphaea, Phlox, Primula, Ranunculus, Sedum, Solidago

PLANTLETS

Acaena, Ajuga, Fragaria, Geranium (some), Rubus, Sempervivum

ROOT CUTTINGS

Acanthus, Anchusa, Echinacea, Echinops, Eryngium, Papaver, Phlox, Primula, Pulsatilla, Romneya, Verbascum

"Stars of the herbaceous border are often a little choosy about rooting."

DIVIDING RHIZOMES

Perennials with rhizomatous roots need to be lifted and cut into sections to propagate. Monocots such as irises cannot regenerate damaged roots as dicots can, so cut any such roots back to the crown.

Lift the plant *Use a fork to lift the whole plant and shake off as much soil as possible. Break into manageable sections by hand.*

Split the rhizome *Cut new, young sections with leaves from the clump with a clean, sharp knife and shorten roots by up to one third.*

Trim the divisions *Dust the cut surfaces of the rhizome with fungicide. Trim the leaves to minimize wind rock, and replant the divisions.*

Dividing stem and root tubers

To successfully propagate plants it is important to know where the plant stores its food supplies, hormones, and dormant buds. Tubers are often considered to have all three, but not all tubers are the same.

These specially adapted storage organs can form along the stem, as in potatoes, or along roots, as in dahlia. These two plants particularly relate to the way my grandparents propagated their stock and demonstrate the different kinds. Propagating from the tuber formed on the stem is simple, as it carries dormant buds – the "eyes" – from which roots and shoots form. Therefore the extra-large seed potatoes that my grandfather bought could be sliced (to save money) as long as each section contained at least a couple of eyes. But my grandmother's dahlias could not be treated in the same way, as the root tuber does not include a dormant bud. Each section of root must have a section of stem attached, containing the dormant bud, if they are to grow into a new plant successfully.

Grafting and budding

Grafting is essentially the process of taking the shoots of one plant (called the scion) and placing them on top of the roots of another plant (called the rootstock), with the aim that the two plants should unite and grow as one. Budding is a similar principle, but involves taking only a bud from the scion plant and inserting this into the stem of the rootstock.

The art of sticking two completely separate plants together is nothing new; evidence suggests that the Romans frequently used the technique to propagate and cultivate their favoured vines. Despite such history, few gardeners today are prepared to experiment with the world of such engineered plants, but with a little care and attention it is a beautifully straightforward process. Take a walk in an unmanaged woodland, where the trees are growing freely, and you may spot nature engaging in her own

Polygonatum (inset) and dahlia
The restrained woodlander and the bold
exotic share a similar root structure. Both
should be propagated in spring when new
shoots appear at the growing points.

grafting as the canopies of mature trees become a dense and sometimes disorganized tangle of boughs. Occasionally two branches will grow to touch one another and, over time, with the friction created by the breeze, bark will be worn away at the point of contact. This exposes the valuable cambium layer just below the bark (*see p.71*), the point in the stem where rapid cell growth takes place. Eventually, the two boughs may fuse, and after several years the scar between the two is healed.

Such a natural demonstration of grafting may have provided the first inspiration for early gardeners, and it still serves to demonstrate the basic principles. The first is that not all plants will graft successfully, as the roostock and the scion must be genetically compatible; the more compatible they are, the more likely a graft is to be successful. In the wild two oak (*Quercus robur*)

Espaliered apple
Apple and pear cultivars on the right rootstock are easily managed and trained into decorative, productive forms.

boughs on the same tree might fuse, or a bough from one might fuse with another from a neighbouring tree of the same species, but the branch of an oak would not fuse with, for instance, that of a beech (*Fagus sylvatica*). This is because a precise union must develop for the two boughs to fuse, with cells permanently bonded and growing together. This is essential if water, nutrients, and chemical compounds such as hormones are to pass between the two successfully.

The details of compatibility are not fully understood, with trial and error guiding growers, but it is generally accepted that the more closely related the two plants are, the more a graft is likely to be successful. For instance, plants of different cultivars but within the same species will usually work together, plants of different species but within the same genus will sometimes unite, and just occasionally plants from different genera will graft well. In the garden this is usually evident in fruit trees, where an apple (*Malus*) cultivar grafted onto an apple rootstock is common but a pear (*Pyrus*) won't unite with an apple rootstock. However just to confuse matters further, the pear will work together with a quince (*Cydonia*) rootstock, and this combination is widely used (*see panel opposite*).

Why use grafting and budding?

One advantage of these techniques is that the wood used as the scion can be from a bough showing signs of maturity, giving an instantly mature plant that can flower immediately. This is why grafted fruit trees set fruit while small in stature, whereas seed-grown fruit trees take years to mature before flower and fruit set – as anyone who has ever grown an apple from seed will testify. The same is true of ornamental plants like wisteria and tree peony, both of which can be encouraged to flower as small plants when grafted. The practice is also useful for creating forms such as standard weeping roses: an upright rootstock provides the stem, and a ground-cover or climbing rose is budded on the top.

Perhaps most importantly, the rootstock can be used to control the vigour and eventual size of the plant. This is because the rootstock acts as the engine powering the plant with water, nutrients, and sugars. A vigorous rootstock will inject plenty of energy in to a scion, creating rapid growth and large eventual size, while a low-vigour rootstock will cause the same scion to grow more slowly and be dwarfed. The rootstock can also be chosen to cope with poor soil or environmental factors; in difficult growing conditions, I opt for a vigorous rootstock to help a tree establish and prosper, while a low-vigour rootstock in such conditions will create very slow and possibly sickly growth. For these reasons fruit tree cultivars are grown on rootstocks specifically labelled to indicate the likely vigour and size of the resultant tree (*see right*).

Micro-propagation for special plants

Also called tissue culture, this relatively recent advance requires specialist laboratories. A small piece of plant tissue is cut into tiny pieces and smeared onto culture dishes with hormones (*see pp.112–15*) and nutrients. In warm, humid conditions, liverwort-like structures develop in a few days. These are either grown on or sliced up and returned to a culture dish to make more plants. This allows growers to bulk up a population to release onto the market from a single bud, far quicker than from seed or cuttings. A further advantage is that the original plants are placed in perfect growing conditions for a few days beforehand to stimulate growth. Rapid cell division at the shoot outstrips the speed at which disease can enter the new cells, so if the meristem (*see p.51*) alone is used, even an infected plant can produce new uninfected plants.

FRUIT TREE ROOTSTOCKS

Vigorous for rapid growth to 4–8m (12–24ft) and poor conditions

Apple	MM111
Cherry	Malling F12/1
Nectarine	Brompton
Peaches	Brompton
Plum	Brompton

Semi-vigorous for moderate growth to 3–4.5m (10–14ft) and moderate conditions

Apple	MM106
Apricot	St Julien A
Cherry	Colt
Damson	St Julien A
Gage	St Julien A
Nectarine	St Julien A
Peach	St Julien A
Pear	Quince A
Plum	St Julien A

Semi-dwarf or low vigour for growth to 3–4m (10–12ft) and good conditions

Apple	M26
Cherry	Damil

Dwarf or very low vigour for growth to 2.5–3m (8–10ft) and good conditions

Apple	M9
Cherry	Gisela 5
Damson	Pixy
Gage	Pixy
Peach	Pixy
Pear	Quince C
Plum	Pixy

Very dwarf or dwarfing vigour for growth to 1.5–2m (5–6ft) and good conditions

Apple	M27
Cherry	Tabel

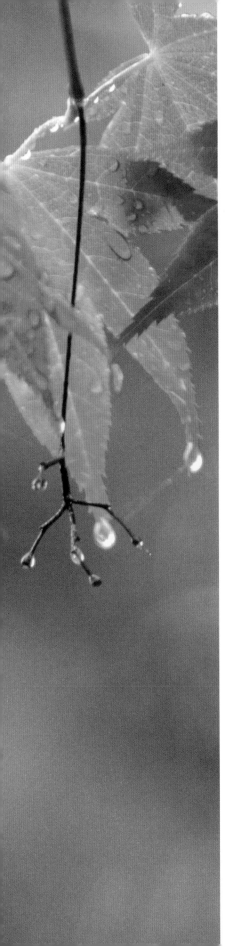

The working plant

Flowers, fruit and foliage may be
responsible for love at first sight
between gardeners and their plants, but
enduring affection can only be assured
by witnessing and closely observing the
complexity, beauty and sophistication
of the thriving plant in full stride.

PLANT CELLS

The sophistication of our plants becomes plain when the details of their cells and the interactions between them are witnessed. Remarkably, it was not until the late 17th century that science was turned on its head by the discovery that all living things were composed of cells, each with a specific function and purpose. Although the size and shape of each cell varies enormously, they follow the same basic method of construction, with specialized components to carry out a range of tasks.

The machinery of the cell

The cytoplasm of the cell is enclosed in a membrane, and within it are the organelles. Each is enclosed in its own membrane and has a dedicated purpose, with seven main specialists present. The most obvious is the vacuole, a large sac that holds water, sugars, and waste products from cells' chemical actions. This fluid keeps the cell in the correct shape and at the right pressure or turgidity; when a thirsty plant starts to wilt, it's because fluid levels in the vacuoles fall and, like a deflating balloon, the cells lose their shape and the whole plant looks deflated. The chloroplasts are minute units filled with chlorophyll that allow plants to manufacture sugars via photosynthesis (*see pp.80–83*). The many ribosomes in each cell convert amino acids (foods produced in the plant from photosynthesis) into proteins, such as enzymes that stimulate all the chemical processes in the cell as directed by the nucleus. Any chemical action produces waste material, dealt with in the golgi body or apparatus, a sort of temporary bin for waste before it is sent off to more appropriate areas. Peroxisomes contain enzymes that break down by-products of cellular activity. Mitochondria exist in varying numbers, and function as generators. In a process called respiration (*see p.83*), they use oxygen from the air and sugars manufactured by the plant to release the energy necessary for cell division.

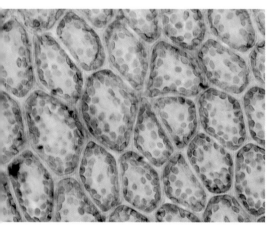

Food factories
The green grains within these cells are the chloroplasts that give the plant its colour and manufacture food.

Inside the cell

The contents of the cell, or protoplasm, has broadly two working parts.
The first is the nucleus, the "brain" behind the cell's actions, the
second a gelatinous substance called cytoplasm, which contains
specialist structures called organelles.

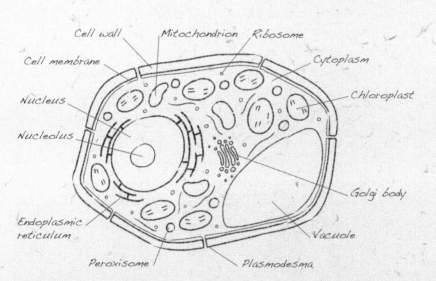

Cell wall · Mitochondrion · Ribosome

Cell membrane

Cytoplasm

Nucleus

Chloroplast

Nucleolus

Golgi body

Endoplasmic
reticulum

Vacuole

Peroxisome

Plasmodesma

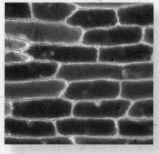

Red onion cells
These turgid cells pack
together like brickwork.
If they lacked water,
their red contents would
shrink from the walls,
leaving large, pale gaps.

Parts of the cell
The nucleus chemically
controls everything that
happens in the cell, while
organelles carry out the
cell's functions.

DNA and chromosomes
Each chromosome is a long
string of DNA. This is
usually relaxed but condenses
into an X shape before dividing.

Cell division

Nucleus divides

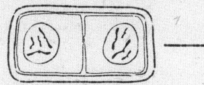

Two identical sets of
chromosomes form "daughter"
nuclei within the cell, and a cell
plate grows between them.

Chromosomes uncoil

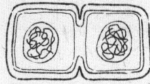

The cell plate is lined
with cellulose, becoming
a wall between two new,
identical cells.

DNA double helix
"supercoils" and
condenses before
division

Chromatid

Centromere

Each chromosome is
two chromatids
joined at a centromere

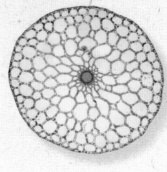

Stem cells
In this aquatic
plant stem, smaller
cells provide a
tough exterior and
air spaces between
larger cells give the
stem buoyancy.

Cell expansion

The cell walls contain cellulose microfibrils that lie in a parallel arrangement.

Internal pressure causes the cell wall to expand. The microfibrils stretch apart on the side walls, but they are woven across either end of the cell, preventing expansion there.

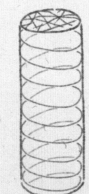

Once a cell has expanded to its maximum size, secondary layers of cellulose are produced in a woven pattern. These thickened walls make any further expansion impossible.

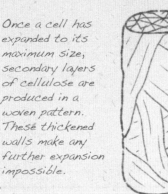

This energy is then temporarily stored and waste products, in the form of carbon dioxide and water, are recycled in other functions or sent to the golgi. The energy is ultimately used for the construction of large molecules such as the cellulose of cell walls, which is why mitochondria are concentrated where rapid growth is occurring, such as root and shoot tips. Finally, there are specially arranged membranes known as endoplasmic reticulum for the transportation of substances throughout the cell, like an internal mail system.

The brains of the cell

The nucleus controls all the activity of the cell's organelles, and contains a nucleolus, which makes the ribosomes. It also contains the chemical deoxyribonucleic acid, more commonly known as DNA, which governs the way the nucleus communicates with all the working components of the cell.

DNA is a large molecule made up of a sequence of units called nucleotides. The sequence is the genetic code of the plant, essentially its characteristics, and is unique in every plant. The string is formed into chromosomes, and every plant has a set number of chromosomes: the tomato has 24, the onion 16 and, for reference, human beings 46 – so theoretically two tomatoes are more complex than one gardener!

Cell walls and bonds

A fundamental difference between our cells and those of our plants is that only a membrane surrounds ours, while plant cells are wrapped in a cell wall to encase and protect the contents. This wall is composed of fine, parallel strands of cellulose called microfibrils, with successive layers added in slightly differing directions. The resulting structure is a fine mesh like a fishing net, critically allowing the cell to expand and contract to take account of both fluid movements and cell growth. This tissue is a major investment for the plant: unlike much of the contents of the cell, the cellulose cannot be recycled within the plant. It contributes to the solidity of the plant, supplemented by the pressure of turgid cells; where greater rigidity is needed, cells specialize (*see p.52*).

Of course one cell, no matter how sophisticated or complex, is of little use unless it is able to play a team part, and this is achieved by the plasmodesmata, numerous meshes that cross the walls between adjacent cells to allow the passage of nutrients and hormones between them. They also control the speed of fluid movements, and their elasticity allows them to maintain the links even when a lack of water causes the cells to shrink.

I have always been fascinated by how all the cells within a plant operate as individuals, but work together as a team. Their individuality is demonstrated by the fact that the bond between cells is loose, relying on a natural glue called calcium pectate to bind them together. It creates a strong but flexible bond that takes account of growth and physical movement, while ensuring that the vital communication links between cells are not broken.

Cell expansion and division

Limited plant growth can be achieved by cell expansion. The vacuoles of young cells are filled with available sap, and the cells increase in length. This elongation continues until the wall is stretched to its limit, with the cellulose layers dictating the direction and proportions of the expansion (*see panel opposite*).

A plant has to multiply its cells to grow beyond this, and does this by a process called mitosis (from the Greek *mitos*, meaning thread). This cell division (*see p.49*) occurs throughout the plant and sometimes at remarkable speed; in a young seedling there may be 20 divisions an hour. Given the tiny size of cells, consider how many must divide to make the lawn grow 5cm (2in) a week.

There are two kinds of growth in a plant. Primary growth is concentrated in root and shoot tips (*see p.57 and p.70*), in areas of rapidly dividing cells called meristems (from the Greek *meristos*, meaning divided). Cell division constantly thrusts these

Kitchen chemistry

You might think you need a microscope and a chemistry set to discern what goes on inside a plant. However, if you are a gardening cook and have noticed that jams and preserves of some fruits set better than those of others, then you have witnessed calcium pectate, or pectin, at work, because it is this cellular glue that causes jams to set. Apples and oranges are high in pectin, making crab apple jelly and marmalade firm, while strawberries and cherries are low and often need extra pectin, which is extracted from citrus skins.

New growth
Meristems at the tip of shoots constantly produce new cells that then become flowers, leaves, and stems.

further out to create additional length on the shoot or root. This kind of growth responds quickly to changing environments, allowing leaves to find the sun, seedlings to move quickly to the surface of the soil, and roots to seek out moisture and nutrients. Of course, a stem cannot simply continue growing up without strengthening its base, so secondary growth is essential, and achieved by slightly slower cell division in linear meristems that extend throughout the length of the stems and roots. This is how stems, trunks, and boughs increase in girth, forming layers of cells seen as the familiar annual rings in a felled tree (*see p. 72*).

Types of cells

Although we refer generically to "plant cells", there are in fact three types of cell that make up most plant tissues, tongue-twistingly named parenchyma, collenchyma, and sclerenchyma.

Parenchyma cells have thin, flexible walls and large central vacuoles, and are roughly cube-shaped and loosely packed. This is the most common type of cell, making up the bulk of roots and stems, the photosynthetic cells of leaves, the soft parts of fruits, and internal tissues of seeds.

Collenchyma cells are elongated, with walls thickened and strengthened with cellulose. They provide structural support in growing shoots and leaves, forming fibrous tissues such as the veins in leaves and the fibrous strings in celery stalks.

Sclerenchyma cells are small, and their walls are specially adapted and thickened with lignin, a substance that lacks the flexibility of cellulose but has incredible durability when laid densely. They are long and tapering, fitting together firmly while maintaining a certain articulated flexibility, and provide structural integrity, like steel girders in a building. They are found in plant parts that are no longer growing, and make up wood, the tough fibres of phormium leaves, and the hard shells of nuts. Sclerenchyma are regarded as dead because they lose their protoplasm once mature, which is why it is often said that most of a living tree is actually dead.

Tailor made

To avoid wasting resources on strong supports that aren't needed, plants make their more specialized cells to order. The walls of collenchyma cells in plants that are blown by the wind or shaken to mimic wind movement can be up to twice as thick as those of the same type of plant when grown in more sheltered conditions. This is why some gardeners brush or blow their seedlings, and newly planted trees should only be supported with short stakes that let them experience some movement. Even music can have an effect, and the stronger the bass beat, the greater the effect. It may dismay some gardeners to learn this, but their plants respond most to heavy rock.

Natural versatility
The shoot meristems of a plant produce
undifferentiated cells, which then diversify
into the tissues of soft fruits and leaves, or
tougher stems and shells of nuts (inset).

Agressive roots
Some trees, such as eucalyptus, have fast-growing roots and should be kept away from buildings, while bamboos may need to be contained by barriers in the soil (inset).

VITAL ROOTS

Roots have three functions: to secure the plant to the ground, to take in nutrients and water, and to store food. Like many aspects of horticulture you really can't cheat here; there is a fine balance between the amount of root and the amount of shoot developed, with plants only ever producing shoots that the roots below can support and supply. A plant will even modify its canopy in later life to compensate for root damage, which is apparent in downsizing of the canopy or conditions like the familiar "stag's horn" dieback that is often seen in mature trees.

"Root actions benefit not only their own plant but both the soil and other plants."

Perpetual thirst

The roots of a plant never stop growing, but constantly divide and extend to seek out new supplies of moisture and nutrients. They make up 80 per cent of the plant as a whole, and even modestly proportioned herbaceous specimens have a staggeringly intricate and fine network of roots.

One of the primary functions of roots is the mass extraction of water from the soil. Obviously the amount taken will vary according to local conditions and microclimate, but on average about 2500 litres (550 gallons) of water is taken up by roots in every square metre or yard of your garden every year. Imagine removing plant roots, especially those of a large, thirsty tree: the implications of surplus water in the soil are staggering. This is why removing mature trees from gardens can cause structural damage to adjacent buildings, and why gradually reducing the canopy is better than simply felling trees.

Taking this water from the soil, particularly soils with heavy clay content, reduces the total water held and so reduces the incidence of waterlogging. This dramatically increases the actions of soil microorganisms that require aerated conditions (*see p.186*), so an important side effect of roots extracting water is to increase the decomposition and incorporation of organic matter, which in turn increases the availability of nutrients and humus to improve plant growth and soil structure.

Struggling survivor
To grow at all in such a bare spot is impressive, but the dieback above is a tell-tale sign of root problems below.

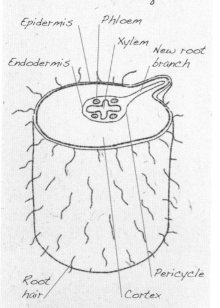

Roots and hairs

The layered structures inside a root operate in a well-coordinated sequence.

Epidermis

Phloem

Xylem

Endodermis

New root branch

Root hair

Pericycle

Cortex

Root hairs

There are an estimated 200–400 hairs per square millimetre, lasting only a few days each.

Breaking and binding soil

The physical action of the roots pushing through the soil opens up the structure and improves air penetration. This is vital, because while growth relies on the internal supply of nutrients, moisture, and chemical stimuli, none of these are effective without a constant supply of oxygen to the root cells to fuel respiration (*see p.83*). This is why the ideal rooting medium for plants has ample supplies of nutrients, water, and air, with soil structure open enough to allow aeration but also firm enough to stabilize the growing weight of the plant (*see pp.160–61*).

The network of fine roots produced by some plants also binds soil particles together, limiting erosion by water and wind. Even when roots die, the tunnels and runs that remain still offer aeration, drainage, and burrows for larger soil organisms.

From the outside in

The outer layer of the root, called the epidermis, is a single layer of cells, often coated with a protective cuticle of cutin. This is a waxy material designed to keep fungi and bacteria out and helps to control the flow of water into the root. The epidermis cells also develop into the fine root hairs on fibrous roots.

Inside the epidermis is the cortex, made up of rounded cells, roughly packed like a badly built dry-stone wall. Far from being a design fault, this loose assembly allows fluid and air to pass through the gaps between cells, a faster and more versatile route than moving through the cells themselves. The thickness of the cortex varies from one species to the next, but is greatest in herbaceous plants and those that rely on underground storage of food reserves. The innermost layer of cortex cells, called the endodermis, are closely bound, forcing fluids to pass through them rather than between them. This gives the plant a second opportunity to control the flow of water (*see pp.122–23*).

Just inside the endodermis is the pericycle, a further single layer of cells essential to the success of the plant. All side roots originate from this thin layer, like dormant buds in a stem, and grow through the outer layers into the soil. Such deep origins offer the new roots protection and gardeners the reassurance that if a root tip is damaged or pruned, further roots will branch out to replace it. Much like pinching the tip out of a stem (*see pp. 70–71*), cutting stimulates the growth of many roots rather than one, supporting the idea that root pruning of plants from an early age to coincide with stem pruning helps to form a robust and self-sustaining plant.

At the centre of the root lies the plant's transport system, a collection of tubes called vascular bundles running from the tip of the root to the tip of the shoots and leaves. Developing into varying shapes in cross-section, these vascular bundles are made up of the xylem and phloem.

Xylem cells transport water up the plant. Their cellulose walls (*see p. 50*) lack ends, allowing them to stack end-to-end like drinking straws and provide an uninhibited flow for fluids, while perforations called pits in the side walls allow fluid to flow out into cells along the xylem. This is why plants wilt from the tips in drought, as any available water will flow into the plant's lower cells before the quantity and pressure and are enough to reach the tip of the plant. Phloem cells are also arranged like straws and operate on a similar principle to xylem, but move sugars made in the leaf down to storage sites such as the roots. Their ends are perforated discs that allow controlled flow of fluids.

Deceptively compact
Even the roots of a modest plant can have a surface area equivalent to 600 square metres (700 square yards).

Both of these cells lose their nucleus (*see p. 50*) when mature; xylem is classed as dead, but phloem cells are still classed as living because they are controlled by minute companion cells that sit alongside them. Separating the two transport systems is a thin line of cells called the vascular cambium. This constantly divides, forming xylem cells on one side and phloem cells on the other.

From end to end

A section across the root only tells a part of the story, with perhaps the most essential aspect of the root only highlighted when the root is cut along the length, specifically at the growing tip. The fine, probing roots of any plant are protected at their extremity by a dense shroud of cells known as the root cap, which allows the root to push between soil particles without incurring damage.

Immediately behind the root cap, in a section no more than 0.3mm long, is the root meristem, the area of most rapid cell division (*see p.51*), and beyond this an area of cell expansion. Together these two push the tip of the root ever further away from the parent plant. Once the cells have divided and expanded, they become differentiated and ordered into immature xylem, phloem, and cortex cells.

Beyond this area, just a few millimetres back from the root tip, is the zone of most dense root-hair growth, perhaps no more than a few centimetres long, where the vast majority of water and nutrients are absorbed. Root hairs, essential for the efficient supply of water, are modified cells that protrude from surface of the root like a fine, white fur, to make the surface area as large as possible. They are capable of drawing water from as far as 10mm (½in) away, but only if they are in contact with soil or soil water – hence the need to firm plants into the ground after planting, establishing contact. It is these delicate roots that are most damaged during transplanting, which is why it is important to move plants with as little soil disturbance as possible. It is also interesting that root hairs do not develop effectively in water, so cuttings kept in jars and bottles of water and seeds that germinate in water-based gels tend to suffer or even die when transplanted into composts.

Further along, closer to the plant, older sections of root become thickened and woody (lignified). This happens through the secondary growth that we are used to seeing in stems and trunks (*see p.70*), and a corky bark provides protection through the waxy chemical suberin in its cells, which reduces the efficiency of water uptake.

Plug plants
Most young plants form a mass of fibrous roots with plenty of root hairs to feed their early rush of growth. Given some room, these roots will expand quickly.

Tap roots and fibrous roots

The roots of plants fall into two broad categories, tap and fibrous. Tap roots principally anchor the plant to the ground, and are usually deep, branching, and wide reaching, reducing in size as they move further from the base of the plant. In some plants the tap root is obvious, like the perfect, slender, inverted cone of a carrot. In others, such as the oak (*Quercus*), the tap roots branch and twist as they push through the soil, reaching tremendous depths when soil conditions allow, but rarely spreading beyond the tip of the leaf canopy above.

Broad tap roots not only offer secure anchorage but also have tissues ideally suited to the storage of sugars and carbohydrates. Under close examination, these can be seen as large starch molecules within the cortex cells. This energy reserve powers the plant into growth in spring, and also provides nutrition for gardeners eating root vegetables.

By contrast, fibrous roots are delicate and fine, a three-dimensional fabric of woven tissue in the soil. They can arise all along a tap root, but are found predominantly in the upper soil, with the majority in the top metre (yard) of soil. Here they scavenge and collect the water and nutrients percolating through the soil. The comparatively warm temperatures and readily available oxygen in the soil pores at this level (*see p.161*) facilitate rapid absorption of water. Fibrous roots are the workhorses of the root system, essential to all plants. Nurseries often excavate around dormant plants and prune tap roots to encourage the development of fibrous roots that will ease the transplant shock experienced by newly planted specimens. This practice can be used when moving established plants in the garden by digging a

Firm anchors
Tree roots can be deep, wide, or both, depending on species and conditions. The roots of beech (Fagus) initially grow down, then spread more widely with maturity.

Fine and fibrous
The fine roots of a camellia are mostly close to the surface, so cultivation around them to the depth of a spade or fork could disturb and damage up to half their roots.

trench one spade wide and deep around the plant in the autumn and then backfilling with sand. This will sever tap roots and encourage the production of fibrous roots close to the crown of the plant. Leave the plant undisturbed till the following autumn, then transplant as normal. This is a sure-fire way of successfully moving even the most mature specimen.

Not all "roots" are roots

Tap roots are not the only mechanism for a plant to hold supplies of food in reserve. In plants such as dahlias, parts of the roots at the base of the stem swell into fleshy tubers to allow greater storage capacity. Other plants use structures that we think of as roots, because they are under the ground, but in fact they are not truly roots. The corms of crocus and the rhizomes of irises are modified, swollen stems, but are kept safely below the surface of the earth, with fibrous roots growing from their bases. Even the tubers of potatoes actually form along the stem, not the roots, which is why potato plants have to be "earthed up", with the stems buried ever deeper, if they are to produce substantial crops.

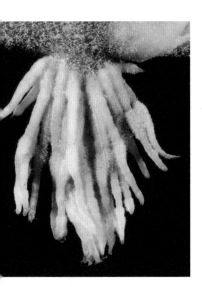

Seeking a hold
The ability to produce roots along the stem enables ivy (Hedera helix) to spread over wide areas with creeping growth, or climb a tree or wall to reach the light.

Contractile roots

The ingenuity of roots is breathtaking, and one of the most cunning modifications of the root is the development of contractile roots. These emerge as branching roots and extend into the soil until they reach a depth predetermined by the plant, at which point they stop growing and start contracting their cells instead. The process is thought to be the reverse of inflating a cell by filling it with sap; cells in contractile roots seem to shrink by removal of sap. This places stress on the plant, and with sufficient contractile roots all reducing in size simultaneously, the plant is able to move.

This is a practice most commonly employed by bulbs and corms to pull themselves not only the right way up in the soil but also to the soil depth most appropriate for protection and flowering. In theory this means that, far from diligently planting bulbs at the commonly prescribed two-and-a-half times their depth, gardeners could just throw bulbs into prepared soil and let nature do the rest – but that's assuming of course that soil conditions are good and the local squirrel doesn't find them first.

Adventitious roots

Adventitious roots occur where a root wouldn't normally be found, such as along the stems of ivy (*Hedera helix*). These specially adapted cells originate deep in the stem, pushing through the outer cells to increase the potential rooting zone. Where conditions are not favourable, the root cells may shrink and die, but still offer a secure climbing hold (*see p.143*).

Think carefully before planting species that produce adventitious roots close to the house; in temperate climates they can cause rising damp in walls, and they always leave debris attached to the wall that makes decorating difficult. In some plants, such as strawberries and *Rubus* species, the root emerges from a dormant bud and can be used in propagation (*see p.41*).

Structural roots

Some plants have a tendency to become top heavy with maturity and fruiting, or naturally grow in unstable conditions, such as wet ground or even submerged under water, and these create additional supports as they age. In herbaceous species, such as tomatoes and sweetcorn, pencil-thick roots are produced from the bottom 10cm (4in) or so of the stems, their emergence seemingly linked to the development of fruit.

On woody species such as figs (*Ficus*), hemlock (*Thuja*), swamp cypress (*Taxodium*), and dawn redwood (*Metasequoia*), roots emerge in response to ageing. They may develop into distinctive "knees" of bark-covered root section that start below the ground but arch upwards through the soil surface to form a buttress, which may be at a considerable distance from the plant. This response is changeable; for instance a swamp cypress grown in or next to water will develop significant knees, but the same species grown in moist but stable soil shows little tendency to produce them. This has led to speculation that these adapted structural roots perform an additional role gathering oxygen for roots below the water line.

Take a hike

A controversial theory amongst botanists is that statuesque plants such as trees exploit contractile roots. Some evidence suggests that when the demise of a mature tree leaves a clearing in woodland, surrounding trees perform a horticultural shuffle, using contractile roots to invade the free and favourable space. The notion of trees walking to a better home is something to worry any gardener guilty of neglect.

Stilt roots
Mangroves are tropical trees adapted to coastal wetlands. Many of them develop these aerial roots, which not only support them but also trap sediments, slowly increasing the land area.

LOOKING AFTER ROOTS

When I worked at a nursery, we encouraged customers to knock plants out of the pots and look at the roots knitting the compost together. The nurseryman's stock phrase was "this is what you're paying for, the shoots and flowers are just the advert". Of course he was right; without healthy roots, the stem, leaf, and flowers all grind to an unceremonious halt. When buying plants today I still knock them out of the pots; if the roots are good I will buy, but if they are spiralling around the base of the pot like a frustrated cat in a cage, or if the compost falls away due to recent re-potting, I walk away.

Get the depth right

Recently questions have been raised about traditional planting techniques, especially the advice to plant trees or shrubs at the same depth as the nursery or a little deeper. The standard practice is to dig a hole half as deep and wide again as the root spread, place the tree in it, and backfill with soil in layers, firming as you go. Studies of long-term growth have shown that in waterlogged or clay soils, the hole fills with water like an underground bucket. Deep roots either rot off or cannot penetrate, and shallow roots sometimes fail to make it out of the hole. The result is that trees often fail to establish – even those that do can be uprooted by wind as the canopy develops above poorly anchoring roots. Problems may appear years later: a windbreak of leylandii conifers that grew next to our nursery for over a decade were felled by a storm, and when they were examined it was obvious that most of the structural roots hadn't escaped the planting hole due to the heavy clay soil and the planting pit effect.

For these reasons, and particularly on a wet soil, gardeners now suggest planting the trees in a shallow pit, half the depth of the root ball, and earthing up a cone around the stem to enclose the roots. The theory is that this lifts the roots out of the waterlogged pit and encourages them to forage widely just under the surface of the soil. Just how successful such techniques are remains to be seen, but it could offer a solution if your ground is very wet all year.

Perfect for repotting
Choose plants with a firm, but not tightly packed rootball: if you can't see the compost for frustrated roots, put it back.

The special case of clematis
Plant clematis 5–10cm (2–4in) deeper than
they were in their pot. They may need to be
cut to the ground if attacked by clematis wilt,
and deep planting aids their recovery.

Buying bare-root

In the nursery many tree and hedging plants sold as "open ground" or "field grown" are now routinely root pruned from an early age. The tap root is severed in the second year and then about every third year till the tree is moved, a practice also called root trimming or undercutting. This practice encourages a proliferation of fibrous roots that enable the plant to be sold as a bare-root specimen in winter and transplant successfully. The severed tap roots are easily seen on young plants as a distinctive stump, but on larger trees they are more difficult to spot, so ask the seller, as root-pruned trees have a survival rate estimated to be 30 per cent higher than that of untrimmed plants.

Other plants benefit from adjustments the other way in planting depth. Plant suckering shrubs, such as salix, clerodendrum, and cornus, so that soil covers the first 10cm (4in) of stem, and they will produce more stems, creating a healthy thicket and a dense canopy. Climbers such as clematis, roses (*Rosa*), and wisteria not only produce a greater number of stems from the base if planted deeply, but also suffer less from nutrient-based disorders.

Acclimatize new arrivals

Pot-grown plants in nurseries are usually given plentiful supplies of slow-release nutrients. There is a growing feeling that they are sometimes so pampered by unrealistic rooting conditions that they suffer transplant shock once in normal garden soil. This shows in a number of ways, from stunted growth in the season after planting to roots staying in the safety zone of the planting pit, or even death. To combat this, acclimatize new plants slowly by leaving them in the container for a season after purchase, so that roots can mop up surplus nutrients. Also, buy small plants in preference to large specimens, because juvenile plants are more able to cope with stress than older ones.

Pampered plants
Coddled to the peak of flowering protection in a nursery, these plants may find conditions in even a well-tended garden a bit of a strain.

Tempt and tease

The planting pit effect is often made worse by the incorporation of composts and fertilizers in the planting hole, which encourages the roots to stay close rather than spread out in search of their own nutrients. To entice roots out of their comfort zone to forage far and wide naturally, water and feed at the edge of the developing canopy, rather than at the base of the trunk. In studies on a wide range of soils, the trees showing the greatest rooting capacity were those in ground that was cultivated to 30cm (1ft) depth and 5m (15ft) diameter before planting. This is beyond what most of us could achieve in our gardens, but it certainly demonstrates the need to think big when considering roots.

There is also some discussion amongst gardeners regarding the practice of "teasing" roots when planting. This means unravelling any roots of perennials, trees, or shrubs that have started to grow in a spiral manner inside pots, and spreading them out in the planting area. The results of growing trials indicate that once a tap root has started to grow spirally it tends to continue to do so, even after planting out, but roots that have been physically unravelled and laid out across the planting pit do tend to grow more normally.

"Widespread feeding, watering, and cultivation are needed to aid root development."

Provide support

Ensuring that the newly planted specimen is secure in the ground is of key importance for the growth of healthy roots. Constant buffeting by wind not only causes the aerial parts of the plant to become agitated, but also rocks the root ball. Obviously the most significant movement is in plants with a large, dense canopy, such as shrubs and trees, particularly evergreens, and in these specimens the young roots exploring the ground are easily damaged and torn free as the canopy moves.

For this reason, firm the ground in layers with your heel when backfilling the planting hole, and use stakes on plants where wind rock is likely. Just remember that the primary function of the stake is to secure the roots, so in most cases a low stake no more than 30cm (12in) high is preferable, with a single tie to the plant. Firm rooting should take no longer than three years on even the most hesitant of plants, so remove the stake once its job is completed. Such short stakes allow movement of the canopy and stem causing cell wall thickening and more resilient growth (*see p.52*).

Solid support
A stake 30cm (12in) high and leaning 45° into the prevailing wind should provide enough support in most conditions.

STEMS AND TRUNKS

The primary role of a stem is as a scaffold, on which the foliage and flowers are hung. Since the success of most plants relies on the efficient placement of these secondary parts, it is essential that the stem can thrust its way as quickly as possible to where the foliage can capture light, and flowers be held aloft for pollination. Two great challenges face any plant attempting to achieve this: firstly, all other plants have exactly the same aim, and secondly, the prevailing conditions, from wind and drought to fire, which influence the approach adopted. So a stem might stand proud like a forest tree, or loll, twine, lean, flop, or creep to achieve its goal.

Whispering stems
Anyone who has ever lain back in a summer meadow agitated by a breeze knows how flexible stems are.

Support and transport

The stem is an essential part of the plant's competition strategy (*see pp.142–43*). It is essential that the plant strikes a balance between the size attained, the energy invested in constructing the stem, the speed of growth, and the flexibility of the total structure, since a lofty specimen of great competitive spirit is of little use if it is destroyed by a slight breeze. The flexibility of plant stems is startling. Even the most statuesque and robust of trees remain tremendously pliable, becoming highly animated as the sail-like foliage of the canopy causes boughs to heave and billow with the slightest air movement. The importance of the stems can be seen in summer gales when leaves, heavy with rain and exerting additional strain on the stems, become a structural liability and are allowed to sever from the plant. Logically it is far better for a plant to sacrifice a few leaves, which can be quickly replaced, than lose a bough that can take years to regrow.

As well as performing an obvious structural function, the stem must allow gaseous exchange to enable respiration (*see p.83*) within the stem, and move nutrients, food, water, and hormones between the aerial parts and the roots.

Reach for the sky

A primary goal for a stem is to place leaves in good light. The straight, vertical growth of these birch trees and the leaning stems of the seedlings (inset) both aim to achieve this.

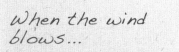

When the wind blows...

My earliest memory of any plant is of an old apple in the meadow behind my first childhood home. Almost as soon as I could walk, I climbed the coarsely textured trunk to perch on the boughs, revelling in the elevated perspective this offered and in the gentle swaying of the canopy. Still unable to resist the temptation to climb trees and enjoy their mesmerizing movement I recently climbed one of Britain's tallest, a handsome Abies grandis measuring a heart-stopping 61m (200ft). Once in the heart of the structure the subtle rhythmic sway became so apparent that after over an hour of climbing I returned to ground to find I had developed sea legs, that persistent swaying experienced after hours of being on water.

The stems of grasses, herbaceous plants and young woody species also often carry chlorophyll in their cells and contribute to the plant's photosynthesis (*see pp.80–83*).

The heart of the living plant lies in the xylem cells, which conduct water and soil nutrients upwards, and the phloem cells, which carry foods made in the leaf downwards. These sit next to one another, forming parallel pipelines called vascular bundles, just as in the roots (*see pp.56–57*). The similarities between the internal structure of the stem and that of the root are essential for the plant's transport systems to be effective. The principle difference is that while the root is largely supported by the soil in which it sits, the stem has to modify its growth to form internal structural supports.

Differing stem structures

One of the principle differences between the monocots and the dicots (*see pp.14–15*) is the structure of the stem. Monocots, such as grasses, bamboos, and palms, are in a sense stripped to the bare minimum. The scattered vascular bundles are each surrounded by a tube-like construction of sclerenchyma cells (*see p.52*), which are largely responsible for structural support. Some stems are even more stripped-down, with the vascular bundles arranged in a ring to form the familiar hollow tube of growth seen in bamboos and grasses.

Young stems of herbaceous and woody dicots have vascular bundles evenly distributed around the outer edge of the stem. The xylem is located innermost in each bundle, and the phloem outermost, and the two are separated by a thin layer of vascular cambium that generates new cells of each. Each bundle is surrounded by a thin layer of supporting sclerenchyma cells, and outside these lie the pith and cortex, composed of mostly parenchyma and some collenchyma cells (*see p.52*). In a non-woody plant it is largely the cortex cells, pumped full of water, that provide the structural support, which is why they wilt so fast when water is lacking.

Stems and trunks

In all plant stems an outer protective or epidermal layer encloses cortex cells and the vascular bundles that carry nutrients and sugars. The nature and the age of the plant dictate the precise organization within the stem.

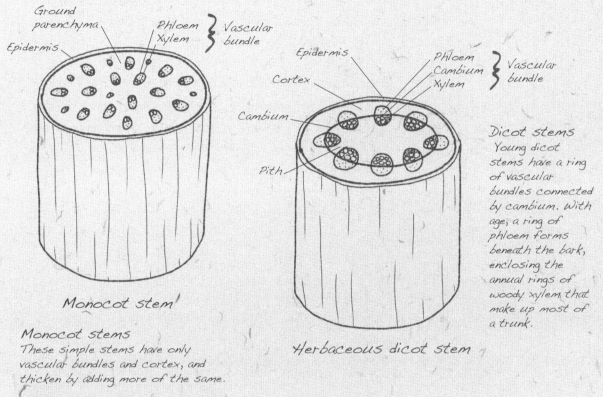

Ground parenchyma

Epidermis

Phloem
Xylem
} Vascular bundle

Monocot stem

Epidermis
Cortex
Cambium
Phloem
Cambium
Xylem
} Vascular bundle
Pith

Herbaceous dicot stem

Monocot stems
These simple stems have only vascular bundles and cortex, and thicken by adding more of the same.

Dicot stems
Young dicot stems have a ring of vascular bundles connected by cambium. With age, a ring of phloem forms beneath the bark, enclosing the annual rings of woody xylem that make up most of a trunk.

Bamboo stem
These stems are hollow, except at the nodes.

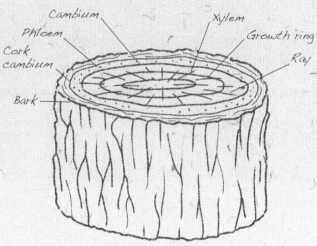

Cambium
Phloem
Cork cambium
Bark
Xylem
Growth ring
Ray

Woody dicot stem

Making new length

Growth in stems takes place primarily in the apical bud, at the end of a stem. This contains the apical meristem (*see p.51*) which renews itself and produces cells that become all the stem tissues, neatly enclosed in a protective wrap of bud scales or modified leaves. The ability to constantly and quickly produce a range of tissues makes a healthy bud essential to many forms of propagation, such as micro-propagation, budding, grafting, and cuttings (*see pp.38–46*).

It is no surprise that the apical meristem with its massive cell division is one of the most vulnerable parts of the plant. Damage by frost, drought, or insects can give rise to distorted and deformed growth, and just a few aphids piercing a bud in early spring can do substantial damage. This is why my grandmother loved feeding the birds in winter: she hung bacon fat and dripping balls from the boughs of her trees and shrubs to entice birds into the garden, and while feasting on fat they also fed on insects trying to over-winter on the buds.

This primary growth is virtually the only kind of growth that monocot stems make: they rarely branch and form no wood, but some are quite specialized. Unlike most plants, which grow from a meristem in the top of the shoot, grasses keep their meristem at the base of the leaf, pushing the leaf further out. This is why grass can be mown or grazed; the position of the meristem enables constant regrowth. The grasses commonly used in lawns even benefit from such trimming, as it encourages them to produce side stems called tillers. These produce further foliage, creating a sward that knits seamlessly together.

Branching out

Only a few monocots, such as cordylines, are able to branch, but axillary buds are found along the shoots and branches of dicots. These have the same potential for growth as the apical bud, but hormones keep them subservient (*see pp.112–15*). They typically grow only once apical buds are already growing, and their cell division is more sedate, giving branching lateral stems rather than enthusiastic vertical shoots. When these laterals are produced the nearest vascular bundle branches to extend transport links into the new growth; these branches of bundles appear as knots in sawn timber.

If the apical bud is removed by climate, pests, or gardeners, axillary buds close to the tip assume dominance, turning upwards and increasing in vigour.

Damaged daisy
Fasciation can take many forms, from flattened stems to dictorted flowers, all caused by damage to the meristem.

This is why pinching out a bud on a single-stemmed young plant, such as sweet pea (*Lathyrus*), results in several shoots of a more upright habit. In trees such as birch (*Betula*), it can give a multi-stemmed specimen; not only are these often more pleasing plants, with greater flowering and fruiting potential, but their ultimate height is also reduced, as the roots' resources are shared between several stems instead of concentrated in one.

A good gardener can also control plants by "rubbing" or removing buds in spring, instead of allowing the plant to waste valuable time and energy producing tissue that is destined to be pruned away later. Rubbing buds was once commonplace, as experienced gardeners could visualize the desired shape of the plant and select the buds required even before bud break.

Staying slim and flexible

Monocot stems add to their girth simply by producing more isolated vascular bundles; no wood is made, and so no secondary thickening occurs. They also lack the layer of cork cambium that produces bark in dicots; instead, parched cells on the surface of the stem shrink to create a tough protective layer.

The distinction between monocot and dicot is perhaps best considered as the former creating a plethora of tiny drinking straws to support the canopy, while the latter builds a single large, solid cylinder. This explains the relative slenderness of monocot stems, and also their greater flexibility: palm trees such as the coconut (*Cocos nucifera*) are the most flexible of trees because they lack woody deposits, and can withstand extreme weather with minimum damage. For the gardener, this makes monocots the ideal plants for a garden buffeted by strong winds.

Middle-aged spread

A large canopy naturally needs strong stems to provide support, water, and nutrients, and this is achieved in dicots by secondary growth. Initially this growth is centred on the vascular cambium

COPPICING SHRUBS

Many plants can be cut back to the base to control their size or habit. Buddlejas are cut back to prevent them becoming gaunt, brittle giants, while dogwoods (Cornus) are cut to encourage brightly coloured young stems.

Young cornus
Allow plants to grow unchecked for the first year after planting. Young shoots have the most vibrant colour; if left unpruned, this coloured growth will be produced only at stem tips.

Winter pruning
After enjoying the coloured stems in winter, cut back to a low base before growth begins in spring. If you are worried about the plant's vigour, cut back just half the stems each year.

Deer damage
Rabbits, deer, grey squirrels, and even mice will all gnaw at nutritious bark, causing damage and in severe cases even death.

Thick-skinned

Just how vulnerable the living phloem layer is was demonstrated to me when called on to inspect a stand of semi-mature birch (Betula) in a client's garden. After several years of vigorous growth, they all started to wilt in the heat. Close inspection revealed the culprit was the client's husband, who had strimmed grass clear of the stems. In the process he severed almost the entire phloem layer, killing nine glorious trees in one afternoon.

between the xylem and phloem, which forms an entire ring around the stem, its cells constantly dividing to produce xylem towards the heart of the stem and phloem towards the outside. These cambium cells become lignified sclerenchyma, or wood, enhancing the flow of water and soil nutrients and providing the central pillar of support for the plant.

It is this large-scale wood production that distinguishes woody plants from herbaceous ones, and also produces the rings in the trunks of felled trees. Each ring represents a season of growth, with many large xylem cells produced during spring to provide for growth spurts in the canopy, and smaller cells produced later in the season as growth slows; during winter, when temperate plants are dormant, there is little cell growth. These rings of growth mirror perfectly the climatic conditions in which the plant is growing, and are therefore most evident in cool climates; in wood from tropical climates, where growth is possible all year round, clear growth rings are absent.

The bark and beneath

In woody stems, division of the vascular cambium into phloem produces of a continuous, narrow band of small, delicate phloem cells, most of which are used to transport food molecules and hormones. These essential cells are immediately below the surface of the stem and are therefore easily damaged by pruning or hungry squirrels and rabbits. To protect this vulnerable layer from pests, diseases, and hapless gardeners, the plant has a second layer of cambium outside the phloem, called corky cambium. This produces the familiar bark of trees, expanding to allow for thickening within the xylem and phloem layers.

This corky material varies tremendously between species, creating beautifully intricate patterns, colours, and textures. It also contains toxins, such as suberin and tannin, which act as waterproofing agents and guard against attack from grazing animals, insects, and fungal infections. The same chemicals are also present in unripe fruit to protect it from attack (*see p.105*).

Tannin is of course a great preservative, and has for centuries been extracted from bark and used in tanneries to preserve leather.

The presence of the cambium and phloem layers immediately beneath the bark in dicots makes budding and grafting of plants possible (*see pp. 43–44*), as the vascular material of the two plant plants is permanently united by these techniques. It also means that the position of pruning cuts to remove boughs is critical, as it is the cork cambium layer that heals the wound: cuts should be close to, but never into, the "collar" of growth around the base of a branch.

Employing a close understanding of the plants' vigour and the nutrients it required, gardeners of old also used to "ring bark" trees to control their growth. The process involves slicing a strip of bark from around the stem, peeling it away, inverting it, and then replacing it. The upside-down tissue acts as a barrier to nutrient and hormones, significantly reducing the available resources to the canopy and thereby bridling the plant's energies.

Waste disposal

As the plant ages, it accumulates toxins and debris from water uptake, air diffusion through the aerial parts, or particles landing on the tissues. Wood continues to be built in the stem, and cellular debris and toxins accumulate in the central tissues. This causes the dark heartwood colour of many trees, while the sapwood, the more recently produced xylem tissue further out, remains functional as a transport system. This ability to absorb toxins has attracted the attention of NASA, who experimented with using plants as air filters and demonstrated that they can harness and lock up many carcinogenic toxins. Such toxins are passed through the heartwood by the plants air-conditioning system, which consists of ribbons of sclerenchyma cells radiating out from the centre of the stem, forming the radiating cracks and splits often seen in drying logs. These ribbons, called medullary rays, stretch from the depths of the heartwood to apertures in the bark called lenticels, where the corky tissue is less dense and allows the exchange of air right into the heart of the plant.

Some species filter and dispose of toxins before they can enter the plant. These plants are used to growing in extreme conditions where dust or salt pollution can literally suffocate them, so periodically the bark flakes off and is replaced. This is clearly seen on tree species such as arbutus and eucalyptus, and helped to make a plane (*Platanus*) the classic London street tree.

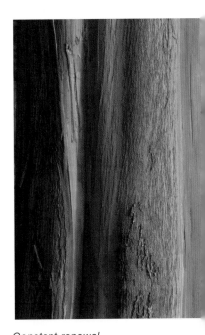

Constant renewal
Trees and shrubs with peeling bark, like this eucalyptus, are a particularly good choice in gardens where pollution is most likely, such as coastal, arid, and urban areas.

LUSH LEAVES

An architect I once worked with felt that plants were great but for their flowers, which arrived unabashed in a palette of gaudy colours to disrupt his tonally considered scheme. This may sound extreme, but it did lead me to attempt a green garden, in which the visual stimulation was provided entirely by stems and foliage, with a few compliant green blooms. Only then did the huge diversity of foliage become plain. Far from having all the appeal of chopped lettuce, the variation in leaf shape, shade, and texture created a visual feast in which, free of other colours, the variety of greens shone out.

Leaf design

Of course, far from evolving to play such whimsical design games, leaves of all shapes, colours, and sizes perform a role, the magnitude of which often seems to escape even the most horticulturally astute of us. Put simply, without plants' foliage we wouldn't be here, because the functions that their leaves perform are as essential to us as they are to the plants. I remember my biology teacher explaining the functions and processes that were taking place in the leaf I was about to dissect, and I thought it was the most perfect and beautiful example of design opportunity, efficiency, and simplicity.

Getting the point
The long pointed tips of some leaves are "drip tips" that will quickly shed rain and any fungal spores or bacteria in it.

The precise details of leaf design vary widely, but the basic working mechanisms are common to all. While we tend to refer to the entire structure as a leaf, it is actually composed of several parts. The leaf blade or lamina, is the large flat panel that turns to the sun, usually supported by the leaf petiole, a stalk that secures the lamina to the stem and continues through the centre of the lamina as midrib. The midrib offers rigidity and a highway for water and nutrients via vascular bundles. The smaller veins differ in dicotyledons and monocotyledons (*see pp. 14–15*): in dicots they branch to form an extensive and fine network, while in monocots they run parallel to the midrib.

Design options

*The broad leaves of a woodland beech
(Fagus, inset) or the wind-tolerant foliage of
carex give plenty of variety in the garden,
increased by the range of coloured forms.*

Surface structure

Covering the surface of the leaf, and particularly evident on the upper surface, is the cuticle. This is a thin, waxy layer of cutin, designed to restrict water loss (*see pp.123–24*). In some plants, such as fatsias and camellias, the cuticle gives the surface a glossy sheen that, like a varnish, helps to protect it from damage by rain. In plants from sunny or exposed locations, such as alpines, the cuticle also may contain pigments to block harmful ultraviolet rays (*see pp.144–45*).

Immediately beneath the cuticle, and enclosing the entire leaf, is the epidermis. As elsewhere in the plant, this is a single layer of unspecialized cells that lack pigments. In sun-loving plants this layer also contains flavenoids to minimize damage from ultraviolet light. Other defensive features are also present at this surface level (*see panel below*), and plants often employ combinations of defences. For example, while both rhododendron and camellia leaves have a glossy cuticle on their upper surface to limit water loss but allow light penetration, rhododendrons have hairs called trichomes under the lamina to limit water loss, while camellias employ a waxy residue. These details of a leaf provide an insight to the precise conditions the species requires to succeed (*see pp.120–21, 126–29, and 144–45*).

Controlling the flow of carbon dioxide, oxygen, and water vapour are the stomatal pores, or stomata. These small cavities form predominantly on the underside of the leaf, where they are protected from becoming blocked by dust and rain. The notable exception to this are the floating aquatics, such as

Microscopic surface features
Hairs that slow airflow, cells that secrete wax or volatile oils, and pores or stomata are vital to leaf defense and function.

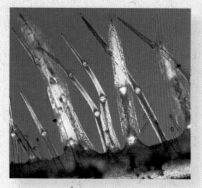

Trichomes

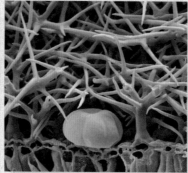

Oil gland among trichomes

Stomata

Nymphea, whose stomata are situated on the top of the leaf. The cavity is protected by two sausage-shaped cells called guard cells. These have differentially thickened walls that cause the cells to curve as their turgidity (*see p.48*) increases, opening the stoma, and straighten as cell turgidity decreases, closing it. The actions of the guard cell are controlled by hormones, which stimulate it to absorb or expel potassium; as the concentration increases, water is drawn in via osmosis (*see pp.122–23*), and when it falls, water leaves the cells.

Inside the leaf

Beneath the epidermis hang lines of loosely packed, elongated cells called palisade mesophyll. These are primarily responsible for capturing the sun's energy, so the number of rows increases with the level of light available. They contain the chloroplasts (*see p.48*) responsible for photosynthesis, and it is here that the rate of photosynthesis (*see pp.80–83*) is greatest.

Beneath the palisade mesophyll lies the spongy mesophyll, layers of large, irregularly shaped cells randomly assembled with large spaces between them. This layer stretches to the underside of the lamina, giving structural support through cell turgidity and providing the cavities behind the stomata. The rather untidy assembly of the cells is to allow carbon dioxide and oxygen to move within the leaf. These gases move from a high concentration to low concentration, and move faster through air than through fluid, so it is essential that the air spaces within the spongy mesophyll are maintained. As the carbon dioxide is used for photosynthesis in the palisade cells, the concentration in this layer falls; in response, further molecules are pulled in, so as long as photosynthesis continues, carbon dioxide is drawn into the leaf.

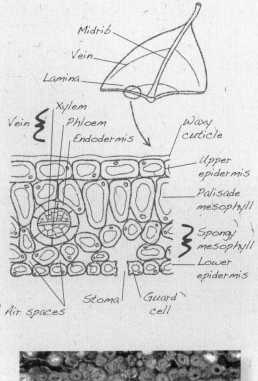

Leaf layers

Leaves work in layers from the upper side, facing the sun and rain, to the protected underside.

Midrib
Vein
Lamina
Vein
Xylem
Phloem
Endodermis
Waxy cuticle
Upper epidermis
Palisade mesophyll
Spongy mesophyll
Lower epidermis
Air spaces
Stoma
Guard cell

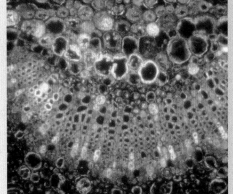

Aquatic leaf midrib

Vascular bundles often form a crescent in midribs. In this aquatic leaf, darker air spaces between cells aid bouyancy.

Transport mechanisms

"There are many comparisons to be drawn between great feats of engineering and the working plant."

As elsewhere in the plant, nutrients, water, and food are carried in the vascular bundles, composed of a sheath encasing pipelines of xylem and phloem cells, separated by a layer of cambium which makes new cells. Linked to the rest of the plant, the xylem delivers water and minerals from the soil, together with root-produced hormones (*see p.115*) to all the cells of the leaf. The xylem fluid holds minerals such as calcium and iron in solution; when infrequent watering or drought causes low xylem pressure, these minerals run short in the leaf and deficiencies become apparent (*see pp.131–33*). The nutrient solution is fed into an ever-decreasing network of xylem cells so extensive that no living cell is ever more than 1.5mm ($\frac{1}{16}$ in) away from vascular tissue. This is because while the solution can move rapidly through the dead cells of the xylem, it moves an estimated one million times slower through living cells, which is far too slow to sustain cell turgidity.

The phloem cells transport the sucrose produced from photosynthesis away from the palisade cells. The sugar solution is pumped into the phloem and reaches concentrations of up to 30 per cent. This causes massive osmotic pressure (*see pp.122–23*) from the water outside the phloem, so these cells are reinforced with hoops to prevent collapse. The network of phloem allows sucrose to be easily and widely distributed throughout the plant to fuel cell division, cell wall building, and respiration, with large quantities transported to the meristems (*see p.51*) of shoots and roots. The organisation behind this is phenomenal, and supply can reach speeds of 50cm (20in) per hour in some species; this is particularly evident in those that are farmed for their sap, such as rubber trees (*Ficus*).

Leaf veins
As well as transporting nutrients, the network of tough xylem cells with their lignified walls is essential in the support of the lamina.

Disposable assets

Faced with the need to shed foliage as it ages, and the possibility that high winds may cause structural damage, a plant leaf has a designed weak point, just as some machines have a shear bolt designed to give under strain. In the plant, this is the abscission layer, a superb engineering solution. Where the petiole joins the stem, the vascular bundle narrows and the cells are weakly connected, so that a stressed leaf can be shed quickly with minimum damage to the stem.

During autumn preparations for winter (*see pp.146–48*), a corky layer of the waxy substance suberin grows to seal the vascular bundles at this point and literally pry the leaf from the plant.

Leaf production

The production of new leaves is genetically predetermined, and starts in the meristem. The edge of this cone of cell division produces small pegs of growth known as primordia, arranged in a distinct pattern that governs the position of the leaf on the stem. Lime (*Tilia*) species produce leaves horizontally and alternately along the sides of the stem, giving it a zig-zag shape, while ash (*Fraxinus*) species are produced horizontally but in symmetrical, or opposite, pairs. Other variations are seen in stachys, which produce opposite pairs on one axis and then at a 90° rotation, and sunflowers (*Helianthus*), which have spiralling single leaves. Such patterns help us to identify plants, but the primary aim for the plant is to place its leaves in the best position to capture sunlight (*see p.142*).

Once a primordium is formed, a carefully orchestrated series of divisions take place at secondary meristems. First the midrib and vascular bundle form, then all along the midrib further cell divisions create the basic lamina shape, followed by growth and expansion of internal tissues to flesh out the lamina and create the distinctive leaf blade. This order of events remains the same from one species to the next, but the duration varies, hence the diversity of leaf types. The long foliage of miscanthus is the result of a long period of midrib expansion and short period of lamina expansion, while broad leaves like those of catalpa result from a moderate period of midrib expansion and long period of lamina expansion. Divided leaves, such as the pinnate foliage of ash, are the result of intermittent lamina expansion, producing a burst of growth for a leaflet, alternating with no growth where the midrib is exposed. Knowing this, take a look at a fern frond and imagine the intricately choreographed meristem dance needed to form a leaf divided with such delicacy in up to four opposing directions.

Identifying marks

The abscission layer is most easily seen on species of Aesculus. In these trees, the scar left by the departed leaf is clearly visible as a semi-circular mark on the stem. The scar resembles a horseshoe in shape, which is one reason behind the common name of horse chestnut.

Pinnate leaves
We often think of trees like ash having leaves grouped on a stem; in fact, each "stem" is a leaf midrib, with paired leaflets. This is shown when they are shed as one piece in autumn.

GREEN ENERGY

In photosynthesis, a plant performs a feat that 21st century science cannot replicate. This process that allows plants to manufacture their own food takes place throughout all green parts, but mostly in the leaves. The ingredients must all be present in the right quantities for efficient photosynthesis; they are readily available, although some are difficult for gardeners to control. The most common problems for plants occur when they are placed where light levels are insufficient or temperatures are too low or too high.

"Photosynthesis is only one of several operations that drive growth, but without the sugars that it provides, a plant simply runs out of fuel."

Simple ingredients

Chloroplasts in plant cells (*see p.48*) need only carbon dioxide, water, light, and the right temperature to produce the sugar to fuel cell division, cellulose building, enzyme production, fluid transport, and all a plant's other activities.

Carbon dioxide, present in the air at 0.04 per cent, enters plants through the roots dissolved in soil water (*see pp.122–23*) and through the leaf stomata (*see pp.76–77*), the latter route being 10,000 times faster. Dense planting and closed glasshouse cultivation can reduce levels of carbon dioxide, so many commercial growers burn propane gas in glasshouses to take carbon dioxide levels as high as 0.1 per cent, increasing the efficiency of photosynthesis.

Water is essential, providing hydrogen for conversion into sugars. Almost as important is the role it plays in letting carbon dioxide into the plant, as the stomata will close on plants when cells are just 10 per cent below their optimum turgidity (*see p.48*). This prevents carbon dioxide from entering the leaf and cuts photosynthetic efficiency by up to half. Once a plant shows signs of wilting, photosynthesis halts.

Sunlight provides the energy necessary to turn these two substances into glucose sugars. The amount of light needed varies from species to species and also from young, efficient leaves to older inefficient leaves. It is measured in units called lux, with a well-lit room like an office typically measuring about 400 lux. Shade-loving species such as yew (*Taxus*), mahonia, and ivy (*Hedera*)

Spiral growth (inset) and leaf mosaic
The importance of light can be seen by the
way plants arrange their leaves to capture
every ray, but always seek to avoid shading
their own leaves with overlapping growth.

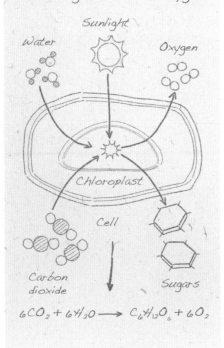

Photosynthesis

Carbon dioxide and water become glucose and oxygen.

Sunlight

Water

Oxygen

Chloroplast

Cell

Carbon dioxide

Sugars

$$6CO_2 + 6H_2O \longrightarrow C_6H_{12}O_6 + 6O_2$$

require only 1000 lux, while the vast majority of sun-loving temperate garden plants require up to 30,000 lux, and tropical sun addicts can absorb around 50,000 lux. Winter light levels in the United Kingdom are 3,000–8,000 lux, so it is not surprising that plant growth slows or stops in these conditions. During winter, keep glasshouses clean of dust, algae, and debris, as research shows that even moderately smeared windows can reduce light levels by several hundred lux.

Commercial growers often supplement natural light, and levels can be boosted in domestic glasshouses to extend the season. Take care when reaching for artificial back-up, however, because the wavelength of the light is critical. Plants use blue or red spectrum light, available from high-pressure sodium lamps and white (colour 29) fluorescent tubes; tungsten bulbs emit a high level of less useful green light, resulting in leggy growth.

Temperature is vital for efficient photosynthesis. The enzymes that accelerate the rate of chemical reactions within the plant are present from 0°C (32°F), but they increase activity in line with temperature and are at their optimum at 25–36°C (77–97°F). Beyond 40°C (104°F) photosynthesis halts in most plants.

From food back into energy

Respiration is the process by which plants break down foods to produce the energy for all their needs. The process is the exact reverse of photosynthesis: glucose and oxygen become carbon dioxide and water, releasing energy. Compare the equation for photosynthesis opposite with that for respiration, and it becomes clear just how intertwined these two processes are.

$$C_6H_{12}O_6 + 6O_2 = 6CO_2 + 6H_2O + Energy$$

The principle difference between the two is that while photosynthesis is largely confined to chloroplasts in the leaf, respiration takes place in the cells in all living tissues, all the time. It occurs most in areas of rapid cell division, such as meristems (*see p.51*), germinating seeds, and rhizomes, bulbs, or corms that are bursting into life, where respiration can be twice as fast as it is in the leaf.

Of course, in theory photosynthesis and respiration balance each other out, with the plant releasing sufficient oxygen in photosynthesis to fuel respiration. However, oxygen is used by most living things, from humans to the soil organisms breaking down organic matter, and in all combustion and oxidisation processes. These additional uses release carbon dioxide into the atmosphere, and so add to the global greenhouse effect.

Storing for the future

At peak production, photosynthesis generates more sucrose than can be used. The surplus is converted into starch and stored in stems, roots, and other storage organs (*see p.60*). The more extreme the seasonal variation a plant experiences, the more critical this process is, as an unsuccessful growing season inevitably results in a shortfall of stored energy to start the spring flush; this is why plants that struggle one year often also underperform in the next.

A good example of gardeners creating problems for the future can be seen when the spring bulbs have faded after a season of joyful colour, and impatient gardeners show their gratitude by trimming off the leaves or, as my childhood neighbours used to do, tying them in knots. This cuts off the sucrose factory from the bulb, and the plant fails to flower the next year, opting instead for foliage growth to redress the shortfalls. My neighbours' bulbs always flowered, but only because I would sneak in to untie the leaves on my way home at night. I still can't walk past contorted bulb foliage without feeling that I should help.

Kept in the shade
Low levels of light beneath woodland canopies mean plants in the understorey have to work on less light or grow before the tall trees leaf out.

Getting the light right
Commecial growers in Japan have succeeded in producing lettuce from seed to standard supermarket size in just six weeks (half the usual time) under banks of red LEDs.

FLOWER POWER

Nothing quite surpasses the tremendous sense of anticipation that comes from growing flowering plants. Such breathtaking beauty and poise evoke strong emotional responses in all generations. It is easy to become lost in the romance and drama of a flower, but next time you gaze into the porcelain trumpet of a lily, or are captivated by the unfurling petals of a rose, remember that as far as the plant is concerned, its flower is no more than a huge advertising hoarding for the reproductive system. At the risk of shocking sentimental gardeners, the flower exists only to be pollinated and create seeds.

Spores before seeds

It would be a mistake to suggest that all plants reproduce by way of flowers, as there are dozens that adopt an alternative strategy. This "choice" is largely a result of evolution and habitat conditions, and the true breadth of reproductive techniques are demonstrated by the primitive plants such as mosses, liverworts, and ferns. These evolved in habitats rich in water, up to 440 million years ago, before there were insects that could aid pollination. Taking advantage of this,

Moss spores
The spores released from the capsules of mosses or the brown patches on fern fronds are single-celled plants in waiitng.

Moss with spore capsules

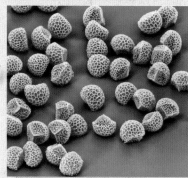

Stag's horn clubmoss spores

Clubmoss spore capsule

they reproduce by releasing spores that are are dispersed widely on wind and water. Each minute, dusty brown "seed" is in fact a single cell, which grows through numerous phases of division into the soft green cushion of a moss or, in the case of ferns, a tiny, short-lived heart-shaped structure. Reproductive cells swim together on these structures to produce the little capsule structure lifted above the cushion, or the familiar fern plant. This generation in turn releases spores, starting the cycle again.

The first flowers

About 350 million years ago the first of the "higher" or flowering plants evolved (*see p.14*); these were the gymnosperms, such as conifers. In these, distinct cone-like flowers form as adaptations of short branches with specially modified leaves. In these cones the cells of reproduction are created. These are male (pollen) and female (eggs), each carrying half of the chromosomes of the parent (*see pp.116–17*). This development is a challenge: separate adaptations are necessary to produce the male and female components, and a way of uniting the two also has to be found. In the gymnosperms the solution was wind, and the pollen is released in the breeze to drift and land on a female flower.

Until 140 million years ago this was the most sophisticated process available; then the angiosperms developed, with their glamorous, often insect-pollinated, blooms. Darwin called this shift an "abominable mystery" because he failed to see the leaps in evolution; these are hard to discern from the fossil records, because soft flower tissues are rarely preserved. Only in the last few years has a feasible and cautiously accepted theory been put forward that angiosperms evolved from an unremarkable shrub known as *Amborella*, now only found on scattered islands in the South Pacific. From this tentative start, continued adaptation of modified leaves around a stem has given us an estimated 400,000 angiosperm species, each with distinctive floral characteristics.

Early flowering
The magnolia family is one of the oldest among the angiosperms, with fossils dating back 95 million years.

Although the intricate details of flower placement and construction seem initially to be of interest only to botanists, it is easy to identify similarities between the blooms of species and from these determine both their family and their likely cultivation preferences.

Young cones
Female cones are soft and often flushed with colour when young, as in this larch (Larix), becoming woody as the seeds ripen in them.

Look closer

Even the most ubiquitous of blooms, when viewed closely, possesses great charm. Take the button-like blooms of the lawn daisy (Bellis perennis), whose habit of opening at sunrise and closing with sunset give the common name of "day's eye". As a child, it struck me as a huge injustice that its reward for determined survival was to be called a weed and be regularly beheaded by my father's mower. If it were a rarity, surely we would celebrate its bloom.

Cone structure

The reproductive process in conifers relies on the production of two separate types of cone. The male, or pollen, cone is a tassel-like structure that houses the developing pollen between scaly adapted leaves; it is generally small and quite easily overlooked. The flexibility of this pollen cone allows distribution of its cargo into the breeze, and once empty it generally falls from the tree. The other cone is the female or seed cone, a corky appendage composed of layers within which are carried the ovules. These are the familiar structures we pick up on woodland walks, and often persist on the tree for more than one season, distributing the seed with wings to aid relocation (*see p.106*).

Flower structure

The flower of an angiosperm is carried on a stalk, or pedicel, that is loosely connected to the stem. Like a leaf petiole, this has an abscission layer (*see p.78*) where it joins the stem, which allows the flower to be jettisoned once flowering and fruiting is complete, or in times of stress. Premature fall of flowers is typically seen on crops like tomatoes and cucumbers stressed by infrequent watering, which sacrifice flowers in favour of keeping the main plant hydrated. Just as in the leaf or stem, the pedicel carries the transportation network of vascular bundles to all parts of the living tissue. At the tip of the pedicel is the receptacle, a broadening of tissues with an apical meristem (*see p.51*) in which the parts of the flower develop in a distinctive whorl.

The entire developing meristem is encased in a protective layer of leaf-like structures called sepals, which form the bud. Take a close look at a large bud like that of the horse chestnut (*Aesculus*) and you will see the multiple layers of sepals creating a diamond pattern. Often the cells of these thickened sepals contain chloroplasts and can photosynthesise (*see pp.80–82*) in the early stages of their development. It is also thought that the green coloration offers a degree of camouflage from insects and particularly birds, such as bullfinches, that peck the buds in search of the nutritious developing embryo. The complete whorl of sepals is referred to as the calyx, which means covering; this may be retained once the flower is open, as it is in the rose, or shed, as it is in the magnolia. The large, downy, grey sepals of magnolia, almost triangular in shape, nearly caused a riot at an arboretum I was visiting, as an elderly couple saw what they thought were severed cats ears on the ground and complained bitterly to the curator, whom they wanted to report for cruelty to animals.

The next ring of modified leaves is the petals. These are typically the most glamorous and showy part of the structure, and may be either a simple ring or modified to form tubes, funnels, bells, and so on. They are the advertisement, designed to announce the presence and ripeness of the flower to potential pollinators. Nothing is ever straightforward, especially when it comes to flowering plants, and some flowers have no clear layers of sepals, only thickened petals called tepals, as in tulips, which gradually change from green in bud to adopt the colour of the flower once opened. Other plants produce "incomplete" flowers that have only sepals and no petals, like those of Persian ironwood (*Parrotia persica*).

The very centre of the flower contains the reproductive parts. The female parts form a single slender growth collectively called the pistil. At its base is the ovary, which ultimately forms part of the fruit and contains ovules that become seeds. On top of the ovary sits the style, a lengthy column that extends to place the stigma, a sticky anvil on which the pollen grain is gathered, in a suitable position. The male parts are collectively referred to as the stamens. These consist of the filaments, which perform much the same role as the female style, often arching or curving to place the pollen-bearing tips, or anthers, where they can touch a pollinator.

Brazen bloom
The lily (Lilium) shows off its reproductve parts, with bright orange pollen-bearing anthers held on filaments around the central style and stigma.

Prime advertising sites

To minimise resources and maximise exposure, many plants carry clusters or inflorescences that may contain hundreds of flowers. These are the distinctive spires, towers, and domes of blooms that grace the garden. The simplest form is a spike, in which individual flowers, each carried on a reduced pedicel,

Strength in numbers
Both the tall spikes of the liatris and the flat heads of the achillea (inset) group many small, relatively insignificant flowers together to achieve greater impact.

are packed around a modified stem to create a tight spire, as in liatris. A stem on which the flowers are carried on longer pedicels is a raceme, seen upright in eremurus and many grasses, or pendulous in wisteria. A stem that branches to allow several flowers to bloom in succession is referred to as a panicle, such as in phygelius. Taking a quite different form, short stems may spread from the tip of a stem to produce a characteristic flat-headed umbel, as in achillea. Perhaps most complex of all are the daisy family, which cluster fertile but petaless blooms tightly together in a dome or disc, with only the outer, often sterile, flowers producing a circle of "petals"; these are known as composite flowers and typical of this style is the sunflower (*Helianthus*).

The arrangement of the bloom is largely down to evolution, but there seems to be a close relationship between the flower location and pollination tactics. The flowers of aspidistras are carried at soil level to catch the attention of the ground-dwelling creatures that pollinate them, while wind-pollinated plants hold their flowers aloft. Foxgloves (*Digitalis*) carry a spike of blooms each broad enough to admit to bumble bees, and flat-headed umbels appeal to insects that might find access to small individual blooms difficult. With a little observation, you can pick your plants to suit your wildlife *(see p.230)*.

"For me, the flower is evidence that in nature, function and beauty are quite inextricably intertwined."

Sun lovers
Most gardeners would like to brighten their shady corners with flowers, but colourful Insect-pollinated plants like this rose put on their best display in the sun, because that is where the insects are.

PICKING POLLINATORS

The chosen pollinator of a plant shapes the design of its flowers. Flowers of wind-pollinated plants, such as many trees and grasses, are generally far less showy than those of the large-blooming insect-pollinated plants. Rather than producing bright petals and fragrance, they rely on the massive release of pollen into the wind, so their flowers are like miniature wind chimes that dance in the breeze. Blooms pollinated by animals are not only flashier, to attract their clients, but also sturdier, because they must be strong enough to support pollinators, and tough enough to withstand their probing.

Plentiful pollen
Shake the bough of a birch (Betula) in full flower, and your hair instantly turns blonde with the quantity of pollen.

Wind pollination

Dull in colour, odourless, and primitive is how the botanists of the late 1800s saw wind-pollinated plants in comparison with the flowers of the insect-pollinated species. Individual flowers might be insignificant, in fact they are stripped to the bare minimum of components, but collectively the inflorescence can be a striking feature. It is true that in evolutionary terms, early plants like the gymnosperms (*see p.85*) and cycads rely on the wind, but the grasses and many trees that also use use wind pollination, such as beech (*Fagus*), oak (*Quercus*), birch (*Betula*), and hazel (*Corylus*), are far from primitive, having evolved after the glamorous petal-producing plants.

Most wind-pollinated trees occur in temperate zones, and their pollen is released prior to the leaves forming, allowing maximum dispersal at a time of year when insect activity is low. As there is no reliance on insects to transport pollen, the plants don't waste valuable energy in nectar production, but instead invest in massive pollen production. This is a risky and energy-sapping business, due to the quantity of pollen that is required to ensure successful pollination. Wind-dispersed pollen is light and does not stick together, and as a result travels freely on the gentlest breeze. The flowers have protruding anthers, and feathery stigmas with a large surface area to catch pollen grains. They exude a sticky sap through the micropyle, the minute hole through which the pollen grain must enter the ovule (*see pp.102–103*). This sap moistens the surface of the stigma to ensure that it captures the drifting pollen grains.

Serious specialists

Individual grass flowers are particularly specialized. They are encased, sometimes singly, sometimes in clusters, in bracts called glumes, which often carry long hairs known as awn. It is usually panicles (*see p.89*) of these glumes and awn that we think of as the flower of a grass and value for their glow in the autumn sunshine. Within the glumes are two further bract-like structures, the large outer lemma and the small inner palea, which encase the developing flower or floret. The floret opens to reveal first three male stamens – flower parts in all monocots are in multiples of three – which are often like dried and curled strips of flypaper, spinning and flicking in the breeze to release their pollen. Once pollen is released, the stamens are withdrawn and the stigma and ovary are exposed instead.

But perhaps the most peculiar of all pollination processes is completed by some submerged aquatic species, such as the tape grass (*Vallisneria spiralis*). The male flowers of this species are carried on long, lithe stems and produce erect stamens, which act as sails, moving the bloom towards the larger female flower. The mass of the female flower is enough to create a depression in the surface tension of the water, so capturing the passing male and enabling pollination.

Visiting insects

Nutrient-rich sap released to moisten the stigma in gymnosperms like the cycads first attracted insects to the plants. While grazing on other flower parts and pollen they harvested the sap, and on moving from one plant to another, they inadvertently transferred the pollen on their bodies. As a result they transformed the way in which some plants opt to distribute their pollen. This was the

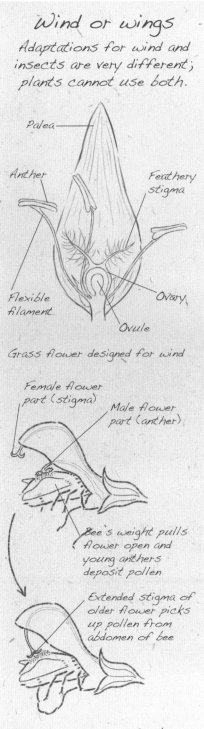

Wind or wings
Adaptations for wind and insects are very different; plants cannot use both.

Palea
Anther
Feathery stigma
Flexible filament
Ovary
Ovule

Grass flower designed for wind

Female flower part (stigma)
Male flower part (anther)
Bee's weight pulls flower open and young anthers deposit pollen
Extended stigma of older flower picks up pollen from abdomen of bee

Salvia flower designed for bees

Planting distances

Although some wind-dispersed pollen grains will travel vast distances from their source, most are deposited within about 100m (109 yards) of the parent plant. In contrast, insect-pollinated plants can often cross-pollinate over several kilometres, as insects like bees will range widely when foraging. This is why wind-pollinated crops, such as sweetcorn (Zea mays), should be planted in blocks for the very best pollen exchange between plants, but you needn't go to great trouble to place two apple or pear trees directly next to one another in the garden.

evolutionary start of a close relationship between insects and flowers, and also the critical opportunity for the development of the angiosperms (see p.85). Insect pollination is a more efficient system than passive wind pollination, as fewer pollen grains are required, and over time a number of modifications took place in the flower to make it more attractive to insects (see pp.95–99). The development of concealed ovules, which are characteristic of angiosperms, prevented grazing insects from eating them, while flowers with both male and female parts allow pollen to be deposited and collected in one stop.

What it is essential to remember, as you browse the garden squirting insects with chemicals to prevent them damaging the blooms, is that these insects are the very reason such diversity of showgirl flowers are present. For about 100 million years the two have lived an ever more interdependent life, the flourishing of the angiosperms perfectly matching the flourishing of insects, with ever more complex and precise adaptations evolving.

Busy bees

Bees are by far the most important group of pollinators. In the 80 million years or so of this relationship, they have developed fused mouthparts that suck nectar; bristles on their legs, known as a pollen comb, to force pollen into baskets at the top of the leg; and bristles on the back of the abdomen that collect pollen. They prefer blue, white, yellow, and violet flowers, mostly with "honey guides", either ultraviolet (see p.96) or visible (see p.98). Some limit their visits to specific flowers, one reason why diverse planting is key; this dependence has led to adaptations such as long-tongued bee species that favour the deep flowers of the foxglove family and short-tongued bees that prefer the flat heads of the composite blooms (see p.89). Nectaries tend to be set deep in the flower, allowing access only to the bees. Flowers pollinated by larger bees, such as the bumble bee, have protruding lower petals to act as a landing platform, as in salvia flowers. The bee's weight opens the bloom and triggers pollination (see p.91).

Perfectly formed
The shape of a flower is tailored to its most preferred pollinator. A broad-winged butterfly cannot enter a foxglove (*Digitalis*, inset), but its long tongue is perfect for scabious.

Butterflies and beetles

Blooms that co-evolved with butterflies and daytime moths tend to have long, tubular flowers suited to the insects' coiled tongue – good examples are hebe, stachys, and buddleja species. These insects are attracted by a combination of sight and smell, so expect rich fragrances and yellow, blue, purple, and pink hues, although some appear able to see reds and oranges too. Honeysuckle (*Lonicera*), evening primrose (*Oenothera*), and nicotiana are typical nocturnal moth-pollinated flowers, with pastel colours and lingering evening fragrance.

Beetle-pollinated plants tend to adopt two strategies, being either large, solitary affairs such as magnolias, lilies (*Lilium*), roses, and eschscholzia, or small flowers in umbels, panicles, or composite forms (*see p.89*) such as spiraea, dogwoods (*Cornus*), and fennel (*Foeniculum*). Although beetles gain food from other sources, they are frequent visitors and have an acute sense of smell rather than good vision, responding to fruity and spicy fragrances. Typically they chew petals and pollen as well as taking nectar, so plants welcoming them tend to hide their ovules well back in the flower, away from munching jaws.

Birds and bats

Bird-pollinated flowers such as hibiscus, poinsettia, and strelitzia produce little fragrance, as birds' sense of smell is not finely developed. Instead they shine in bright colours, usually oranges and reds that appeal to the birds' red-bias sight. They also produce large reserves of concentrated nectar to replenish the energy the birds expend while visiting the flower, a very different approach from insect-pollinated flowers, which provide dilute nectar in modest amounts.

About a quarter of the worlds' bat species feed off pollen and nectar from plants like passionflower (*Passiflora*), mango (*Mangifera*), banana (*Musa*), and many bromeliads and cacti. Like the bird-pollinated blooms, these are robust, to prevent the weight of the pollinator causing damage, but to attract these keen-nosed nocturnal flyers the colours are pastel shades that shine out in low light, and the fragrance is very high, usually fruity or musky. The flowers also stand well clear of the leaf, tending to hang down from the branches or trunks.

Grown in gardens beyond their native range and far from their natural allies, these plants will still often be pollinated by experimental local wildlife; most flowers have something to appeal to more than one passing pollinator.

"Given the purely utilitarian designs of flowers, it is interesting to consider what a flower designed and created by humans would look like."

OFFERING INCENTIVES

The critical adaptations of plants to attract pollinators included the development of modified leaves that we now know as the petals to announce the rewards on offer, and floral nectaries to provide a fast-food outlet. Having made these basic adaptations, flowers have developed a wide array of advertising strategies to lure pollinators to their flowers in preference to others, and reward their visitors once they arrive. Different tactics are needed to attract diverse pollinators, and it is illuminating to look deeper into the mechanisms behind these inducements.

Flying colours

Perhaps most obvious in flowers is the range and combinations of colours in the petals. These are designed to act as beacons to attract the attention and entice potential pollinators. Colours are visible because pigments in the plant reflect that part of the spectrum, so a delphinium appears blue due to a pigment in the petals that absorbs all parts of the spectrum except blue, which is reflected. All flower colours are produced by a small number of pigments, which are present in all vascular plants but occur in large quantities in angiosperms.

The pigments fall into three main categories: the green-reflecting pigments of chlorophyll; xanthophylls and carotenes that show as yellow and orange; and flavonoids that block harmful ultraviolet (UV) radiation (*see pp.144–45*) but selectively admit blue-green and red light for photosynthesis (*see pp.80–83*). Other pigments include betacyanins, fragrant compounds that shows as a deep red in the beet family and as a cerise pink in bougainvillea. All petal colours are provided by subtle combinations of these pigments, governed by changes in cellular pH and in the structural elements of the flower. The same compounds come into play as fruit ripens and autumn colour washes through the leaves of many deciduous plants.

Brash bracts
These brightly coloured "petals" are modified leaves called bracts: the true flowers are clustered in the green centre.

For their eyes only

The colour seen by gardeners isn't necessarily the colour seen by the pollinator: bees are known to be attracted to, and can therefore presumably experience, colours beyond the human eye in the far blue spectrum, but they cannot see reds. Bats and moths are thought to respond to pale hues and white, while birds are thought to view into the far-red spectrum and are attracted to reds, but also to vivid contrasts.

Several pigments, such as flavonol and carotene, reflect UV light. In the cuticle of plants growing in high sunlight they play a protective role, but they also often form elaborate patterns that act as runway landing lights to insects, indicating where to set down, and in which direction the pollen and nectar are to be found (*see panel below*).

Sweetening the deal

Although rarely written about, the consumption of pollen itself by pollinating insects, beetles, and even bats is commonplace and acts as a vital food source. It is never a complete food, and foraging bees, for example, also need sugar-rich nectar, but it adds protein to their diet. These proteins, incidentally, are one reason why pollen causes hayfever allergies in people.

Nectar, the main reward for pollinators, is often considered to be a simple sugary solution designed purely to entice pollinating insects to the flowers,

Unseen petal patterns
Invisible to our eye, the patterns seen by insects become apparent when a flower is photographed using special ultraviolet film.

Daisy family

Dandelion (Taraxacum)

Evening primrose (Oenothera)

but research suggests that plants evolved nectaries prior to flowers, possibly to dispose of excess fluid and sugars at times of high photosynthetic activity. Over 2,000 species of plants have nectaries outside the flower, including members of the rose, willow, mallow, and daisy families. These extra-floral nectaries are usually on the leaf petiole or lamina (*see p. 74*), and are, for example, the familiar purple spots on broad bean foliage. Here, nectar released by modified trichomes, or hairs, is often gathered by beneficial insects such as ladybirds and ants that also eat pests (*see pp. 220–21*).

Floral nectaries, recessed in the bloom at the base of the petals and stamens, are similar in construction. They are linked to the vascular tissues and surrounded by cells that fill the nectar with sucrose, glucose, and fructose, amino acids, vitamins, protein, minerals, and antioxidants. This is what made the tubular flowers of deadnettle (*Lamium*) that we picked from the hedgerows as children taste so sweet when sucked. Secreted nectar either remains on the nectaries for insects to collect or drips onto flower parts, as in aquilegias, where its evaporation attracts insects.

Nectar drops
Turn up the flower of a crown imperial (Fritillaria imperialis) *and you will see glistening drops of clear liquid poised on the white nectaries.*

Catering to all tastes

Different type of nectar appeal to specific insects, with sucrose solutions being favoured by long-tongued insects, such as butterflies, moths, and some bees, while fructose and glucose are high in plants pollinated by short-tongued bees and flies. As a general rule, plants pollinated by long-tongued insects have watery nectar, to allow easy uptake through long mouth parts, while thick nectar, which insects often have to chew, is produced by exposed nectaries. Intriguingly, the concentration of sugars in some nectar is so high that it ferments, producing a heady sap that intoxicates the visiting insects. In some species of lime (*Tilia*) and *Aesculus*, alcohol concentrations can reach 50 per cent, causing bees to literally fall out of the trees drunk – so sunbathing close to a flowering lime isn't a good idea.

It is also thought that plants might use the nectar to dissuade pollinators: there is little benefit to the plant in being visited by insects once it has been pollinated, so pollen grains fall into the nectaries of some flowers as they age and create a sour solution that persuades insects to go elsewhere.

Guide lines
The streaks in the throat of a penstemon
or the whiskers on the face of pansies and
other violas (inset) guide insects to the pollen
and nectar at the heart of the flower.

Protecting the assets

Nectar production varies between plant species, but appears to be stimulated by light, temperature, and moisture levels, and aimed at guiding the right pollinator to the plant. It is a costly business, as almost 40 per cent of a plant's photosynthetic activity can be directed into nectar production. With so much at stake, it is vital for plants to time their flowering and nectar production to the optimum moment.

This is why rising spring temperatures trigger the start of the flowering season, with most of our insect-pollinated plants blooming in the warmer months, when their customers are plentiful. A few flower in winter, like sarcococca and hamamelis: this might at first seem a poor strategy, but there are always a few insects around and the flowers that open earliest will have less competition, so the investment pays off often enough for these plants to have succeeded. Winter flowers have strong scents that carry well, to alert the few insects around to their presence.

Even when the general conditions are right, passing weather conditions can lower the chances of success. Most pollen is very robust, but if damp it can be attacked by moulds and also may not be so easily transferred onto a pollinator. Some flowers, such as osteospermums, are notorious for slamming their petals shut at dusk and even on cool, dull days, a response that protects their pollen from night condensation and rain. Others, like African hemp (*Sparmannia*), hang their flowers upside down, the brush of stamens protected by an umbrella of petals. This flower has another trick up its sleeve: if stroked, the stamens will gently fan out to give the insect that appears to have landed better access.

In fact, many plants adjust the arrangement of their anthers or stigma when touched to improve pollination, but few are so visible. Usually they make a one-off change from presenting the anthers prominently to pushing the stigma into a favourable position. Perhaps the most dramatic of all are trigger plants (*Stylidium*), which take their name from their habit of flicking pollen onto insects from a "trigger", a fused style and stamen.

Acid colours

One of the flavonoid pigments, called anthocyanin, is largely responsible for determining flower colour in the red and blue spectrum, and is pH-dependent. If the plant sap is alkaline, anthocyanin turns blue, while acidic sap creates a pink or red colour. This pH dependency is responsible for several cultivars of hydrangea changing from blue to pink in alkaline soils. My grandmother periodically threw a handful of nails under her hydrangea plants, as the iron released from the corroding nails adjusts the chemical composition of the soil, simulating the high iron availability of acidic soil and turning the florets blue. Another gardener I know diligently saves all their tea leaves, throwing them into a water butt and using the resulting "tea" to water their plants, as it will similarly release iron and aluminium.

PRECISION POLLINATION

Once flowers are produced and the season is progressing the urgency for them to become pollinated becomes clear. The pollen grain is, like a seed, designed to withstand environmental stress, often lasting several years before breaking down, but it must land on the stigma of a suitable female flower to finally fulfil its purpose. Ensuring the right pollen gains access to the right ovules is a further feat of engineering, and only after passing a strict entry examination can the pollination process be successfully completed.

"All the efforts made by plants to cast their pollen onto the wind or deposit it on a pollinator will be wasted if it does not find the right female flower."

Identifying pollen

The shape and pattern of pollen grains can used to identify the parent plant several million years after the plant was fossilized. The dense, fatty outer wall is often highly etched and sometimes flushed with colour. It is as distinctive in plants as fingerprints are in humans, so much so that bee keepers know which plants that their bees visiting simply by examining the pollen in the hive. The reason for this is that it is essential that a plant doesn't make a false start by responding to alien pollen. Plants can generally only cross-pollinate

Pollen design
Pollen carried on the wind is smooth – literally aerodynamic – while that carried by animals is barbed to help it stick to them.

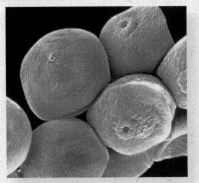

Grass pollen

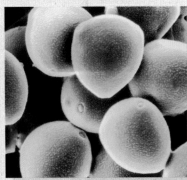

Hazel (Corylus) pollen

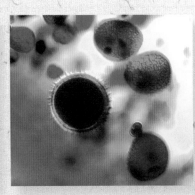

Adhesive pollen for insects

others of the same species, and each has devised a chemical map on the surface of its pollen grains to help identification. Pollen from incompatible species is blocked, while that of the correct species is allowed to proceed to pollination.

Avoiding self-pollination

Flowers also need a mechanism to avoid being pollinated by their own pollen, as this would defeat the object of flowering, which is to mix genes (*see pp.116–17*). Plants adopt different strategies to encourage cross-pollination and prevent self-pollination. A grass might unfurl its bracts to release and gather pollen repeatedly (*see p.91*), and its pollen grains also contain antigens to prevent self-fertilization; these antigens are thought to be irritants that contribute to hay fever, so any sufferers should steer clear of flowering grasses in their gardens.

Ovary and anthers may also ripen in a set sequence (*see p.91*), as in cherries and plums (*Prunus*), which are moderately self-fertile but fruit best if two different cultivars are grown. In apples (*Malus*) and pears (*Pyrus*) the stigma suppresses the progress of pollen that matches its own genetic profile, so cultivars of these fruits are best pollinated by another cultivar that flowers at exactly the same time – which is why the pollination groupings so often referred to in planting guides really do matter.

Gender separation

In extreme cases, such as conifers, holly (*Ilex*) or sea buckthorn (*Hippophae rhamnoides*), plants are "sexed" and produce either male or female flowers. These plants are called dioecious, and usually the male flowers are less showy and elaborate structures. Growing these plants for their fruits requires identifying their gender, which is not always an easy process: the holly cultivars 'Golden Queen' and 'Silver Queen' are male, while 'Golden King' is female. Sea buckthorn doesn't suffer the indignity of inappropriate names, as all the plants are sold as the species.

Pollinated pips

Should you be tempted to grow the pips of your favourite apples, you would have a long wait and a disappointing result. Most domesticated fruit trees will not "come true" from seed because of the genetic mixing during pollination. Oranges however, can be grown from the pips in your fruit, because they have some specialized cells in each ovule besides the egg, that can develop without being fertilized. One orange pip may produce several seedlings: as a rule, the most vigorous will be cross-pollinated and variable, the weakest will fail, but the ones showing middling growth may well be natural clones of the parent and worth growing on.

Sexing young plants is tricky unless you have both types in front of you, so it is best to make sure several are planted: one male plant in or near your garden will usually provide for fruit on several females. Unless you want a particular cultivar, also check that your supplier is propagating from seed, and not cuttings (*see pp.38–39*); the former will produce mixed plants while the latter will produce a clone of the same sex as the parent. Some plants bear male and female flowers on different parts of the plant, usually in sequence to avoid self-pollination. These plants, called monoecious, include walnuts (*Juglans*) and hazel (*Corylus*), and also curcurbits like cucumbers and courgettes, in which production of male flowers is usually linked to high temperatures.

Occasionally flowers will accept their own pollen. This can be the result of artificial breeding programmes, or simply a last ditch attempt to salvage something from the flowering process; some foxglove species allow pollen to enter the ovary of the same flower when chemical inhibitors are switched off prior to petal loss. This is a high-risk strategy, as without fresh genetic material the offspring may be less vigorous, but producing some offspring that may find other pollinators when their turn to flower comes is better than nothing.

Fruitless flowers
Skimmias have male and female plants: this male cultivar, 'Rubella', is grown for its abundant winter buds, but will never bear fruits.

The pollination process

Simplistically, we often think that pollen "meets" eggs and fertilizes them to form seeds. In fact, each grain of pollen is like a Russian doll: the tough outer layers enclose one cell, and inside this is a second, smaller cell. When pollen lands on the stigma, a variety of factors provoke it to germinate, springing into growth like a seed. The grain absorbs water and swells, pushing out the cell membrane and cytoplasm (*see pp.48–49*) through an opening in the wall.

The larger, outer cell now grows into a tube, burrowing down through the style to the ovules thet hold the eggs. The cells of the style produce substances called adhesins that help the tube to stick to their surfaces and extend its length. There are many things still not understood about this process: nobody knows, for example, why no two pollen tubes ever head for the same ovule.

Inside the tube, the second cell ripens to form two sperm. These move down the tube as it extends, always close to the tip. When they enter the ovule, one fertilizes the egg and the other merges with another cell in the ovule to become tissue that nourishes the embryo plant in the seed (*see p.12*). All is now in place for the development of the seed and any fruit that surrounds it.

Pollination of a poppy

Pollination begins when pollen lands on the stigma of a compatible flower, and is complete when the pollen tube grows into an ovule and the sperm unites with the egg cell inside. This triggers the start of fruiting.

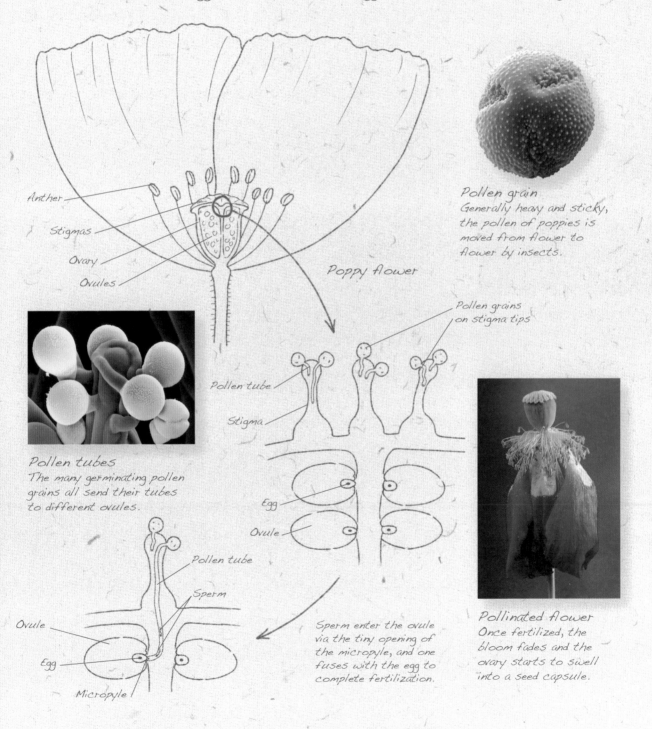

Anther

Stigmas

Ovary

Ovules

Poppy flower

Pollen grain
Generally heavy and sticky, the pollen of poppies is moved from flower to flower by insects.

Pollen tubes
The many germinating pollen grains all send their tubes to different ovules.

Pollen grains on stigma tips

Pollen tube

Stigma

Egg

Ovule

Pollen tube

Sperm

Ovule

Egg

Micropyle

Sperm enter the ovule via the tiny opening of the micropyle, and one fuses with the egg to complete fertilization.

Pollinated flower
Once fertilized, the bloom fades and the ovary starts to swell into a seed capsule.

COMING TO FRUITION

Once an egg is fertilized, the parent plant devotes considerable resources to ensuring that it ripens and is dispersed with the maximum chances of success. While ripening is broadly the same process in all plants, the results range from the juicy contents of the fruit bowl at home to the dry, inflated capsules of nigella. This wide diversity of forms reflects an equally broad range of seed dispersal methods. Just like pollen, fruits are carried by wind, water, and animals, and again each method influences the design of the fruit.

Constant cropping
If you want runner beans all summer long, keep picking throughout the season. Once any pods ripen, the plants will stop producing more.

The end of flowering

The first effect that developing fruit has is on flowering. Flowers require a huge investment or energy, with as much as 60 per cent of the total energy of some plants being targeted at the flowers. No plant can afford to sustain such high energy outgoings unless in full health or when the flowers are no longer needed. Once seed production starts, hormones significantly suppress the production of further flowers and the plant's energy is concentrated on seed development instead. Dead-heading, the practice of picking flowers off as soon as the withering of the petals indicates the end of flowering and start of seed

Fruit development

Cytokinin produced by the developing ovule promote the inward flow of nutrients from the plant for storage in the seed. It also stimulates cell division and thickening in the ovary wall.

Cytokinin

Next the seed produces gibberellin and auxin. These are cell enlargement hormones that promote development of the fleshy fruit as the ovary wall cells enlarge and mature.

Gibberellin and auxin

production, prevents release of flower-inhibiting hormones and forces the plant to continue flowering freely. There are exceptions, including F1 hybrid impatiens and begonia cultivars that have been bred to form seedless fruit and keep flowering, but for most plants deadheading is a worthwhile activity.

Fruit development

Fruit means not just the fleshy types like apples, or pods familiar to us from peas and beans; even the seeds of flowers in the daisy family are enclosed in a dry, tough wall. It is the defining characteristic of angiosperms (*see p.14*), and the only seeds not enclosed in a fruit are those of gymnosperms like conifers.

A fruit is basically the ovary of the flower, which houses the fertilized ovules (*see pp.102–103*). As the ovules develop into seeds, the ovary swells and takes on its mature form. The development is controlled by a series of hormonal messages (*see pp.112–115*) crossing back and forth from the embryo within the developing seed and the parent plant. The developing embryo produces hormones that promote the flow of nutrients into the developing seed, the expansion and thickening of the ovary wall, and the production of carbohydrate-rich flesh (*see panel below*). Because the flesh will only swell around or near a ripening seed, poor pollination can result in corn cobs with empty spaces among the kernels and some bizarrely misshapen strawberries. Once the seed is ready, the plant produces hormones to trigger the shedding of the ripe fruit and keep the seed dormant until it has left the plant and found itself in suitable conditions to germinate (*see pp.23–27*).

"Gardeners who dead-head their plants to prolong flowering exploit the willingness and enthusiasm of the plant to set seed."

Abscisic acid

Abscisic acid produced by the plant is transported into the fruit. This hormone helps to keep the ripe seed dormant, preventing it from germinating too early.

Ethylene

Ethylene, produced in most tissues of the plant and fruit, causes fruit to ripen and be shed. The fruit changes colour and begins to smell attractive, its flesh softens and becomes sweet and juicy, and it drops off the plant.

Coping with excess

Some species self-regulate the investment in flowers and fruit. The irregular production of beech (*Fagus*) mast and biennial cropping of many fruit trees and even grapes (*Vitis*), is due to the plant responding to unusually heavy

Thinking ahead
An abundant fruit crop might seem cause to celebrate, but to ensure a good harvest the following year, reduce the strain on the tree by thinning.

crops in one season by becoming shy of flowers the next. This process is governed by hormones released from the ripening fruit that are returned, via the phloem into the stem tissue (*see p.68*) where they suppress the development of flower buds. It is popular practice amongst commercial growers, and advisable for those growing fruit at home, to thin fruit to moderate levels from early to midsummer, as this will create reliable annual crops rather than feast and famine. Some species are capable of performing this themselves, particularly stone fruit such as peaches, plums, and apricots (*Prunus*).

These perform what is termed "June drop", a self-thinning exercise of immature fruit, which is why you can leave thinning these plants till after midsummer.

Rather different is the case of trees, usually fruiting, that produce a bumper crop in one season and then die the next; I have lost count of the number of times I have been asked to advise on the reason. The simple answer to this lies in the fact that the plant, sensing it was under threat, usually after years of neglect or deteriorating health, opted to make the ultimate horticultural sacrifice and push all its energies into flowering and fruiting, to the point where it was unable to function adequately the following season and so died. This shows the importance of seed production to the success of the species.

Passive passengers

The first requirement for fruits distributed by the elements is that they should be light, to help them travel. The familiar parachutes of the dandelion "clock" are some of the most distinctive seeds of this type, but most seeds of the daisy family are carried by some kind of aerial sail, known as a pappus. Garden plants with airborne seeds include trees like poplars (*Populus*), and clematis, with the silky seedheads of *Clematis tangutica* being among the most striking.

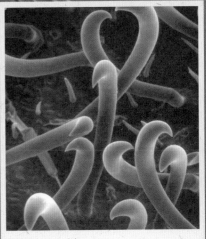

Catching a ride
The burrs of larger seedheads are obvious
enough, but some small seeds, like those
of cleavers (Galium aparine), also have tiny
hooks barely visible to the naked eye (inset).

Shock treatment

Fruiting plants often suffer a raw deal in the garden, being hard pruned, trained, and even deprived of nurtients to encourage fruiting rather than leaf growth. Possibly the most vicious example of cultivation techniques I have experienced was practised widely in the walled gardens of the late 1800s. Pear and apple trees (*Pyrus* and *Malus*) were dug up in autumn and root pruned by up to one third before replanting. This pruning kept the vigour of the plants low while stressing them sufficiently to encourage panic in the plant. Fearing the end was near, they then concentrated on a flower flush. Such harsh treatment isn't possible every year, and is best done every five to allow the plant a recovery period.

Many trees opt to use a rigid wing instead, as seen on seeds of gymnosperms and maples (*Acer*), which twirl away from their trees on the wind like prototype helicopters.

The seeds of aquatic plants, of course, are most readily dispersed by water. They usually have pockets of air inside them, making the "sink or float" test of viability (*see p.21*) meaningless. It is not only plants that grow in the water that use it to distribute their fruits, however. The invasive *Impatiens balsamifera* spreads rapidly along rivers, colonizing one stretch of bank after another wherever seeds wash up. Seeds can be carried amazing distances on water, not just from the upper reaches of a river downwards, but in the case of coconuts (*Cocos nucifera*) and "sea beans" like coco de mer (*Lodoicea maldivica*), across entire oceans.

There are also seeds that are distributed passively by animals. Rather than putting energy into fruit, plants such as acaena, bidens, geum, and many weeds surround their seeds with hooks. These will attach to the coats of passing animals and gardeners, so we distribute them whether we like it or not.

Fleshy fruits

Enclosing the seed in a sweet, juicy package designed to be eaten enables plants to use birds and mammals for wider distribution. Different plants approach fruit design in different ways. In many the ovary wall swells, and in the compound fruits of raspberries and blackberries (*Rubus*) each of the juicy sacs is a swollen ovary. In apples and pears (*Malus* and *Pyrus*) the petal and sepal bases form a tube around the ovary, and it is this tube that swells to become the flesh. Strawberries (*Fragaria*) carry multiple ovaries upon a receptacle and it is this that swells into a "fruit": in fact, the fruits are the pips on the surface, each containing a seed.

If you grow your own fruit – and home-grown fruit always has a quality and flavour unmatched by bought produce – storing the fruit as it ripens can be a challenge. Try harvesting bracken fronds, drying them and then wrapping both fruit and root vegetables in them before placing in a tray in a cool dark place.

Although rarely used today, the advantage of bracken is that it allows cushioning and protection while not leaving a tainted flavour, as is often evident in fruit stored in newspaper, straw, hay, and sawdust.

Industrious ants

You may not appreciate ants in your garden, but several of your plants do. The seeds of cyclamen, corydalis, and violas are all distributed at least in part by ants. If you have cyclamen in your garden, take a look at them after the coiling stem brings the seed capsule to earth (*see p.19*). One day the spherical pod full of seeds is there, then the end splits open and with startling speed the seeds disappear. The agents of this vanishing act are usually ants, which carry off the seeds and eat the nutritious coating. Lest you think you should try to beat them to it and do the sowing yourself, be aware that once exposed to light cyclamen seeds can rapidly plunge into a dormancy (*see pp.23–27*) that is hard to break. With a relationship developed over the ages, the ants will probably do a more successful job than you, and if you happen not to like where they sow the seeds, you can always move the young plants later.

Removal team
Many seeds have a coating or even a fleshy appendage, called an elaiosome, to attract foraging ants.

Strange fruit

All this leaves one question: if fruits are basically just a delivery mechanism for seeds, how on earth do we have seedless bananas and grapes? There are in fact two different processes at work here producing the same result. Bananas can be produced without pollination, the egg cell in the ovule (*see pp.102–103*) dividing on its own. Many reproductive cells can do this in the laboratory, but only a few manage it in nature; other examples are the pineapple and the navel orange. Seedless grape cultivars, on the other hand, are pollinated, but the embryo is not viable and the seeds fail. These biological oddities of course are useless for reproduction and would not persist in the wild, but because we like the convenience of seedless fruit we propagate them (*see pp.38–45*) – and I for one fervently wish that the pomegranate came in a seedless version.

Designed for life

Every single plant is a wonderfully designed organism, refined and honed to thrive in a specific habitat niche, collectively broader than can be tolerated by any human being. This means there truly is a plant for every situation in your garden, or in any garden. So why do gardeners complain that nothing grows in a certain spot, or despair at their difficult garden? Usually it is because they have chosen the plant before considering the place. Change that starting point, and you change everything.

NURTURE AND NATURE

Over millions of years, plants have adapted to cope with everything the environment can throw at them. Some adaptations are so commonplace that we hardly give them a second thought. For example, why are some plants evergreen, why do others have hairy leaves, and what lets some of them live with their roots underwater while others survive in parched soil? Some adaptations are genetic, and part of a plant's core nature: cacti are always cacti, and plants of acid soils will never grow on limestone. On the other hand, some responses to stress can be switched on and off, and the growth of individual plants is tailored to their circumstances by hormones.

Shaping the plant

There are several major plant hormones, but the workings and even existence of some are still a matter of argument – some kind of chemical signal certainly stimulates flowering, but botanists have yet to discover exactly what it is. From a gardener's perspective, probably the most important hormone is auxin; like most hormones this has several forms, so may be referred to as either auxin or auxins, but for the purposes of gardening the terms are interchangeable. One of auxin's key functions is to tell the plant which way is up, since it is produced by young leaves and then moves towards the roots. The concentrations at the bottom end of a cutting (*see pp. 38–39*) stimulate root formation, so if a cutting is completely buried upside down, it still grows roots at the "right" end; but this is not an efficient or recommended method! Auxin's role in rooting has led to the use of synthetic auxins as rooting aids. Early enthusiasm for hormone rooting compounds was a bit misplaced, and we now know that choosing the right material is at least as important as any chemical assistance.

Auxin promotes the growth and development of the vascular cambium (*see p. 68*). The effects depend strongly on the level of concentration, and very high concentrations will cause excessive growth and ultimately death. This has led to another use of synthetic auxins as hormone weedkillers.

Genetic destiny
Many adaptations are genetic and unchangeable: a cactus cannot be acclimatized to grow in a swamp.

Responding to the world
Hormones cause the branches of a tree kept upside down to "weep" upwards, and the faces of sunflowers (Helianthus, inset) to track the sun across the sky.

The effects of auxin

Auxin is the most versatile of the growth hormones. As well as ensuring that the main stem is where the main growth occurs (apical dominance), it also controls how a plant grows in response to light (phototropism), gravity (geotropism), and touch (thigmotropism).

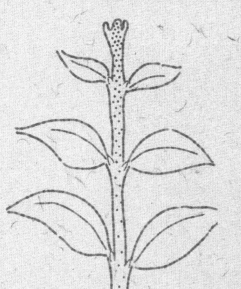

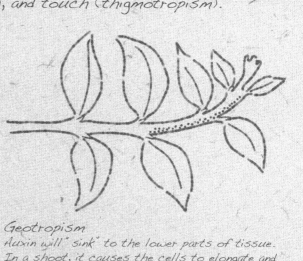

Geotropism
Auxin will "sink" to the lower parts of tissue. In a shoot, it causes the cells to elongate and the shoot to bend upwards. With less auxin, buds on the upper side are more inclined to produce shoots and flowers, which is why we train the branches of fruit trees horizontally.

Apical dominance
Auxin produced by the shoot tip inhibits growth in axillary buds along the stem, maintaining the dominance of the apical bud.

Phototropism
Light causes auxin in the plant tissues to migrate away to the shady side of the stem. Here it causes greater cell elongation, resulting in the plant stem bending towards the light source.

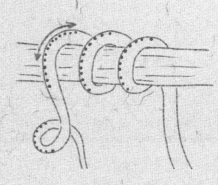

Thigmotropism
In twining stems and tendrils, auxin distribution causes the cells on the side that is not touching the supporting object to elongate more. As a result, the stem or tendril grows in a spiral around the object.

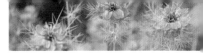

Natural auxin also performs another important function: maintaining apical dominance (*see opposite and pp. 70–71*). A cunning way to persuade a single side shoot to grow, often used in training fruit trees, is to "notch" or remove a little piece of tissue just above a bud to isolate it from the auxin coming from above.

Growth and maintenance

Other plant hormones include gibberellins (tricky for those of us who aren't even sure how many c's are in broccoli) and cytokinins. Gibberellins are crucial to a bewildering variety of functions, some of them not at all well understood. They are involved in breaking dormancy in seeds and plants that need winter chilling (*see pp. 24–25*), transition from juvenile to adult growth (*see pp. 36–37*), and in flowering: artificial doses of gibberellin persuade plants that normally flower only in the long days of summer to bloom in short days. Together with cytokinins, they seem to be all-purpose stimulators of cell division and growth, a role exploited in horticulture by the development of a range of chemicals to block synthesis. Known as growth-retardants, these are used to encourage pot plants such as chrysanthemums and poinsettias to flower while still compact – which is why these plants never seem to perform as well for you the next year.

Ripening and age

Ethylene is a bit of an oddity among the plant hormones: unlike all the others, it's a gas. Like gibberellin, ethylene seems to have a diverse range of functions in plants, including both triggering and suppressing flowering (in different species). It is widely exploited commercially, being used used to promote flowering in pineapples and other ornamental bromeliads, while flower growers devote a lot of effort to reducing ethylene levels during storage and transport of cut flowers. For the gardener, ethylene's chief importance is in promoting fruit ripening and the ageing or senescence of cut flowers. Ripening of produce left at the end of the season can be accelerated by storing with ripe tomatoes, apples, or bananas, although high temperatures are also important. And if you want your cut flowers to last, stand them away from the fruit bowl. Ethylene also triggers the loss, or abscision, of leaves in autumn, a role once attributed to the misleadingly named abscisic acid, which in fact slows growth in autumn (*see pp. 146–48*) and keeps seeds dormant (*see pp. 24*).

Follow the leader
Ripe red tomatoes produce ethylene, encouraging the ripening of other fruit on the plant – but only if they are not harvested, of course.

Talking plants

One of the most intriguing questions raised by studying hormones is "can plants talk to each other?" Certainly most plants produce a hormone called methyl jasmonate in response to attack by pests or diseases. It seems to warn other parts of the plant that trouble is on the way, and they respond by producing defence chemicals that slow the growth of fungi or reduce the feeding of caterpillars. Methyl jasmonate is volatile, and there's some evidence that it escapes from the plant and alerts neighbouring plants to the problem. It may have a promising future in improving the shelf life of stored fruit, but perhaps the most appealing thing about it is the contribution it makes to the smell of honeysuckle and jasmine.

Genetic strategies

Genetics can get complex, but in essence inheritance is governed by genes, lengths of the DNA in chromosomes (*see p.50*). Most plants have pairs of chromosomes, one from each parent, and so two copies of each gene, one from each parent. A kind of cell division called meiosis, from the Greek "to reduce", splits these chromosome pairs during reproduction, reducing the number to half in egg and pollen cells. When these fuse in pollination (*see pp.102–103*), the pairs are restored, with one chromosome from each parent again. This botanical line-dance creates new, potentially more successful combinations in each generation.

Mendelian inheritance

The consequences of all this were worked out 150 years ago by a Czech monk called Gregor Mendel, studying peas. These are normally self-pollinated, giving rise to "true-breeding" lines that show the same traits in every generation. The leading theory at the time was that traits were "blended" during sex (like mixing paint), so that crossing purple- and white-flowered peas would give pale purple flowers. But when Mendel made the cross, he got first all white-flowered plants and then a mix (*see opposite*).

Mendel was lucky (or clever) in choosing traits determined by a single gene rather than several, and with complete dominance. If he'd used red- and white-flowered snapdragons, the offspring would have been pink. Not due to blending, but because flowers with only one red gene have less pigment than flowers with two. Self-pollinate the pink snapdragons and you get quarter red flowers, quarter white flowers, and half pink flowers.

Plant breeders sometimes copy Mendel, breeding two lines of plants very closely and discarding variants until their offspring are consistent, like Mendel's peas. When these are crossed, the first generation (F_1) has a predictable combination of the parents' traits. This is why highly consistent F_1 seeds and plants cost more, and why their seeds produce variable offspring.

Mendel's pea flowers

This gene for colour is written W for purple and w for white. The pattern Mendel found in first (F1) and second (F2) generations from known parents is the same for any trait controlled by a single, simple gene. His genius was to see that this proved discrete "particles" govern inheritance: it was another century before these were identified and named genes.

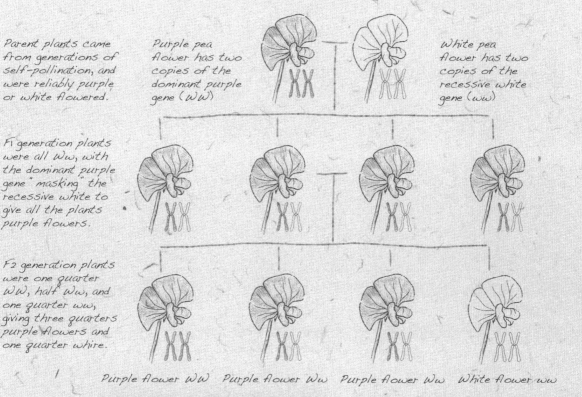

Parent plants came from generations of self-pollination, and were reliably purple or white flowered.

Purple pea flower has two copies of the dominant purple gene (WW)

White pea flower has two copies of the recessive white gene (ww)

F1 generation plants were all Ww, with the dominant purple gene "masking" the recessive white to give all the plants purple flowers.

F2 generation plants were one quarter WW, half Ww, and one quarter ww, giving three quarters purple flowers and one quarter white.

Purple flower WW   Purple flower Ww   Purple flower Ww   White flower ww

Ever present Recessive traits, like the white flowers of peas and foxgloves (Digitalis) show up in a minority of plants but at a consistent level.

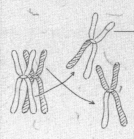

Each egg or sperm carries a random selection of traits from its parent

How traits are mixed
Chromosomes pair up and then split during meiosis to form sex cells, the egg and sperm, which each have only one part of the chromosome pair.

Shelter and warmth
To mitigate the effect of wind, seen obviously in wind-pruned trees (inset) and cold, the Incas of Peru built terraced "greenhouses" that gave shelter and trapped the sun's heat.

TEMPERATURE AND WIND

While books frequently allocate plants to hardiness zones on a map, and magazines tell us what to do each month, much of this should be taken with a good pinch of salt. Many factors modify the climate where you live and the times when you do things. On a large scale, climates range from continental, with hot summers and cold winters, to maritime (more equable); Britain, for example, is more maritime than most of mainland Europe. Even within this small island, some Cornish valleys are practically subtropical, and parts of East Anglia are almost steppe-like. Altitude, slope, and aspect are all important, and there is little you can do about them without moving.

Hot and cold gardens

If you garden at a high altitude, on a steep slope that receives little sun, you may be a hardiness zone (or even two) colder than the map says. Gardening on a slope or in a valley inevitably encourages cold air to flow to the bottom of the slope, potentially creating frost pockets that will both damage growth and limit plant choice. If you garden on a slope, you could always replace any wall at the lower edge that will trap the cold air with a hedge to allow the cold air to drain away. In colder regions you would be ill advised to try a lush garden of tropical plants, but a range of shrubby Mediterranean plants, including rosemary (*Rosmarinus*) and some lavenders (*Lavandula*), can do quite well provided that sharp drainage keeps them dry. It is cold combined with wet that will finish them off.

At the other end of the temperature scale are city gardens. Cities are major heat islands and really big ones, like London, practically have their own local climate, being several degrees warmer than the surrounding countryside. Even within a city, proximity to buildings is crucial. Plants growing close to buildings will benefit from the heat they radiate during the night. During a heatwave, city gardens will of course be even hotter; these are the places where a garden of subtropical and tropical plants may not just be possible, but necessary.

Winter performer
The leathery, glossy leaves of hardy evergreens such as mahonia are not damaged by frost or a coating of snow.

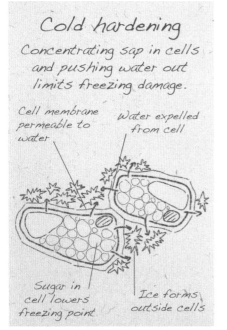

Cold hardening

Concentrating sap in cells and pushing water out limits freezing damage.

Cell membrane permeable to water

Water expelled from cell

Sugar in cell lowers freezing point

Ice forms outside cells

What makes plants hardy

Across the whole globe, from tropics to poles, there's little doubt that plants are governed chiefly by temperature. Freezing causes damage to plants as water inside cells turns to ice and expands: plants that can survive low temperatures are capable of cold hardening. This mainly involves increasing the concentration of sugars and other chemicals in the cell contents (*see panel*), which lower the temperature at which the fluid freezes – the process is precisely analogous to adding antifreeze to the water in your car. The cell walls also become permeable, allowing excessive water-based sap to be forced out of the cells, because if it freezes in the spaces between them, it does less harm.

Of course, plants from cold regions also suffer in hot climates: not only are they ill prepared for the heat of summer, but their suffering is also partially caused by the lack of a cold winter which would normally have prepared them for growth, flowering, and fruiting (*see p.149*).

Overexposed gardens

Wherever you garden, don't overlook the effect of wind. It causes direct physical damage, breaking branches in extreme cases, but it also has a significant drying and cooling effect, which will slow plant growth in a windy garden. Movement itself also apparently has an effect, since research shows that plants that are regularly shaken or brushed remain smaller than those that are not.

Plants vary in their tolerance of wind. Small alpines and many of the plants from coastal areas have evolved to hug the ground in their wind-scoured habitats, while grasses and other monocots have leaves and stems that bend with the wind rather than breaking (*see pp.68–71*). Even these plants, however, will suffer checks to growth if exposed to strong winds, while tall, lush herbaceous plants can look very sorry indeed. Most vegetables are very sensitive to wind, and if you have any ambition to have a kitchen garden, it will pay to select (or create) a sheltered spot.

Tender tropicals
Plants from frost-free climates, such as this Musella, have never evolved the necessary mechanisms for cold hardening. They cannot be be acclimatized to the cold, even slowly.

Wind also affects temperature. We all know that the faster the wind is the cooler it feels; our plants experience this too, but they don't have the luxury of being able to step out of the wind. Bearing in mind that most plants in a temperate climate grow best at 12–25°C (54–77°F), it is sobering to know that at an air temperature of 12°C (54°F) a wind of 32kph (20mph) reduces the effective temperature to around 1°C (34°F). This affects plants at all times of the year, but is particularly noticeable in early spring as they come into growth, with protected plants coming into growth earliest.

Creating shelter

The reduction in the effects of wind gained by using one plant or group of plants to shelter another is particularly obvious – on a large scale this is why we plant windbreaks. Not all plants serve the purpose well: open plants with few branches and sparse leaves, such as shrub roses (*Rosa*), do little to impede wind, while dense plants like *Thuja plicata* can be too effective. Evergreens are generally better than deciduous plants and provide year-round protection, but the solidity of the plant is critical, as the wind is ideally slowed rather than stopped, a consideration that applies all the more to walls and fences. This is because a solid barrier causes the wind to rise over or round it and accelerate, creating more wind in a smaller space, resulting in speeds up to 40 per cent greater than the prevailing conditions. Solid windbreaks also create a wind "void" immediately in their lee, and wind racing over the top tries to fill this, creating violent eddies. The ideal permeability of either a fence or a plant for an effective windbreak is about 30 per cent, restricting 70 per cent of the wind; a practical example is a hedge of beech (*Fagus*).

Shelter can extend to 15 times the height of the windbreak, but is greatest within 3.5 times the height, so a 45cm (18in) high hedge around your vegetables can offer significant protection for over 1.3m (4½ft). The sheltered plants suffer less physical damage, and have a slower transpirational rate (*see pp.123–25*).

Shop locally

My grandmother's habit of helping herself to cutting material from over her neighbours' fences wasn't just economical, but made sound horticultural sense. Plants that flourished in the gardens around her were evidently suited to the local conditions, and so had the best chance of settling happily in her own garden. Looking at your neighbours' successes is one of the best rough guides to what you can grow, because even if you don't want exactly the same plants you will will know what type to look for. This is also worth remembering when you fall for a plant in a far flung garden or spotted on holiday: however beautiful it may be, is it growing in conditions anything like those in your own garden?

WATER OF LIFE

The importance of water to plants is obvious: plants are up to 95 per cent fluid, and we all recognise that water from rain or irrigation is vital to keep them happy. However, recent research suggests that of all the plants in our homes and gardens suffering a premature death, over three quarters are due to watering issues. The most obvious factor in our plants' water supply is rainfall, which can vary even from one side of the garden to another, as plant canopies and structures all affect the amount of rain making it to the soil. Once on the ground, the type of soil and quantity of organic matter present controls the speed at which the water percolates through the soil.

"The process a plant uses to absorb and move water is, like so many functions, beautifully simple."

From roots to leaves

The passage of water through plants can be divided into three phases: uptake, movement, and loss; understanding how these work is key to good watering. Plants take up and transport water by a process called osmosis. This relies on the fact that water molecules move from a dilute into a concentrated solution. As water percolates past plant roots, the water molecules pass into the root through the cell wall because the plant keeps the solutions in its cells at a higher concentration than that of the soil water. The molecules, which are small, pass into the plant cell, while the larger molecules in the concentrated solution inside the cell cannot travel out. This gives rise to the term "semi-permeable membrane" used to describe the cell wall.

Once across in the cell, the water molecules and their dissolved nutrients fill the cell vacuole, until the cell is turgid (*see pp.48–49*). Water continues to enter the cell via osmosis, but now an equal quantity of water is forced out along the path of least resistance, between the root cortex cells (*see pp.56–57*). In this way the epidermal cells of the root pump the water into the heart of the root. Here the endodermis operates in exactly the same way as the epidermis, using a concentrated solution in the endodermal cells to draw water molecules in from between the cortex cells and then pumping it into hollow cells of the xylem, from where it flows up through the plant. A good example of this root pressure is clearly seen when a plant is felled in summer and the stump continues to weep sap.

The combined actions of the endodermis and epidermis are thought to create sufficient pressure to pump water to the foliage of low-growing annuals and herbaceous plants, but lifting water to the top of a tree canopy requires a further system. The secret to this lies in the fact that water moves in long "threads" of molecules joined together. When a molecule of water evaporates away from the surface of the leaf it is immediately replaced by another, and all the molecules move up one place. Scientists can replicate this, but the laws of science do not allow water to be drawn more than 10m (33ft) in unbroken threads in laboratory conditions, so quite how mature trees lift water to their crowns remains a mystery. The upward pull of water is also experienced in flower stems, and once cut from the plant air is pulled into the xylem. If it reaches the bud it often causes the flower to fade prematurely, so before you arrange cut flowers, shorten the stems by cutting under water.

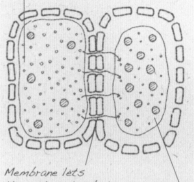

Osmosis

This cell sap is dilute, so water molecules are pushed out through the selectively permeable membrane

Membrane lets through water but not larger solutes

Water entering this cell will dilute the concentrated sap to the same level as in the neighbouring cell

Using and losing water

The process by which the plant loses water through the leaf is called transpiration, and it is largely controlled by the stomata (*see pp. 76–77*). These respond to a number of factors, opening in light and closing when turgidity drops or levels of carbon dioxide increase significantly. Broad-leaved trees have up to 40,000 stomata in every square centimetre of leaf, and in a single day a mature oak tree transpires around 1000 litres (220 gallons), while even a modest tomato plant loses about 1 litre (1¾ pints). This represents about 98 per cent of all the water that the roots take up, with the remaining 2 per cent used in the construction of cells and in photosynthesis.

This might sound wasteful, but the water is used along the way to keep cells turgid and in chemical reactions in the cells. It also carries nutrients to every cell in the plant, so the more a

Shedding excess water
Occasionally surplus nutrients and water congregate in the leaf, especially in humid conditions. The plant exudes nutrient-rich water as droplets of sap on the leaf tip or along the margins, a process known as guttation.

plant transpires, the more nutrients reach the cells. Even water evaporating from the leaf is not wasted; it helps to cool the air immediately around the leaf, allowing foliage to experience high levels of heat from the sun unharmed.

While rapid transpiration places the roots under increased pressure to take up water, it also helps to protect the plant from infection. The stomata offer high-humidity access points to fungal spores seeking a place to germinate and spread infection. Plants transpiring at high levels have a constant stream of water molecules leaving the leaf, making it difficult for fungal spores to invade the stomata; if humidity around the leaf increases, transpiration slows and fungal spores may be able to gain access. This is one of the reasons that low humidity levels and constant air flow are essential around plants that are prone to fungal attack, such as roses (*Rosa*), vines (*Vitis*), top fruit, and seedlings. So while damping down the glasshouse, as practised by my grandfather, does increase humidity and lower water loss, it also inevitably increases the risk of fungal infections.

Keeping the balance

Understanding osmosis offers guidance not just on watering, but on choosing plants and feeding them. For instance, a plant is only able to take up water and nutrients while the solution within the root cells is more concentrated than that in the soil, and while some plants can adjust the concentration of the solution slightly, these adjustments are small. Apply too much fertilizer, and there is a danger that the solution outside the plant will become more concentrated than that inside, reversing the normal passage of water so plants find themselves uncontrollably losing water, wilting, and dying – just one reason for using modest applications of fertilizer. This is also one of the drawbacks of repeatedly sprinkling slugs with table salt or using rock salt to clear ice off frozen winter paths; salt increases the concentration of soil solutions. Some plants have evolved to maintain especially high concentrations of solution in their cells to cope with naturally salty conditions. Maritime plants and those of

Coastal conditions
Maritime plants have a range of adaptations to cope with salt, from leaf surface and shape to the sap in their cells.

coastal flats and margins maintain the concentration of their cells beyond that of salt water, allowing them to succeed in soils rich in sea salt that would kill other plant species. This is why these plants will also grow in a non-maritime environment, but non-maritime plants quickly perish in saline soils.

Emergency closure

If a water shortage is likely, a mass of rapidly-transpiring foliage quickly becomes a dangerous liability, so plants have learned to respond to the earliest hint of drought, acting quickly to head off potential trouble before it becomes serious. As soon as the growing root tips encounter drying soil, they send a chemical signal to the leaves in the form of abscisic acid (*see p.115*), which has the immediate effect of closing the stomata. This drastically curtails not only water loss, but also growth, leading to the severe "check to growth" which is so familiar to gardeners who are careless enough to let their plants go short of water. The problem with such a check is that because it is caused by a hormone, its effects are quite persistent and are not quickly reversed, even by the restoration of adequate water supplies. The lesson is that to achieve flourishing plants, even a brief period of drought should be avoided.

Vineyard

The check to growth caused by drought can be exploited. Many grape varieties tend to produce stem and foliage at the expense of fruit. Australian growers irrigate each side of a row of vines alternately, letting the other side dry out. The dry side stimulates abscisic acid production, which slows growth, and the watered side ensures that the plants don't actually go short of water.

Saving water

Adaptations to leaf shape, thickness, and surface reduce water loss.

Air flow passes over hairs

Hairs trap still air and reflect sunlight

Hairy leaf

Waxy cuticle

Hairs slow airflow

Epidermis

Thick leaf holds water

Water-storing cells

Photosynthetic cells

Succulent leaf

Adapting to drought

A major challenge for plant design is balancing water absorption and loss. If water is short, steps must be taken to reduce water loss, but transpiration cools the leaf, so reducing water loss can easily lead to overheating in dry, sunny habitats. The responses of natural selection have been to reduce leaf size and to trap moist air around the stomata by siting them in grooves or pits, or rolling up the whole leaf with the stomata on the inside, or frequently coating the leaves in a dense layer of hairs (*see panel*).

Ultimately, in the driest places, some plants have lost their leaves completely, or at least reduced them to spines or hairs. Cacti are the most familiar example. Of course cacti still face the temperature problem, which is why many are so densely covered in spines or woolly hairs. In fact, cacti are so obviously well adapted to drought that it's easy to ignore their less visible adaptations like their specialized photosynthesis (*see p.144*).

Reaching deeper

How far roots can penetrate into the soil has a fundamental effect on a plant's ability to harvest water and nutrients. Most fine roots develop where microorganisms are breaking down organic matter to release nutrients, within 1m (3ft) or so of the surface. Well-structured soil (*see pp.160–62*) aids both moisture retention and root penetration; if possible, roots will penetrate to more significant depths in search of water and food, following soluble nutrients leached to lower levels by rainwater.

Some plants, such as carrots, potatoes, comfrey (*Symphytum*), and rheum are capable of rooting to depths in excess of 2m (6ft). Having worked briefly with a champion vegetable grower who grew root crops in drainpipes to achieve the longest possible roots, I now am no longer surprised at the depths roots can penetrate – the longest carrot reached over 5m (15ft). Shrubs and especially trees of course achieve great depths. Such long roots give not only the ability to forage deep for nutrients, but

also steadier water supplies. Deep roots also spread wider, so even the modest tomato which roots to 1m (3ft) deep would, under ideal conditions, like to extend its roots as wide as 2m (6ft), giving a potential rooting zone of 2 cubic metres (2½ cubic yards). Look at the plants you keep in pots at home, which probably have no more than 0.5 per cent of their potential rooting zone; suddenly their reliance on you for water and food becomes understandable.

Water-wise gardening

Soils that dry out during the summer, due to a lack of vegetation cover, low organic matter content, or lack of surface mulch (*see pp.201–202*) significantly reduce the supply of moisture and nutrients (*see pp.130–33*). But bad watering can be worse than none at all. Occasional sprinkling encourages roots to grow close to the surface, where they become prone to drought. The fine root hairs responsible for the majority of water and nutrient uptake are most vulnerable here, as their simple construction gives them no buffering against drought. If the soil becomes dry, root hairs quickly die and the water uptake of the plant is severely compromised. Far better is deep watering, applying high levels of water over a long period to encourage thorough wetting of the soil at depth.

Water is lost from the soil not only through the plant roots taking it up and gravity pulling it down, but also by evaporation from the surface. Hot sun, winds that carry moisture away, and low humidity all increase loss through evaporation. Just as in a plant leaf, once a molecule of water is lost from the soil, another moves upwards to take its place, causing a rapid and continuous loss of water during hot summer days. However, in very warm conditions water molecules at the surface evaporate too fast for surface tension to replace them and the chain is broken: at this point the surface of soil dries, but crucially, no more water is drawn out of the soil below. Research has shown that once the top 20mm (¾in) of soil is dry, little soil water is lost through evaporation. So if you allow your soil surface to dry in a hot summer you will be saving soil water, until it rains or you irrigate the surface, at which point the chain is restored and evaporation begins again. This is why granular mulches retain moisture, and water is most efficiently delivered via buried leaky hoses or a pot sunk into the soil. It is also why we avoid digging or hoeing soil in dry conditions, as this removes the dry layer from the surface and exposes the threads of molecules; in dry weather, just trim the tops of any weeds and then hoe the day after rain.

"Deep roots give the security of being buffered from the fickle conditions in the soil's upper levels."

Watering tips

A saying trotted out with regularity by old allotment growers is "water in the evening, weed in the morning". Plants absorb water better in the cool of the night than in the heat of the day, and if you water the ground in the evening it is soft and pliable in the morning, making the removal of weeds easier. Water temperature can also have a dramatic effect on plants. I found that with tomatoes, flowering and fruiting can be advanced by as much as three weeks by warming irrigation water to 18°C (64°F). One of the best ways of doing this naturally is to place water containers inside the glasshouse (as with those outside, ensure that they are covered to keep infections out). Seed germination rates and times can be improved by warming compost (which has high water content) by placing filled pots in a propagator at around 20°C (68°F) overnight before sowing.

Adapting to flood

At the opposite end of the spectrum from drought, excessive water causes another set of problems for plants. Here some adaptations to drought become disadvantages: hairy leaves can become waterlogged, preventing photosynthesis and eventually killing the leaf. Instead, leaves of aquatic plants like water lilies have waxy coatings that shed water better than a duck's back: synthetic copies of these are being developed for use on surgical implements. However, most mechanisms for coping with flood are in the roots, where they regulate water uptake and air supply.

If water is pumped into the leaves from the roots faster than it can exit through transpiration, leaf cells will swell and rupture; this is particularly evident on lettuces and pelargoniums, when dark green patches and cell death occur on the foliage tips. Most plants control the flow by adapting the endodermal cells in the heart of the root, coating them in a waxy, impermeable layer. Obviously the greater the covering of wax, the less water is taken up, while less wax means more water can be drawn in, and this is one of the control measures used by plants to cope with their natural environmental conditions. Plants from arid regions tend to have less wax on the endodermis, while plants from wetlands have more. This trait is genetic: plants native to wetlands cannot harvest sufficient water when grown in drier soils and so suffer wilting, while plants from arid regions are literally swamped with water if grown in wet soils.

Roots also need a constant supply of oxygen, normally obtained from air-filled pores in the soil (*see pp.156–57*). If the soil is waterlogged, most plants stop growing very quickly and soon die. Plants adapted to waterlogged habitats, however, produce a special internal tissue called aerenchyma. This is a system of interconnected, gas-filled spaces that conduct oxygen to the roots. Plants with this trait can respond to local conditions: for example, some flood-tolerant plants, such as willows (*Salix*), produce hardly any aerenchyma tissue if grown in well-aerated soil, but can produce aerenchyma when they need to.

Aquatic adaptations

The water-repellent leaves of Nelumbo (inset) are a visible adaptation to a wet habitat; below the surface, aquatic and marginal plants also have specially adapted roots.

NUTRITIONAL NEEDS

The necessity of providing nutrients to plants is accepted by most gardeners. To function, grow, and crop effectively, a plant harvests nutrients largely from the surrounding soil via the roots. In the wild, the success of plants depends on their growing in an appropriate habitat, where the minerals they require are present, and on natural processes providing for their needs as part of the rhythms and cycles of life and death. In the garden, demands from the gardener for growth, diversity, and performance are significantly higher than those in the wild, and are coupled with the regular removal of plant material in crops, and regular clipping, trimming, and tidying that are all part of gardening in the ornamental garden.

"It is no wonder that our plants sometimes go a little hungry and require the addition of supplements."

Nutrient sources

At least 15 elements (including carbon, hydrogen, and oxygen) are vital for plant health, supplemented by several others of lightly lesser importance. Essentially plant nutrients are inorganic minerals. Their origins are diverse and their functions within the plant equally so – in some cases they are not fully understood, although deficiencies can have severe repercussions. Nutrients are divided loosely into high-demand nutrients, referred to as "major", and low-demand nutrients, unsurprisingly called "minor". As ever, there are variations in terminology, so on fertilizer packets expect to see the terms macro and micro, and even macro and trace.

Plants harness the majority of their nutrients through their roots from the soil, where they originate from the decay of living organic material, droppings from animals, the breakdown of mineral-rich soils by bacteria, and from the atmosphere itself. Just because the minerals are present in the soil doesn't necessarily mean that they are readily available to the plant: chemical and environmental conditions can impede uptake, and a lack of moisture has significant effects on the plant's ability to feed because water is the vehicle used to transport the minerals (*see pp.122–25*).

Major nutrients

Nitrogen in the soil comes largely from plant debris, and sometimes from dung, when it is in the form of protein or amino acids (*see panel, p.132*). It plays a key role in the development of nucleic acids, the cell's messengers, and also in the manufacture of chlorophyll (*see pp.48–50*). It makes up as much as 50 per cent of cells' dry weight, and is highly water-soluble. Deficiency is seen as slow, stunted growth, short internodal distances, and leaves that are reduced in size and, critically, pale and lacking in chlorophyll. Such pale growth, called chlorosis, is most evident in older foliage, where the tissues between the veins become pale and blotched; this is because the older foliage is sacrificed by the plant in favour of the continued supply of nutrients to the new growth. This lack of chlorophyll often allows other pigments in the leaf and young stems to come to the fore, with bronze or purple flushes common, as if autumn has come early.

Phosphorus originates from mineral-rich rocks, and is not rapidly leached in temperate gardens. However, because of chemical reactions only about 1 per cent of soil phosphorus is available to plants. Even more frustratingly, extra phosphorus applied to the garden can be rendered unavailable within weeks. It is therefore one of the most commonly lacking nutrients. Phosphorus forms a part of the chemical responsible for transferring the energy produced by mitochondria in the cell (*see pp.48–49*) and large amounts are concentrated around the meristem (*see p.51*) and in seeds and developing fruits. When supplies run short, cells cannot grow effectively and growth at the shoot and root tip slows or even halts; the lack of root growth is the most noticeable symptom, particularly on seedlings. Stunted leaves and stems retain their green colour, aside from a bronze edge to the leaf.

Potassium is derived from igneous and metamorphic rock such as granite and slate, and tends to be highly available in soil over these rocks but low in soils over chalk or limestone, from which it is often easily leached. It is easily dissolved in water and so is very mobile and keenly taken up by the plant.

MAJOR NUTRIENTS]

Nitrogen (N)
Phosphorus (P)
Potassium (K)
Calcium (Ca)
Magnesium (Mg)
Sulphur (S)

MINOR NUTRIENTS]

Boron (B)
Manganese (Mn)
Copper (Cu)
Iron (Fe)
Molybdenum (Mo)
Zinc (Zn)
Cobalt (Co)
Chlorine (Cl)
Silicon (Si)

Chlorosis
Yellowing between the veins, here on the leaves of a choisya, is a classic sign of nitrogen deficiency.

Nitrogen cycle

Nitrogen enters the soil from a variety of sources and is made available to plants by soil bacteria.

Lost as gas

Animal droppings

Eaten by animal

Dead animal

Rain

Dead leaves

Soil nitrogen

Leached into soil

Occasionally, uptake is too efficient after heavy applications of potassium fertilizer, and it is absorbed to the detriment of other minerals such as magnesium. The precise role of potassium isn't yet fully understood, but it is often linked with both rooting and flowering performance. It is also one of the principal agents in controlling osmosis (*see pp.122–23*), and is known to play a part in defending the plant from stresses such as winter cold, drought, and disease attack. Deficiency often produces brown, scorched patches on the leaf tip, causing many leaves to roll and curl downwards. Like nitrogen deficiency, this damage is most noticeable in older foliage.

Calcium and magnesium levels in soil are generally high, as these are derived not only from limestone- and chalk-based rocks, but also igneous and metamorphic deposits. Calcium is a key constituent of plant cell walls as calcium pectate (*see p.51*), and is also highly concentrated around root and shoot tips where cell wall production is at its most rapid. In plants growing on deficient soils, cell walls are weak and young leaves become pale and distorted, usually curling downwards, and in extreme cases the growth tip may die out. In bulbs and herbaceous plants the stems become bent, while blossom end rot in tomatoes and bitter pit in apples are the results of calcium deficiency in crops. Magnesium, by contrast, is highly mobile in the plant and an essential part of chlorophyll production in the chloroplasts (*see pp.48–49*). Its deficiency is therefore most notable in old foliage which shows pale yellowing, similar to nitrogen deficiency, and even reddening.

Of the sulphur available to plants, 90 per cent is bound up in organic matter and made available to roots by microorganisms as a part of the decomposition process (*see pp.166–68*). Sulphur is a key player in the formation of chlorophyll, and as a relatively static mineral its deficiency is noticed first in new leaves, where the poor chlorophyll production results in a yellowing of young foliage.

Minor nutrients

Boron is in rock minerals and although rarely talked about, is essential in the plant. It helps seeds to break dormancy and is involved in moving plant sugars. When deficient, tissues become disorganized, causing stems to rot and hollow out (sometimes seen in brassica crops), leaves to distort, and fruit to split.

Iron and manganese are both widely available in most soils and derived from the weathering of rocks. They are essential in stimulating chlorophyll production, and deficiency shows as yellow or even white shoots.

Copper and zinc are both essential components of protein and enzymes produced by the ribosomes (*see pp.48–49*) and used in tissue development in the plant. Deficiency causes distortion and twisting; copper deficiency also causes dark green foliage and premature withering, while zinc deficiency results in the production of small, pale leaves.

Molybdenum is required in small quantities by the plant, playing a part in the uptake of nitrogen; without it plants develop symptoms of nitrogen deficiency such as yellowing and, in extreme cases, death between the veins. This tends to occur first in old leaves, where it is accompanied by the rolling of the leaf edge.

Alternative energy
Carnivorous plants have evolved an impressive range of traps, from sticky surfaces and pitfalls to the snapping jaws of the Venus flytrap.

Living on less

In principle, plants faced with nutrient-deficient soil could either try harder to extract more nutrients from the soil, or make do with less. In practice, the latter solution is less risky and has been the one favoured by millions of years of natural selection.

Perhaps the most intriguing adaptations for a low-nutrient environment are seen in carnivorous plants. Growing mostly in marshy areas, with plenty of water and sunlight but low nutrient levels, these plants supplement their diet with nutrients from insects and even mammals. A surefire way to kill one of these plants is to pot it in a high-nutrient compost and feed it regularly.

Meadow annuals grow in bursts and cram a whole lifecycle into one year (*see pp.148–49*). Other plants take the opposite approach: they grow slowly, are generally long-lived, and have long-lived parts, most obviously evergreen leaves. These traits

More than one way to go
Meadow annuals exploit poor soils where grass cannot grow strongly, racing from seed to seed within a year; the evergreen monkey puzzle (inset) grows slowly instead.

have the twin virtues of requiring fewer nutrients, and helping plants to hang on to those they already have. Plants short of nitrogen and phosphorus can ill afford the luxury of making a whole new set of leaves every year and then throwing them away. In fact, the more deficient the soil, the longer-lived the leaves. The leaves of the bristlecone pine (*Pinus longaeva*) last up to 40 years, while those of the monkey puzzle (*Araucaria araucana*), another slow-growing conifer, last about 25 years. These are exceptional, and most evergreen leaves don't live nearly so long; holly (*Ilex*) and Scots pine (*Pinus sylvestris*) both manage about three years. But as a rule, evergreens grow more slowly than related deciduous species. If you have shrubs in your garden that need frequent heavy pruning to keep them within bounds, I would guess not many of them are evergreen.

Although evergreen leaves started out as an adaptation to infertile soils, their effect is to remove the ability to grow fast even under ideal conditions. Because they are thick, tough, and built to last, less of the leaf matter is available for photosynthesis (*see pp.80–82*), with the inevitable consequence of slow growth. You could design a bullet-proof racing car, but in a race it would always lose to one not weighed down by armour plating.

Nutrient shortages in the garden

To earn their place in our gardens, plants have to perform at a very high level. Flowering, fruiting, and seed setting require tremendous investment, and plants performing these roles will have high nutrient demands. Supply needs to be tailored to demand, so think about what you grow: plants that grow rapidly require more nutrients than slow-growing ones, and herbaceous perennials that burst from ground level in spring to statuesque heights remove high levels from the soil, while slow-growing shrubs take comparatively little. Our gardening practices can also be unhelpful: constant cropping, such as the removal of leafy material from the vegetable garden, repeated lawn mowing, and pruning of herbaceous plants, results in the loss of organic-matter nutrients such as nitrogen and sulphur. Wherever possible, compost what you remove (*see pp.172–75*) and return the nutrients to the soil.

Bristlecone pine
The world's oldest known plant, with living specimens that are almost 5,000 years old, this is also the slowest growing tree.

Soil type (*see pp. 154–59*) and condition are also important factors to consider. Light soils where drainage is rapid are most likely to be deficient in water-soluble nutrients such as nitrogen and potassium. Gardens in which fertilizers and organic matter are never, or only sporadically, applied are also likely to suffer nitrogen and potassium deficiencies. Soils that are rich in organic matter (*see pp. 165–69*) tend to suffer less from loss of nutrients than poor soils, largely due their ability to lock in nutrients.

Costly display
Garden plants tend to flower more and for longer than wild species, therefore reward their efforts.

Water and nutrient supply are closely linked. Heavy rains, flooding, or excessive irrigation can all lead to shortages of soluble nutrients, especially nitrogen. At the other extreme, drought causes a reduction in availability, because nutrients reach the plant as a water-based solution. Sporadic watering interrupts the flow of nutrients to the plant, particularly the less mobile nutrients such as calcium and phosphorus – hence the problems with blossom end rot on tomatoes that have been poorly irrigated. Container-grown plants that are highly irrigated are also likely to suffer a loss of soluble nutrients; with the plant roots confined and no ingress of nutrient-rich soil water possible, plants in pots are totally reliant on the nutrients provided in the potting compost (*see pp. 176–80*).

Identifying nutrient problems

Pinning down which nutrient is lacking, even when it is a major player such as nitrogen with its classic interveinal yellowing, isn't always straightforward. It is also worth remembering that overfeeding plants can do as much harm as underfeeding (*see pp. 198–99*). Symptoms of deficiency vary between plant species, and often the uptake of one nutrient may be affected by either a surplus or a deficit of another.

Narrow down the likely candidate by considering where the symptoms are occurring, for example on old or new foliage, together with the range of other environmental and management factors, such as soil condition and water supply, that might be affecting nutrient uptake.

The special case of soil pH

With the right balance of nutrients in a well-managed soil, it should be fairly straightforward for plants to get the nutrients they need; however, the chemical composition of the soil has a startling effect on the way that roots perform. Without the right chemical balance in the soil for both the nutrients and the plant, adding fertilizer could be wasted.

Nutrients are made available to plants through a simple reaction in the soil called cation exchange. Soil particles, particularly clay particles, carry a negative electrical charge that attracts the positively charged nutrients. These are locked onto the soil particle, preventing them being washed from the soil, but the electrical binding is not so strong that it prevents plant roots from taking the nutrients. Critically the type of nutrient and quantities in which they are held dictates the acidity or alkalinity of the soil: iron, aluminium, and hydrogen produce an acidic soil while magnesium, calcium, potassium, and sodium give alkaline conditions.

Unlocking the nutrients from the soil particles involves a cunning piece of science in which the soil water "swaps" a hydrogen ion for a nutrient; the hydrogen is attached to the soil particle and the nutrient is dissolved in the soil water and so becomes available to plants. The more hydrogen ions attach themselves to the soil particle, the less room there is for the nutrients to become attached, and instead they are either collected by plant roots or, more often, washed from the soil. In the long run, the hydrogen ions bound to soil particles cause the soil to become acidic, unless the rock beneath releases calcium, magnesium, sulphur, and potassium to counter it. Any soil in temperate rainfall climates will eventually become more acidic if it is left unmanaged for long periods.

The amount of hydrogen present in the soil is measured on the "potential hydrogen" or pH scale. This is graded from 1 to 14, with 1 being extremely acidic, 7 neutral, and 14 extremely alkaline; most garden plants exist in the range of 4 to 8. The most important influence of pH is that it governs the availability of nutrients to the plants. Most nutrients remain accessible at a pH of 6–7.5, but critically, outside this range their availability decreases.

Acid blues
Plants in the genus Vacciunium, like blueberries and cranberries, will thrive only on acidic soils.

Room to spread
Plants that can survive at the extremes, like heather and ling (Erica and Calluna) often establish impressive colonies with little competition.

Living at extreme pH

Iron and manganese are unavailable in alkaline soils and present in potentially toxic amounts in acid ones. Lime-loving, or calcicole, plants manage to extract them from alkaline soils by secreting large amounts of citric and oxalic acids from their roots. Acid-loving, or calcifuge, plants lack this ability, and show yellowing called lime chlorosis when grown on limy soils; if you garden on alkaline soil but love rhododendrons you will have to resign yourself to growing them in containers using ericaceous compost (*see p.180*).

An even more fundamental problem is phosphorus, in short supply at both extremes of pH. There isn't a lot that plants can do about this, except evolve to survive with less, so inevitably plants adapted to either extreme of pH tend to grow rather slowly. They are also strongly reliant on helpful fungal networks or mycorrhizae, which grow around their roots and help them to get hold of more phosphorus than they could on their own. All these adaptations to extreme pH are out of sight, out of mind: there is no way you can tell whether a plant will grow on acid soil by looking at it.

Using fertilizers

The range of supplements for the garden in nurseries and garden centres is dazzling. Although all manufacturers are required by law to provide the nutritional data of their products on the packaging, it is often hidden away in small print on the rear, so whatever you buy be prepared to search for the information. Some gardeners prefer to review their plant fertilizers by the service they provide rather than by product, allowing a close check to be kept on what is being added to the soil.

There is no set guide to applying sources of nutrition to the soil to create good growing conditions. The type of plant, soil conditions, climate, and speed of growth all affect the likely requirements, and no one type of feed is likely to provide for all a plant's needs through all its stages. Consider the plant's growth, and match this with the type of nutrients it is likely to require at each point.

For instance, in the initial stages of seed growth only low levels of all the major nutrients are required, because the tender roots are easily scorched. As growth becomes established, young plants often have a high demand for nitrogen to fuel healthy leaf and stem growth, plus good supplies of phosphorus, but lower requirements for potassium. Once the plant is ready to bloom, flowers can be promoted with potassium- and phosphorus-based food. Remember that woody plants that flower early in the season usually start forming their flower buds a season or so earlier, and that is when they will require a little extra feeding. After any stress, such as heavy pruning, division, or transplanting, use phosphorus and nitrogen to stimulate recovery. As a guide, generally available fertilizers break down like this:

Feed in advance
Spring-flowering trees such as magnolia need feeding when they form flower buds at the end of the summer.

Nitrogen-based: Ammonium sulphate, dried blood, or hoof and horn.
Phosphorus-based: Rock or superphosphate, bone meal.
Potassium-based: Sulphate of potash/potassium sulphate, wood ash.
General: Growmore formula, poultry or farmyard manure, or fish, blood, and bone meal.
Minor nutrients: Dolomitic limestone (calcium, magnesium), gypsum (calcium), Epsom salts (magnesium), nettle tea (magnesium, sulphur, iron).
For increasing alkalinity: Ground or dolomitic limestone.

Nutrients in compost heap materials

If you are an avid composter, and I know many who spend almost as much time putting together their compost as they do planning their floral displays, then the raw ingredients placed on the heap will inevitably affect the nutrient levels of the garden compost.

Ingredient:	N%	P%	K%
Tree leaves	1	0.1	0.1
Banana skins	0	3	41
Coal ash	0	0.4	0.5
Coffee grounds	2	0.3	0.2
Sweetcorn stems (ash)	0	0	50
Grass trimmings	4	0.1	0.3
Poultry manure (fresh)	1	1.5	0.5
Eggshells	1.2	0.4	0.1
Feathers	15	0	0
Wood ash	0	2	10
Pond dredgings	1.3	0.2	0.2
Legume pods	0	1.4	9
Conifer needles	0.5	0.1	0.03
Potato skins	0	5	27
Clover	2	0.5	2
Leafy vegetables	3.6	1	1

Using organic fertilizers

Traditionally food requirements were satisfied using organic fertilizers – that is, anything derived from a living organism. While today you have the option of laboratory concoctions of precisely formulated and concentrated nutrients, there are advantages to using traditional organic sources, not least the contribution they make to improving soil structure (*see pp. 165–69*).

These fertilizers can be divided into slow-release and quick-release. Think of the slow-release types as a hearty meal for marathon runners and the quick-release as a high-energy snack for sprinters. Slow-release fertilizers rely largely on the actions of soil microorganisms to break down and deliver the nutrients in a measured manner, something that can take several seasons and ensures a trickle flow with potentially little wastage; by contrast, quick-release fertilizers rely on pumping a water-based solution into the soil for immediate uptake, with any nutrients that are not rapidly absorbed being easily washed from the soil.

Using the two in combination allows the speed and length of nutrient delivery to be matched to the fluctuating nutrient demands of the plant throughout the growing season. For instance, short-term bedding plants can be provided with a slow-release feed at the start of the growing season to get them established, and then switched to a quick-release feed to keep them at the peak of performance throughout the summer. Trees can be treated to a dose of slow-release at the start of the year with perhaps the addition of further targeted slow-release feeds later in the season to aid flower or fruit development.

Slow-release organic fertilizers

Farmyard manure (N7:P3:K6)

A bulk organic matter base product. Very variable if bought from the farm gate but my grandfather used to swear by it on his dahlias; good as a general dressing around borders.

Bone meal (N3:P17:K0)

Great as a slow-release form of phosphate, hence the traditional use of throwing in a handful when planting new trees and shrubs and for plants in grown in containers long term. Interestingly, monks from monasteries were frequently buried under the orchard fruit'– presumably to enhance the trees' performance.

Dried blood (N13:P0:K0)

Provides a relatively rapid hit of nitrogen for use either as a compost activator (*see p. 174*) or to boost the growth of leafy specimens. Avoid using it after spring on those specimens you wish to encourage to flower.

Fish, blood, and bone (N5:P5:K6)

Faster acting than bone meal, and providing a more rounded supply of nutrients, it is at this ratio the organic general-purpose fertilizer.

Hoof and horn (N13:P0:K0)

Faster-acting than bone meal, but slower than dried blood, this is used at the start of the season, especially for leafy vegetables, or as a top-dressing on poor soil.

Poultry manure (N4:P2:K2)

A variable product, and one not to buy from the farm gate as it is far too rich to apply straight to plants: a steel trailer of ours on the farm, used to fetch fresh chicken manure, rotted through within four days, so imagine what effect it will have on your plants. However, the dried and composted form available from suppliers is good for spring applications, especially to encourage foliage.

Wood ash (N0:P2:K10)

Variable if home collected but a great source of potassium for top-dressing flowering and fruiting trees and shrubs. The potassium is very soluble, so don't allow the ash to get wet or this will be lost.

Quick-release organic fertilizers

Seaweed (N1:P0:K10)

A rapid-acting fertilizer often used as an instant tonic for unhappy plants. The nutrient ratios vary according to supplier but most are biased towards potassium and therefore great for boosting flowers and fruit. Best applied as a liquid feed; it can be watered onto bedding plants for concentrated flowering.

Comfrey tea (N3:P0:K10)

Made by infusing 3kg (6½lb) fresh comfrey leaves in a barrel of about 45 litres (10 gallons) of water for a month, giving variable ratios. Allow to stand – and my advice is to stand well back too, as the mix has a distinctive aroma! Water in undiluted to baskets and tubs or plants requiring a tonic.

Nettle tea (N2:P0:K5)

My grandmother used to love brewing this easy-to-make traditional tea. It varies in its ratios, but will always deliver high potassium and low phosphorus levels and is very high in trace elements. It is most rich if done before the nettles flower. Steep 1kg (2lb) of nettles in 20 litres (5½ gallons) of water for two weeks, and use undiluted.

Don't rush it
Manure should only be applied when well rotted, with no straw evident and virtually fragrance free. This barrowload will need to rot down for some months before it is used.

LIGHT AND SHADE

Plants have evolved to thrive in a wide range of light levels, from alpines that sit in sunshine all day to woodland ferns that shy away in the shade. Some adaptations are hidden at a cellular level; plants even photosynthesize in different ways. Others, especially in the leaf, help you spot the right plants before you begin to read the labels. Adaptations to compete for light are also some of the most visible in the plant world, be it elbowing the neighbours out of the way, scrambling over them, or a less aggressive timesharing approach.

Race for the light

Mountain air
With no chance of being shaded out by tree canopies, alpines hug the ground under the open sky and sun.

All plants need light to fuel photosynthesis (*see pp. 80–82*). In places where trees cannot take hold, like mountaintops, scrubland or desert, and grasslands, relatively small plants can bask in the light. But unless cleared by fire, grazing animals, or human action, trees eventually dominate everywhere there is soil enough to support them. Their secondary woody growth (*see pp. 71–72*) allows them to reach lofty heights, always trying to spread their branches above those of the surrounding trees. Look up in a woodland in high summer, and you will see how the leaves capture every available ray of sunshine.

Plants growing beneath this shady roof have some cunning strategies to get the light they need. Some appear and flower in the early spring, before the trees come into full leaf, and then become dormant in the summer; even woodlanders that flower after the canopy unfurls, like bluebells (*Hyacinthoides*), have had their own foliage stretched out for weeks beforehand, when there is more light. Others use the trees as a support, and climb up their trunks to reach brighter levels (*see opposite*); the classic planting advice for clematis of "head in the sun, feet in the shade" reflects this growth pattern. Some plants leave the ground altogether, and grow on the branches of the trees as either parasites or "air plants" nourished only by rain and airborne nutrients. In the end, however, some plants simply have to make do with less light than others, and this is where another set of adaptations comes into play.

Hitching a ride

Rather than investing energy in a woody trunk of their own, some plants reach the light by scrambling up the trunks of others. Climbers employ a wide range of techniques to achieve this: even thorns are used, by plants like bougainvillea, not only for defence but as grappling hooks.

Once a support is found, the stem will twine around it

Stem grows in wide sweeping arcs, called nastic movements, until it touches a potential support

Adventitious roots
Arising all along a climbing stem, these offer a secure foothold and the chance to absorb water and nutrients.

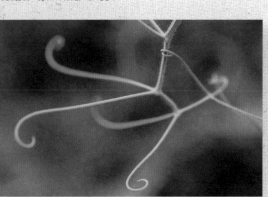

Tendrils
Rather than twining with their whole stem, some climbers use their leaf stalks or special tendrils to grasp their supports.

Sticky pads
These are less damaging to their hosts (living or brick) than adventitious roots, but cling on with impressive strength.

C3 photosynthesis
This is used by most plants in temperate zones that have adequate water, like ferns.

C4 photosynthesis
This is used by plants from hot, dry habitats, such as the grass Panicum virgatum.

CAM photosynthesis
This is used by cacti and succulents adapted for prolonged, searing heat.

Making more from less

All plants contain chlorophyll and photosynthesize (*see pp.80–82*), so why is it that some plants thrive in the shade while others, even if they have superficially similar-looking leaves, sit and sulk? The answer is that while all plants photosynthesize, they do not all do so in the same way.

Most temperate plants and those that grow in lower light levels, such as understorey and woodland species, work on a slow-burn system known as C3. This produces carbon compounds in the leaf that contain three carbon atoms. These plants cannot make use of light levels above the norm, and glucose production remains at an even level – it has even been suggested that excessive light actually inhibits efficiency.

Other plants, particularly those from tropical regions and habitats with high light levels, work by C4 photosynthesis, creating compounds that have four carbon atoms present. This allows them to break down carbon dioxide more efficiently during the day, but poor light levels inhibit this efficiency and compromise growth. This is often why tropical specimens grown in glasshouses and houses at the correct temperature but low light levels fail to perform, and why proper grow lamps (*see p.82*) improve performance.

A third style of photosynthesis, called crassulacean acid metabolism or CAM, is specific to cacti and other plants from deserts, where extreme light and heat levels can cause plants tremendous stress. Open stomata allow carbon dioxide in, but also allow water vapour out; this is part of the essential water transport system (*see pp.123–24*), but clearly excessive water loss is dangerous in such climates. These plants therefore close their stomata during the day and open them at night, when they harvest carbon dioxide and turn it into malic acid. This is stored in the plant till daylight, when it is broken down to make glucose. The drawback of this process is that plants cannot store much malic acid, so glucose production is low and growth is very slow. This is why the cacti collection given to me by my grandmother when I was at primary school is still little more than knee high.

Wear sunscreen

For those plants that do receive full light, sunbathing carries risks; this is as true for plants as it is for us. One adaptation is the ability to produce large

quantities of red or purple pigments, such as carotenoids and flavonoids in leaves. The function of these pigments appears to be to protect the tissues from damage caused by ultraviolet (UV) light. All plants seem capable of producing them, but to markedly varying extents, and they are particularly common in the young leaves of plants from relatively shady habitats, such as Japanese maples (*Acer*) and pieris. Plant breeders, of course, have seized on this trait and used it to produce plants with particularly intense colours. At the opposite extreme are plants selected for their yellow foliage, which tend to have cultivar names like 'Aureus'. These have low levels of protective pigments, and are easily damaged by strong sunlight, one reason why they are seen far more in gardens than in the wild. Other protective mechanisms include the waxy bloom or silver hairs seen on the leaves of many alpine, scrub, or desert plants: as well as conserving water (*see p.126*), these also provide a blanket of protection from the damaging rays.

Protective colouring
Flavonoids are antioxidants and help to protect plants from many forms of damage, including that from the sun.

Using light and shade in your garden

It should now be clear why gardeners are so often advised to photograph or plot where sunlight and shade fall in their gardens at different times throughout the year. This isn't just to help you pick the best place for your deck chair, but also to find the spot where exotics like cannas and dahlias can flourish in the sun or the shade that will prevent your woodland plants from being scorched and shrivelling to nothing.

Assessing where the shadows fall is straightforward, but what is probably less well considered is the total amount of shade that a plant can cast. The human eye can adapt and cope with light changes, but the restriction of light by the overhead canopy is dramatic for plants. For instance, a birch (*Betula*) in summer leaf reduces the total light beneath it by up to 75 per cent, a lime (*Tilia*) by 80 per cent and a sycamore (*Acer pseudoplatanus*) by up to 95 per cent. Even in winter these deciduous trees reduce light by 50 per cent, 55 per cent and 60 per cent respectively. These are perfect conditions for many spring-flowering bulbs, but trying to establish sun-loving exotics or meadow annuals in the same place is a waste of time and money; in some cases, the seed won't even germinate (*see pp.26–27*).

Darker than it looks
The shade of a single tree like this seems slight to our eye, because we can see the light all around; plants cannot.

SEASONS AND AGEING

One of the most rewarding and even therapeutic aspects of horticulture is the way time seems to pass differently in a garden from elsewhere. While we can cheat a bit, using cold frames and raising seedlings on windowsills, a garden is still governed by the seasons and every year has its cycle of awakening, growth, retreat, and winter slumber, a rhythm that puts our daily stresses and weekly pressures into perspective. In the longer term, we watch our plants grow to flourishing maturity, and eventually age and fall into decline – and for a gardener, the passing of an old favourite always presents the consolation of a space for a new experiment.

Preparing for winter

The workings of plants in temperate climates are best understood by starting in autumn, rather than with the start of growth in spring. Most of our familiar temperate trees lose their leaves in autumn (*see pp. 78–79*), sometimes with a swansong of autumn colour as the loss of chlorophyll reveals other pigments and we see colours more familar in flowers (*see p. 96*). Herbaceous plants jettison all their summer growth and retreat underground. The ultimate reason for this is low winter temperatures, but the actual trigger for leaf fall is not temperature, but day length. This is because day length is a much more reliable signal of the changing seasons than is temperature. The dangers of relying on one factor alone can be seen from studies that have grown trees in regions with longer days than in their normal range. Because they needed a shorter critical day length than they actually received, the trees carried on growing into winter and were then seriously damaged by frost.

Leaf fall is only the most visible sign of preparation for winter dormancy. Look more closely and you may see resting buds on twigs, tightly sheathed in glossy scales and kept dormant by abscisic acid (*see p. 115*) until spring comes. And beyond the reach of the naked eye, plants prepare for the cold by "hardening" at cellular level (*see p. 120*).

Sleeping beauties
Most trees in temperate climates save energy by giving up their leaves and staying dormant for the winter. When spring comes, they are often the first plants to flower (inset).

Seasonal changes

Behind the first gauzy haze of green on trees in spring or the coloured
leaves and abandonment of herbaceous stems in autumn lies a welter of
hormonal activity, priming the cells for a season of growth or slowing
activity and storing up reserves for the winter.

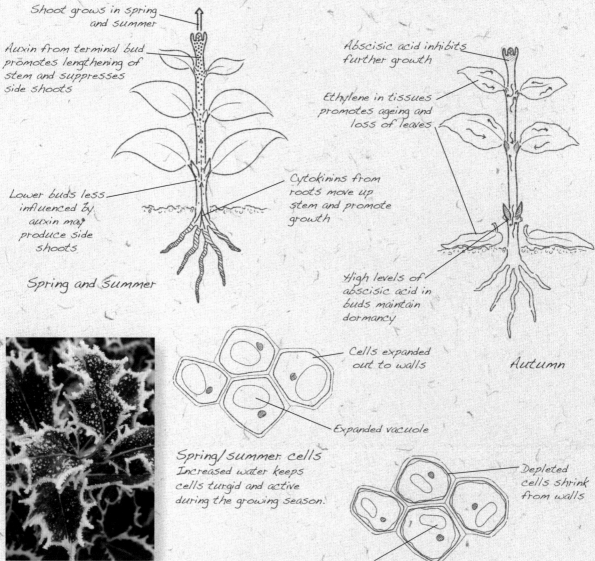

Shoot grows in spring
and summer

Auxin from terminal bud
promotes lengthening of
stem and suppresses
side shoots

Lower buds less
influenced by
auxin may
produce side
shoots

Spring and Summer

Cytokinins from
roots move up
stem and promote
growth

Abscisic acid inhibits
further growth

Ethylene in tissues
promotes ageing and
loss of leaves

High levels of
abscisic acid in
buds maintain
dormancy

Autumn

Cells expanded
out to walls

Expanded vacuole

Spring/summer cells
Increased water keeps
cells turgid and active
during the growing season.

Depleted
cells shrink
from walls

Reduced vacuole

Autumn cells
Reduced water and increased
sugar concentration in cells
improve winter hardiness.

Ticking over
Even evergreens like this
holly (Ilex) conserve their
energy in winter, waiting
for spring growth.

Breaking winter chill

Once winter dormancy is fully established, most temperate trees will not resume growth until they have been exposed to a minimum period of low temperatures. "Low" means below about 10°C (50°F), although 1–7°C (34–45°F) normally works best. This requirement for low temperatures is a serious barrier to growing some temperate fruit trees in climates with warmer winters, such as apples (*Malus*) in California. One solution has been to spray the trees with chemicals to break dormancy, but increasingly, new cultivars with a lesser chilling requirement are being grown. Once dormancy is broken, growth may start in response to rising temperature, increasing day length, or a combination of both. The importance of temperature is shown by the earlier arrival of bud burst in recent years, as a response to a warming climate.

Trees are not the only plants that need a period of winter chill to encourage normal development. Many plants of all types will only flower after a period of chilling. Foxgloves (*Digitalis*) kept at too high a temperature during the winter will not flower, but remain as leafy rosettes. Biennial vegetables such as carrots and beetroot also need chilling before they can flower. In some older varieties, small plants or even seedlings are able to respond to chilling; a number of these will bolt and become inedible in their first season if sown too early. If you encounter this in your kitchen garden, try more modern varieties. These have been bred to have a long juvenile period during which they are insensitive to chilling, avoiding the problem.

Annual events

Some plants simply avoid dormancy by cramming their entire life cycle into one year. It's not immediately obvious why annual plants exist: germination and seedling establishment are by far the most dangerous time in a plant's life, so why survive that stage and then throw it all away by flowering and dying?

The answer lies in the plant's expectation of surviving for more than one year. Annuals typically come from habitats where some kind of regular natural catastrophe, such as drought, flooding, fire, or cultivation, brings matters to an

Desert flowers
Many desert regions bloom in spring. The plants cannot survive the long summer, so set seed before it sets in.

Cutting back woody plants about 30–60cm (12–24in) from the base can provoke even very old wood to produce fresh, juvenile growth in some species. This kind of renovation pruning is worth a try on any prized but declining plant that you might otherwise dig out, although it would be wise to try and root some of the prunings as cuttings, just in case.

Renovating evergreen shrubs
Evergreens, with their relatively slow growth (see pp.133–35), are often best renovated over two or three years. Cut back half the stems in the first year, half the remaining stems in the second year, and the rest in the third year.

Renovating deciduous shrubs
Some deciduous shrubs, such as lilac (Syringa) can take quite drastic pruning in one year when dormant. Make straight, clean cuts across all the main stems. The following winter, thin the resulting shoots to a strong new framework.

abrupt and unavoidable conclusion. In this case, the slow-and-steady approach of most perennials, involving the gradual accumulation of resources and development of a substantial root system, is a recipe for disaster. Far better to get a move on and then blow everything in a single burst of reproduction before the catastrophe happens. Climate and soil fertility are also factors; it's hard to be an annual if supplies of everything are short. This is why there are few annuals in cold arctic regions or on high mountains, and the typical alpine house is full of perennials.

Live fast, die young

The division between annuals and perennials seems clear, but it's worth pointing out that many of the plants grown as annuals in temperate gardens are actually perennials that cannot survive cold winters. Runner beans are perennial, and it's quite possible to save the roots and start them into growth next season, although – trust me – the effort isn't worth it.

In fact perennials vary enormously in natural lifespan. Some of them, particularly those that spread vigorously via their roots or shoot growth, are effectively immortal, but others can be quite short-lived. The beautiful Himalayan blue poppy (*Meconopsis betonicifolia*) has an unfortunate tendency to behave as an annual if it is allowed to flower in its first year. The survival of all such problematical perennials is greatly improved by prompt and thorough dead-heading; a plant is much more likely to be happy dying once it perceives that it has achieved its main ambition of producing a few seeds.

The cause of death in annuals and short-lived perennials is usually all too obvious. Such plants normally convert all their shoot meristems (*see p.51*) to reproduction, withdraw any spare nutrients from their roots and few remaining leaves, and then expire. In fact many annuals, by the time that their fruits come to maturity (*see pp.104–105*), are little more than a dead stick with some seeds carried at the top. In these plants, death is clearly a pre-programmed event.

Slow burn plants

In contrast to these rapid-hit annuals and short-lived perennials, it's quite hard to find any signs of senescence at all in long-lived plants. Age is a cellular process, much more than skin – or bark – deep. With time, the material of the cells eventually loses the ability to divide (*see p.51*), the repeated division and recombination of DNA (*see p.50*) introduces genetic errors, growth slows, and resistance to disease falls. In animals, this affects the whole body, but in plants the process is not so simple.

The tops of tall trees grow very slowly, with stunted leaves and all the outward signs of old age. However, if cuttings (*see pp.38–39*) are taken from the shoots at the top of a tree, the new plants produced show all the signs of juvenile vigour. Some grapevine (*Vitis vinifera*) cultivars have been propagated this way for centuries in vineyards, and the plants that are growing today seem no different from when the original plant was young. In fact, as long as you carry on taking cuttings, there seems to be no reason why most woody plants shouldn't effectively live forever.

Tenacious trees
This English oak (Quercus robur) is at least 600 years old, and is split into three parts, but still healthy.

Living Soil

Most gardeners claim to be struggling against their soil. So often the statement "I garden on ..." is spoken with an air of burden, as if the garden exists in spite of the soil, not because of it. Imagine if the response was "It's great – I garden on ..." Celebrate your garden soil: no matter how apparently unforgiving, it has characteristics perfect for a precise range of plants. As gardeners, all we need to do is identify our soil type, appreciate the implications, and then find the right plants – simple!

GET YOUR HANDS DIRTY

Soil is the life-blood of the garden, the source of the nutrients and minerals that allow our plants to thrive, and amongst the most valuable of all garden resources. We might dig it occasionally, throw a little compost on it every season or so, and wander over it to tend the plants, but only consider its ability to hold water either when it sticks to our boots with enthusiasm in winter or when plants adopt an exhausted, flaccid state after summer sunshine. Let's be honest: the vast majority of us haven't taken the time to acquaint ourselves properly with our garden soil, but if we did, all plants would benefit.

Good grounding

Typically gardeners distinguish their soil by describing it as either clay or sand, with little reference to other textures. However, the vast majority of soils have a blend of particles that produce an overall tendency or identifiable character.

Getting to know your soil
Soil structure and texture are often talked about, but how many of us actually get out and feel the soil?

We expect sand to be warm, free draining, and easy to dig, and clay to be heavy, wet, and hard to dig, but the consequences of the soil's texture run far deeper than this. The colour, the length of the growing season, water-holding capacity, rooting zone, and nutrient availability of soil are all dictated by the types and ratios of particles present and their arrangement within the soil profile (*see pp.161–62*). Identifying the nature of the soil in which your plants live leads to understanding of its possibilities and limitations.

Of course, to create the perfect garden we all need not only an intimate knowledge of the nature of our soil, but also a generous helping of realism; this is essential to prevent that age-old gardening condition of coveting plants that you know simply won't grow well in your soil. If you are prepared to work with your soil type rather than against it, the results can be truly amazing, and I speak as a gardener who gardens on clay – honestly.

Mineral particles

Soil contains a complex range of ingredients. Mineral particles, organic matter, microorganisms, invertebrates, fungi, water, air, nutrient compounds, metals, and simple plants are all likely to be present in just a handful of soil. However, the basic character and personality of the soil are governed by its mineral particles.

These originated, in most cases, from rock. Over millennia, bulky boulders are broken into ever-smaller particles by water, wind, ice, chemicals, and sheer pressure. During this weathering process some of the rock particles are totally decomposed, others are chemically altered, some even react to create new substances, such as clay. The type of weathering and its influence differs depending on geographic location, and the type of soil present in the garden tells a tale of its origin. Silica, found in many rocks, weathers rapidly in tropical conditions and is often washed from the emerging soils by rainwater, but in cool, humid climates, the same mineral weathers slowly, forming sand particles. Other minerals, such as feldspar and mica, weather quickly in cool, humid conditions, releasing calcium, iron, magnesium, and potassium, all key plant minerals. Perhaps even more important, especially to those gardeners with clay on their boots, is that in such a climate mica and feldspar are split into their alkaline components, which then react with dissolved aluminium to form clay particles. This is why cool, maritime Britain has so much more alkaline clay than the dry, continental interior of Europe.

The original rocks might be local – literally under your feet – but it is more likely that the soil in your garden has travelled a long way, transported by rivers, streams, glaciers, and the wind. Soil is constantly shifting as particles migrate downhill, settling in crevices, hollows, undulations, and ultimately in river valleys and flood plains, where the soils are often deepest. Such actions are even taking place on a minor scale in your garden as you read this. These diverse and disparate origins of the soil results in a cocktail that governs how your soil behaves and consequently how your plants perform.

Sampling surprises

With any form of sampling, remember that anomalies creep in. Take an average of six samples within a section of the garden, ignoring extreme results. Whether your garden is in a recent housing development or has been gardened for years, it isn't unusual to find remnants of previous activities. I know of wells, walls, and builders' rubble being discovered. I even worked in a garden where, whilst taking soil samples we unearthed an industrial chest freezer, which had apparently been used by an enterprising gardener as a pond. This, however, pales into insignificance in comparison with the activities of my great uncle, who on discovering that the engine in his car had expired, dug a hole in his garden and pushed his old coupé into a horticultural grave. I never did discover what effect this had on his runner bean crops!

Particles and pores

Soil texture is based on the size and shape of the particles. Exact analysis requires a laboratory, but it is possible to make a reasonable assessment in the garden. The shape of soil particles is the key to many of the soil's characteristics, because it influences the way the particles pack together and so the number and size of the pore spaces that hold air and water.

Flat particles stack like saucers

Water is held in small pores

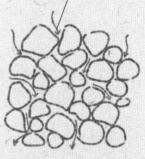

Water passes through slowly

Clay soil
Particles of clay are smaller than 0.002mm. They pack in horizontal layers with many small spaces between them.

Silty soil
Silt particles measure 0.002–0.02mm and are rounded. They pack with small spaces.

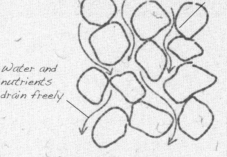

Rounded particles stack like grapefruit in a bowl

Water and nutrients drain freely

Root hairs
Root hairs seek water and nutrients in the pore spaces between the soil particles.

Sandy soil
Sand particles, from 0.02–2mm, are rounded and stack with few but large spaces between them.

Particles and pores

Despite horticulturists' fascination with the texture, shape, and mineral content of the particles, the spaces between are almost as important for the roots that are trying to penetrate the soil. Mineral particles of any kind cannot directly absorb water and dissolved nutrients (*see pp.130–33*), and the fine hairs of plant roots (*see p.58*) cannot break them down. Roots forage in the spaces between the particles, known as pores, and the more pore space, the better the potential rooting. In most normal garden soils, the pores between soil particles account for between 30 per cent and 70 per cent of total volume. Sandy soils, with their large particles, have up to 40 per cent pore space, silty soils up to 55 per cent, and clay soils offer up to 70 per cent – so that's good news for gardeners of clay soils.

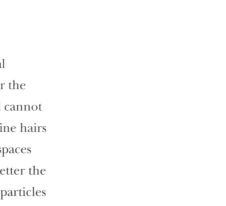

The size of the pores has a fundamental effect on their usefulness to our plants. This is where organic matter, water, and air collect, and roots seeking these can penetrate. Because pore size is dictated largely by the size and shape of the mineral particles surrounding it, the relatively few pores in sandy soil are large, while the relatively many pores in clay soil are small. This affects the passage of water through the soil, with the large pores of sand draining rapidly and small pores of clay slowly, in part explaining why clay soils stay wet for much of the year and sandy soils stay dry.

Perfect for clay
Meadowsweer (Filipendula) likes moisture and abundant rooting space and will grow well on even heavy clay.

Surface tension and soil water

Each particle of the soil retains a thin film of water against the pull of gravity by the force of surface tension. To see this, dip an apple into water, then allow the water to drip off. Once gravity has done its work, a patchy film of water remains on the skin of the apple: this is held by surface tension. Imagine millions of particles of soil in your garden holding water like this, and you will get an idea of the potential water available to plant roots, known as "field capacity". A pot plant plunged in a trough of water and then allowed to drain,

SANDY SOIL

To determine texture, crumble dry soil in the palm of one hand. Add water a few drops at a time and mix well until the soil absorbs no more water and becomes pliable but not sludgy. Now feel and try to mould the soil.

Gritty texture Gravel is large and obvious to the eye, while sand sounds crunchy and feels like coarse sandpaper or castor sugar.

Crumbles under pressure Roll the soil into a ball: if it falls apart, it is a sand. A sandy silt will make a ball, but not a sausage (see opposite).

Digging sandy soil Sandy soils are easy to dig, but avoid working them in hot, dry weather because water evaporates from them quickly.

or a garden soaked with rain then allowed to drain, is said to have reached field capacity. This is the optimum condition for most plants, as the large pores between soil particles are full of air, while the small pores and particle surfaces hold water.

The size of the mineral particles and the pore spaces in a soil dictate the amount of water held in it. Transmission or macro pores, found mainly in sandy soils, are too large to hold water permanently. They become flooded after heavy rain or irrigation but soon drain clear and become filled with air. Storage pores, found in silts and clays, hold water by surface tension, preventing it from being pulled down by gravity but still allowing it to be taken up by plant roots. Tiny residual pores, found in some clay soils, have such high surface tension that even plant roots cannot remove the water. So soils with small pore spaces, such as clays, have a high surface tension and may stay at field capacity for several weeks, while sandy soils, due to the large particles, tend to remain at field capacity for only a few hours.

Pore size affects not only the retention of water falling from above, but also water pulled up through the soil from the natural water table – the level at which soil is permanently saturated in water. This upward movement, capillary action, is also caused by the surface tension of soil particles pulling a thin film of water up. Small particles and pores exert a greater pull than large ones, which means that a sandy soil could pull water up about 20mm (1in) above the water table, while a clay soil can move water up 1.5m (5ft) or so. This means that even in times of drought the roots of plants in a soil with small pores have access to water drawn up from below.

Gardening with your soil

The aim of gardeners is to create soil that provides plants with optimum growing conditions, combining as many of the positive effects of the soil particles as possible while minimizing the negatives. The "good garden soil" that texts often refer to, which gives optimum conditions for the majority of garden plants,

contains about 30–50 per cent sand, 10–30 per cent clay, and 30–50 per cent silt. In practice there is little we can do to alter the mineral particles of our soil, although gardeners on clay soils add coarse particles of grit and sand to open the soil pores, while those on sandy soils add silts and clays to close the pores down. No matter what the soil texture, as long as mineral particles are detectable (that is to say, you are not gardening on pure organic matter already), the regular addition of organic matter (*see pp.165–69*) will enhance the performance of the soil and therefore the plants growing in it.

• **Sand or gravel provide less space** for plant roots, limiting uptake of nutrients and water; expect to apply more of each annually, or modify your plant choice to those that thrive in such well-drained conditions, avoiding fleshy-rooted plants and crops. Because silt and clay soils have a greater total pore space than sands, they offer a greater rooting zone.

• **Large particles absorb heat** from the sun, meaning that the soil warms quickly in the morning and retains the heat into the evening, and that soil temperatures increase quickly in spring and cool slowly in autumn. Because even a modest increase in temperature increases plant growth, the result is that gardening on sand entices plants into life earlier and provides a growing season up to eight weeks longer than gardening on clay. Exotic crops like tomatoes and flowers such as agapanthus will flower and fruit earlier grown in a coarse-textured soil.

• **Water warms more slowly** than the mineral solids in the soil, so the higher the water content of a soil, the cooler it will be. This not only slows plant root growth but also shortens the growing season; in winter it can even jeopardise the life of plants, particularly tender ones. Water carefully, especially plants in pots.

• **Clay soils retain water best** in the summer months, due to the high proportion of small pores. These smaller pores can become waterlogged in winter, and so roots die as they are unable to access air. The high proportion of large pores in sandy soils means that in winter months rainwater is unable to flood all the pores, so roots still have access to essential air.

SILT AND CLAY SOIL

If your soil holds together too well to be a sand (see opposite) or if its basic texture feels much finer, it will be a silt or a clay. Determine which by moulding it further: clay is the most malleable of all soil types.

Smooth to the touch Silt particles have a texture similar to icing sugar, while fine clay feels like plasticine between the fingers.

Holds together well If the soil can be rolled into a sausage and formed into a ring it is a clay; silt will make a sausage but not a ring.

Digging clay soil Clay soil in particular is heavy and sticky to dig. Avoid working it when it is wet, as the structure is easily destroyed then.

STRUCTURE AND LEVELS

Soil structure relates to the arrangement of mineral particles, organic matter, and microorganisms. In an ideal situation, particles will be in close proximity, with no large pore spaces where roots will dry out, but plentiful smaller pore spaces to accommodate roots and moisture. This will maximize water availability, aeration, and rooting potential, and consequently good growth. It is particularly important for new plants or seedlings that are establishing themselves in the garden. Wind, rain, sun, and frost all batter and erode the surface of soil, while at lower depths their effects are moderated, so the finest particles tend to be near the top, while larger fragments lie deeper. This is typical of most soils, except where erosion is marked.

Assessing your soil structure

Soil structure is judged largely on its physical appearance, and can be assessed by simply cultivating the soil and observing the way it crumbles. At one

Cracked soil
As water from poorly structured soil evaporates, particles move closer, causing shrinkage cracks and root damage.

extreme is a "grain" structure, in which there is little union between particles; they will fall into single grains, become dusty, and erode easily when water runs over them. This is usually found in soils that have undergone prolonged flooding, washing, or have insufficient organic matter, and is typical of imported soil used around new developments. The result is a soil that bakes hard in summer and often waterlogs in winter. At the other extreme is "massive" soil, in which all the particles bind together into a mass with little evidence of cracks and weak fracture lines. It is usually due to heavy compaction while the soil is wet, and is also typical of soils around new developments, particularly clays, where the constant trafficking of machines has compressed the soil particles. As a result, the soil is poorly drained, offers little opportunity for root penetration, and can bake hard in summer. The optimum soil structure in gardens is referred to as a "crumb", largely due to the resemblance to crumble topping: fine, rounded or slightly angular clusters of particles or "peds", which don't fall into individual grains. This demonstrates high quantities of organic matter (*see pp. 165–69*), good pore space (*see pp. 157–58*), good drainage, and plenty of opportunities for roots.

Levels of the soil profile

The development of soil creates a potential habitat for plants, which not only push their roots into the soil, but also deposit organic matter, which in turn stimulates the soil organisms that break it down to improve soil structure. The result of these actions is the development of a soil "profile", or cross section, with distinct layers or horizons of soil.

The uppermost level consists of organic matter, newly deposited or newly decomposed, with very little evidence of mineral particles. This may be only a few millimetres thick, as in the case of the thatch on fine mown lawns, or it may be several centimetres thick, as it is in ancient deciduous woodland. In some cases the dried organic matter, which will ultimately benefit the soil, can restrict rainwater entering the soil. This is often the case on lawns where the clippings are left after mowing, or where evergreen shrubs, conifers, and some large trees such as sycamore (*Acer pseudoplatanus*) deposit organic matter in large quantities, and is a good lesson to gardeners to apply organic matter in frequent, small doses rather than one heavy application.

Below this lies the upper topsoil, comprising a blend of mineral particles (*see pp. 154–59*) and fine organic matter. Because of the presence of organic matter this layer is darkest in colour, experiences high levels of activity from soil organisms, and is where the crumb structure develops. Oxidization of iron in the soil often enriches this layer with hues of red and russet. Well-drained and aerated, this is where the vast majority of the plant roots are, harvesting nutrients and water, but due to the good drainage and root penetration, water soluble nutrients and minerals are likely to be leached from this horizon as rainwater percolates through.

Topsoil and subsoil
Topsoil is dark, rich in organic matter, and formed from fine particles; subsoil contains less organic matter, so is paler. It may also contain larger mineral particles.

Slippery when wet

Poor structure is especially associated with working soils when they are wet. Water held in the soil acts as a lubricant between the particles, so that under pressure from boots, wheelbarrows, or machinery the particles will slide into their most compact state, compressing the pore spaces between them. This is particularly problematic in clay soils, where the plate-like particles move from being randomly arranged when well-structured, to being tightly stacked, impeding the movement of roots, air, and water. This is precisely why gardeners of clay soils are best staying off the soil as much as possible, especially when it is wet.

Beneath the upper topsoil is the enriched lower topsoil, where the nutrients from above are deposited. Less organic matter and fewer soil organisms and roots are to be found here, and as a result the soil structure is less well established, with peds being larger and more blocky than the crumb structure of the upper topsoil. This relatively poor structure means the soil is less consistent in water retention and more prone to damage from mismanagement, such as working it when wet. It is often this soil that is left around new building developments, the fine grade topsoil having been removed, and this is why gardeners in new properties commonly struggle to get plants established.

Deeper still is a final layer that grades into the largely unweathered, unstructured parent material. Sometimes called subsoil, it is likely to be heavily littered with large fragments of parent rock. Although often containing nutrients, this layer is of very little value to plant roots. It tends to lack the rich colouration of the topsoil and is composed of coarse, blocky, angular peds.

While in theory the layers of the soil profile should be easily and readily visible in the garden, in practice they are not always quite as evident. It is quite common to find the two layers of topsoil indistinguishable, usually as a result of deep cultivation, and layers can differ enormously in thickness even within the confines of one garden, so affecting the choice and performance of plants. This is just one reason why getting to know the personality of your soil is key to soil improvement, plant selection, and successful gardening.

Damage to soil structure

A poorly structured soil is generally the result of major physical interference. This can be physical activity from machinery, cultivation, and construction, but can also be natural events from rain dripping from tree canopies to floods. Dripping rain results in the surface of the soil losing its structure, creating a "pan", which water or plant roots and shoots cannot easily penetrate.

Seeds fail to germinate, and bulbs emerge with distorted and contorted foliage and flowers. Break surface pans prior to planting and avoid heavy overhead irrigation, which can cause them. A high water table is likely to cause deep structural compromise, and it is possible to create a subterranean pan.

In sandy soils, this is usually caused by a fluctuating water table oxidizing iron in the soil, usually forming a dark, rust-brown layer of dense material a few millimetres thick at variable depths. On clay soils, cultivation and machines are the most common causes of a pan in which the particles are compacted with a distinctive horizontal layering. This may be caused by pressure on the surface being transmitted down to a level where there is enough water to lubricate the soil particles; hence the depth of the pan varies from one place to another depending on conditions. Machines such as rotavators can cause a pan, the rapidly spinning blades wiping through wet soil and smearing it, almost like the outside of a terracotta pot, into a smooth, impermeable layer. So rotavate clay soil only when it is dry, or dust off the spade and start hand digging.

Detecting trouble below the surface

Dig down through the soil and damage becomes evident, but there are other signs that should alert you as you wield the spade.

• **Often a solid pan prevents water percolating** through the soil, so waterlogging or a raised water table may be evident.

• **Soil immediately above the pan** may be grey, because iron in the soil cannot oxidize and turn brown due to the water present. However, plant roots in the soil above the pan are often closely surrounded by distinctive rust, as they allow air into the root channel and so iron oxidization occurs around them.

• **Roots are physically impeded,** often forming a horizontal mat along the top of the pan, which leaves plants prone to stress from waterlogging, drought, and nutrient deficiency.

• **Trees and shrubs** are prone to wind damage, as their roots are prevented from anchoring deep in the soil, and are often levelled in strong winds.

• **Earthworm and microorganism activity** is limited to the upper soil, reducing the incorporation of organic matter that would improve structure.

• **Trees and shrubs show signs of drought** in summer and may rot at the roots during winter. In addition small leaves, reduced vigour, and nutrient deficiency may be evident.

Well-structured soil
A good depth of even, dark topsoil with deep roots and plenty of worms is the gardening ideal.

Smeared clay
Clay particles lubricated by water and then squeezed together readily form a dense barrier to roots and water.

Improving soil structure

An absence of a fine crumb structure, poor soil profile, and even the presence of a soil pan doesn't spell disaster in the garden since there are several ways in which structure can be improved.

• **Break pans,** either by digging through them, a tough but worthwhile activity or, on a large site, using a pan-breaking attachment on a cultivator.

• **Harness the power of nature:** digging the ground prior to winter exposes clods of earth to the freeze-thaw action of frost. This constant expansion and contraction breaks apart compacted soil particles.

• **Use plants:** if you can afford to be patient and wait a season or two to see results, try sowing temporary crops onto bare ground. The penetrating roots the clovers and other members of the pea family (Leguminosae), can soon start to open and refresh compacted ground, after which they can simply be dug in (*see pp.181–85*).

"Improving structure means that gardeners' impatience to plant has to be restrained in favour of work on the soil, but the long-term results are worth it."

• **Try double digging,** if you are prepared for a little hard labour in the name of a beautiful garden. This involves cultivating to twice the depth of the spade to relieve compaction and improve soil structure by mixing organic matter deep into the soil profile. You'll be glad to hear that this is usually completed only once in the life of a bed or border, and after you have exerted yourself it will become plain why Victorian gardeners called it "bastard trenching".

• **Employ the services of both nature** and the billions of microorganisms present in the soil by spreading organic matter across the soil (*see pp.170–71*). This mimics leaf fall in autumn, a process that has served to enrich soils for millions of years. The most enticing aspect of this approach is that, as long as the right organic matter is used, it can simply be spread on the soil surface. Soil organisms do all the hard work of incorporating and blending it, and as a bonus, in the process their energetic activity further enhances the structure.

FREE SOIL CONDITIONER

If ever there was a single golden rule for gardening it must be "apply organic matter". The term organic matter refers to all organic elements of the soil, whether living, dead, or decaying; all have a profound effect on the fertility, behaviour, and productivity of the soil, and I know of few cases where a generous application of well-composted material won't improve growing conditions. Rapid plant growth, early seasons, and moderation of drought and flood are all due to high organic matter content.

Permission to be untidy

Nature of course has rather conveniently been supplying organic matter to the soil for millennia, principally in the form of leaf fall, but also from stems, boughs, and bark. In truth, every part of every plant is destined to become basic organic matter. They join animal dung, insects, invertebrates, and everything else that was once living, including expired gardeners, in creating a product that enlivens and enriches our soils. Without it, plants struggle to survive.

Nature does it best
The deposits of leaves on a woodland floor increase the soil depth by an estimated 5mm (¼in) every year.

Most organic matter in the soil is derived from plant remains, so the current tendency amongst gardeners to incessantly tidy, sweep, and clear stems, leaves, and flowers almost as soon as they are faltering goes against nature. Tidy gardens aren't gardens rich in organic matter, unless the organic matter that has been removed is composted (*see pp.172–75*) and then returned to the soil in a more decomposed state. Every garden has a source of organic matter; from grass cuttings to vegetable peelings, any and all matter of organic origin has a part to play.

The process of breakdown

The moment a fallen leaf touches the soil, the process of breaking it down begins. First the macro soil organisms, such as earthworms and ground beetles, eat it. They are remarkably plentiful, with an estimated 2 million per hectare (80,000 per acre); they are also ravenous, consuming 100 tonnes a year.

Microorganisms such as fungi and bacteria also play a part during these initial stages, but they are most active after the work of the macro organisms. Even more plentiful, the microorganisms are estimated at 7 million per gram (21 million per ounce) of soil, tirelessly feeding on organic matter. They thrive on the sugars, starches, and cellulose, breaking them down into carbon, hydrogen, and oxygen, which they use for energy and growth. They also use nitrogen compounds in the dead matter, such as proteins and amino acids, to fuel the production of their body protein. Populations of microorganisms explode with the addition of organic matter to the soil, but after an initial frenzy of activity they decline unless more is added, so continual applications of organic matter as mulches (*see pp. 201–202*) and compost are needed to maintain high levels. Populations can also be aided by ensuring that the soil holds enough water and is well aerated, and that the soil pH is maintained between 5.5 and 7.5 (*see p. 137*).

Sources of organic matter

All living things are potentially a source of organic matter, but inevitably some are more useful than others. This is largely due to the requirements of the microorganisms to feast on the right blend of foods. Their cells are composed of six parts carbon and one part nitrogen; if the organic matter they feed on reflects this, the population thrives, but if the ratio of carbon to nitrogen alters significantly, populations cannot increase and decomposition is reduced. It is therefore important to supply the right organic matter, with a carbon to nitrogen ratio as near to 6:1 as possible.

Soil organisms can deal with high-carbon material, but to compensate for the high levels of carbon they must raid nitrogen from the soil: this has a fundamental effect on plants, which rely on the nitrogen as a key nutrient (*see p. 131*). This is why gardeners should never apply large quantities of fresh, undigested organic matter to their plants: it is far better to compost it first.

CARBON TO NITROGEN RATIOS OF PLANTS

These are approximate carbon to nitrogen ratios for fresh plant material. The difference in ratios explains why conifer needles take longer to decompose than grass cuttings.

Legumes	15:1
Grass	18:1
Broad leaves	30:1
Straw	50:1
Coniferous leaves	90:1

Annual harvest
The crop of autumn leaves should never go to waste. Raked up and stacked in a simple mesh bin (inset) or even a black bag, they break down into perfect soil conditioner.

To illustrate the point, my grandfather was a great rose enthusiast and used to religiously apply fresh horse manure to his specimens as mulch. Over several years the plants became weak and pale, losing the enthusiasm to flower. The reason was the high carbon to nitrogen ratio of the fresh manure, about 40:1; if only he had used well-rotted manure, with a ratio of about 12:1.

Humus and humification

Following this breakdown of organic matter, what is left is humus, a resilient and stable series of compounds based on carbon, hydrogen, and oxygen. Humus is a fine, spongelike, usually dark brown material. Importantly it carries a negative electrical charge, which binds positively charged plant nutrients (*see p.137*) and it is thought to be up to ten times more efficient at retaining nutrients than clay. This is just one reason why organic matter increases the nutrients available to our plants and makes more efficient use of the fertilizers we add.

In addition to retaining nutrients, humus is also responsible for the building of good soil structure. Filling the pore spaces, it acts as a buffer or shock-absorber between particles, especially those of clay, preventing them from bonding together when they are compressed, and improving drainage, aeration, and root penetration. It also makes soil easier to dig and reduces the chances of soil pans forming (*see pp.162–63*). Due to its sponge-like structure, humus can retain 2–5 times its own weight in water, about half of which will remain available to plant roots. The soil of most well-managed gardens contains about 5 per cent humus. This may not seem much, but the effects are startling; this amount can improve the water-holding capacity of a clay loam by 30 per cent and a sandy soil by 50 per cent over the same soils without humus.

The rich brown colour of humus gives most temperate soils their distinctive dark brown colour, which increases the growing season of the soil.

Natural decay

All broken down organic matter contributes to humus, which is found primarily in upper soil levels.

Leaf litter

Worms, beetles, and others start breakdown process

Dark soil rich in humus

Less organic matter in lighter coloured, less rich soil

Microscopic bacteria and fungal mycelia complete breakdown into humus

Research suggests that a soil darkened by 5 per cent humus warms faster in spring and cools slower in autumn, effectively giving a 1–3°C (2–6°F) rise in temperature to a depth of 15cm (6in), perfect for most garden plants.

Soils rich in humus are also generally more efficient at breaking down and releasing plant nutrients. This is in part due to the conditions that high organic matter content creates – good drainage and good aeration – which allow soil organisms to thrive and release a steady stream of plant nutrients. This efficiency can however be compromised by alterations in moisture level, compaction, major changes in pH outside of the optimum 5.5–7.5, and the addition of organic matter with a high carbon to nitrogen ratio, so once established a well-structured soil should be managed and worked carefully.

Commercial soil conditioners

For those gardeners who cannot generate enough of their own organic matter, help is at hand. These products are all used as soil improvers, supplying a limited range of nutrients but a high dose of organic matter.

• **Spent mushroom compost** This is a composted, straw-based waste product from commercial mushroom farming, which provides high levels of organic matter. It is also highly alkaline, so can be used to moderate pH, but must not be used on ericaceous plants.

• **Farmyard manure** High in nutrients, especially nitrogen and potassium, this is a rich organic-matter product that is best when composted with material that has a high carbon-to-nitrogen ratio, such as straw. Due to the high fertility, it is essential that manure is effectively composted before it is added to the garden, to prevent scorch of plant cells.

• **Wormcasts** Once popular in gardens, the commercial production of worms for large-scale composting has resulted in a resurgence of interest in this product. High in humus, it has a very high water- and nutrient-holding capacity. One of the great benefits of wormcasts is the high percentage of active microorganisms, which are beneficial for root development. This improves soils significantly not just through the addition of organic matter but also by increasing the release of nutrients already in the soil. The disadvantage is that those organisms have a shelf life, usually six months in a packaged product, and they are vulnerable to sunlight and drying out, so open and use any commercial product quickly, forking it into the soil as you go.

Turning in
Whether you add wormcasts or your own compost, organic matter is usually forked into the surface layers of the soil.

Digging in compost
Earthworms actively pull organic matter into the soil, where they ingest and digest it up to six times over.

To dig or not to dig?

I am always mystified by gardeners who make gardening hard work. I prefer to let nature make a generous share of the effort while I direct and gently guide. That's not to say that I don't break a sweat, or feel the warmth of exercised muscles, just that hard graft isn't my main reason to be in the garden. So I am always interested in methods that use natural processes, like the incorporation of organic matter. The annual addition of rotted material is hugely beneficial, but I have always doubted the benefit of digging it in. Who, I asked myself, is digging in the wild? Answer: millions of microorganisms. Spread organic matter on the surface in autumn, and by spring almost all will be gone. Fungi, earthworms, beetles, and bacteria have revelled in dragging it into the soil, and I have revelled in the beauty of my garden without back-breaking work.

There is more to this than laziness. Many plants have fibrous, shallow roots (*see p.58*), easily damaged by digging or even light forking. Also, 80 per cent of soil microorganisms, sensitive to light, temperature, and moisture levels, live in the upper 5cm (2in) of soil; disturbing their stable habitat heavily depletes numbers. Turning the soil also brings high numbers of dormant weed seeds to the surface, where they will germinate (*see pp.26–27*). Perhaps most worrying, though, is the potential loss of humus. Agricultural research suggests that soil turned annually for 50 years can lose 55–90 per cent of its humus, most of it in the first decade. This is because cultivation exposes organic matter to moisture and aeration, resulting in oxidization. The effects are most severe on sandy soils and in warm areas, such as many of the soils of East Anglia in Britain and around Lake Erie in the United States. They occur despite the addition of organic matter, and result in the loss of soil structure, seen in poor drainage, poor nutrient retention, and poor buffering from cropping on these soils.

Reduced digging

The aim in the garden is not to avoid digging totally. Digging in annual weeds, crop residues, or green manures, and digging to relieve compaction, are worthwhile, but most of us relish the idea of reducing it where possible. This method ironically involves, at least at first, digging. Dig a trench about 30cm (12in) deep – less if subsoil (*see p.162*) is near the surface – and spread a 5cm (2in) layer of well-rotted compost in it. Dig a second trench next to this, using

the soil to backfill the first trench, then add compost and backfill this trench from the next. Critically, unlike "bastard trenching" or "double digging" (*see p.164*), the soil layers are not turned. The compost boosts organic matter in the soil, and further material is left on the surface in autumn.

In the vegetable garden, where seeds and young plants are constantly planted, add 10cm (4in) or so of compost on the soil surface in autumn and sow into the remains or upper soil in spring. Even crops such as potatoes can be grown using this technique: place tubers on top of the compost and cover with at least 10–15cm (4–6in) of compost and then a layer of straw. As the shoots grow, add straw to a depth of 30cm (12in) or so. Plenty of compost is required, but if your garden generates enough then try it. Crop yields are about the same as for a dug garden or bed, but heavy labour is much reduced.

Bale gardens

If you can't wait to throw the spade away, the bale garden may be for you. This is based on experiments by commercial growers, using bales as a compost heap and raised bed. High-nitrogen hay is best, but straw will do. Box in four bales, stacked with the "grain" running vertically, then water until sodden. Add a 5cm (2in) layer of high-nitrogen fertilizer such as fresh chicken manure, mixed with fresh lawn cuttings. Some gardeners add urine to stimulate decomposition, but the source of nitrogen you choose is a matter of taste! Add 15–20cm (6–8in) of well-rotted compost and bone meal, water well, and cover with plastic.

In four weeks decomposition will be generating heat, and crops can be sown into a layer of loamy soil spread on the block. Crops with high nitrogen demands, such as brassicas, do well in this first phase, as do early crops of cucurbits. Once sown or planted, cover the soil with a mulch of straw and water the bale frequently, although this can be reduced by using a cloche frame over the plants. After the first harvest, re-dress the bale with a little more well-rotted compost and you can sow or or transplant again immediately. Well watered bales should last up to three years, leaving at the end a rich compost.

Raised beds
These were used in early monastic gardens, with beds narrow enough to reach the middle from the edges.

MAKING COMPOST

Compost is a rather generic name for a composition of mineral and organic matter particles. It refers to both the medium used for potting, but also the steaming heap of prunings and trimmings at the bottom the garden. However, the term composting refers specifically to the decomposition of organic matter. This activity is an essential part of retaining beneficial material in the garden, and a source of free nutrients and soil improver. It is a key way of using raw organic matter from the garden so that the carbon to nitrogen ratio stays balanced, while maintaining a managed-looking garden.

Choosing and siting a compost bin

The secret to making good compost lies in the site, ingredients, and microorganism stimulants used. Despite myriad compost recipes and advice, I have always found the traditional methods the most effective.

Start by selecting the right location, remembering that the success of the compost heap relies on the soil organisms being active for as long a time as possible, and for this they require a sheltered and warm environment. Avoid both full sun, which causes the heap to heat too quickly and become too hot, and frost pockets, drafts, or cold shadows. Cast aside the notion that a compost heap is for the area of the garden where nothing grows, and think of it instead as perfectly placed where you would like to sit! Fork the ground over on your chosen spot, incorporating fresh grass cuttings or green vegetable trimmings, and place an open-bottomed compost bin on top. Cultivating the ground exposes soil organisms to the base of the compost, and the green trimmings provide a ready meal, announcing the presence of great pickings and enticing all the likely agents of decay into the heap. This is why freestanding heaps not in contact with the ground often struggle to create great compost, although you can add topsoil that will bring with it composting microorganisms.

The precise construction of the compost bin is of little relevance, be it plastic, wood, or just makeshift; of more importance is the size. Wooden bins

Plastic compost bins
These inexpensive, compact bins are popular but require more careful management than larger heaps.

1m square by 70cm high (36in by 28in) allow easy layering; taller, narrower plastic bins also make good compost but layering can be fiddly. Use a lid to maintain the essential moisture levels of the heap; this may be an integral part of the bin or simply a piece of thick old carpet. For an average-sized garden of mixed ornamental and vegetable planting, work on creating two heaps. This allows one to be filled while the other is composting. It is also worth having temporary storage areas for organic matter when there is a glut, for instance of grass cuttings in summer or dry stems and leaves in autumn and winter. This allows the material to be added to the compost heap when it is needed, rather than when the garden provides it, leading to more efficient composting.

Hot and cold composting

Two types of composting are commonly used. Gardeners who use "hot" or "rapid" compost heaps exploit the soil organisms' ability to multiply rapidly when given plenty of fresh green material rich in nitrogen and moisture, such as grass cuttings. The organisms reach fever pitch, becoming wildly excited and, as a result of rapid and plentiful respiration, generate incredibly high temperatures. It is not unusual for these heaps to reach 50–60°C (120–140°F),

Compost bins
If your garden and household generate enough waste, this is the ideal: three large bins, one to use, one to fill, and one to hold spare matter.

"The benefits of good compost to the garden make it worth the sacrifice of a potential seating area."

which will kill most weed seeds and garden diseases. Hot heaps demand not only a plentiful supply of green material, but also good aeration to avoid the heap becoming anaerobic – that is, running out of the oxygen these organisms need to thrive. For this reason the occasional layer of hay or straw is added, but apart from this no dry or coarse material. Hot heaps can provide fine compost in a few months, but they are fickle to manage, especially when green material in temperate gardens is in short supply in winter. They also don't accommodate all the surplus organic matter a garden generates.

More appropriate for most gardens is the "slow" or cool compost heap. This is set up in exactly the same way but the range of ingredients is mixed, with high-fibre brown material of a high carbon-to-nitrogen ratio (*see p.166*) as well as fresh green material of a low carbon-to-nitrogen ratio. In these heaps the soil organism populations don't soar, the temperature remains at around 40–45°C (104–113°F), and composting takes nine to twelve months. The process can be speeded up by adding small quantities of water to the heap to aid soil organism activity, and also by adding material high in nitrogen.

Commercial compost activators work because they are high in nitrogen; as a free alternative try adding leaves of nettles (*Urtica*) and comfrey (*Symphytum*) or peas (*Pisum*), chicken manure, and ammonium fertilizers, or even urine, all of which are naturally rich in nitrogen, creating a carnival atmosphere amongst the soil organisms.

Microscopic bacteria in compost
Just as in the soil, breakdown in the compost bin is carried out by a range of organisms including fungi, bacteria, and microfauna.

Fungi fruiting body

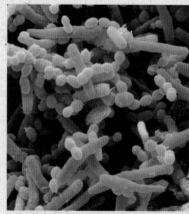

Saprophytic bacteria

Turtle mites

Making your heap

The art of creating good compost is similar to the art of making a good cake. Start with good quality ingredients, add them in the right quantities, and then be patient while it takes shape. Use the wrong ingredients or quantities, and the result is sludge.

The ingredients dictate the success and also the speed of decomposition. Generally anything that is organic in origin is fine, with the obvious exceptions of cooked foods, meats, and dairy products, which attract vermin, pet faeces, and diseased plants. It is also good to avoid perennial weeds and those that have set seed. I have always found success with adding alternate layers of green material (fresh cuttings, leaves, vegetable waste) and brown material (dry leaves, herbaceous stems, hay, paper and cardboard). Limit each layer to about 5cm (2in) in depth over the whole heap, and avoid pressing down, because this causes compaction, reducing airflow and inhibiting soil organism activity. If you feel that the material is too coarse, try shredding it or running the lawn mower over it, collecting the shreddings in the grass box. This reduces the breakdown task of the soil organisms and speeds up composting. The only foliage I avoid adding to the heap in large quantities is that of evergreens, as these are difficult to break down; better to shred them and over time combine them with green material to be added to the heap.

Add worms to compost
Macro- and microorganisms naturally migrate into compost heaps, but you can help by adding worms and old potting compost from pots.

In a well-structured heap turning the compost shouldn't be required, and is best avoided as exposing the inside of the heap allows it to cool. Simply fork off the top un-composted layer, placing it in the bottom of the next heap, and remove the perfect compost below. When ripe, the material should be dark brown, crumbly, and fine, with no discernable smell or uncomposted organic matter. This material is ideal for using as a soil conditioner around the garden. It tends to be low to moderately high in nutrients, particularly nitrogen, and should be lightly forked into the soil, as the microorganisms tend to perish quickly in sunlight.

Don't worry if, after nine months of waiting, your compost is imperfect, as it does take a while to get the right balance. If it is dry and little of the coarse matter has decomposed, add more green material and a little more water or compost activators. If fluid is oozing from the base and a there is a pungent smell, reduce the green material and add more brown material. Experiment to find the right balance for your heap.

POTTING COMPOSTS

Although called composts, these are perhaps more appropriately termed growing media, since this is their primary role. They contain organic matter, mineral particles, and fertilizers, blended to suit the requirements of particular plants at different periods of their life. Mixing your own requires space to store ingredients, time, and care. Commercial compost avoids all this and delivers a more consistent product, as long as it is used appropriately. How many times when sowing seeds, pricking out, or potting on have you reached for the nearest compost rather than one designed for the purpose?

"There was a time when gardeners jealously guarded their own potting compost recipes, adding secret ingredients to boost productivity and growth."

Compost recipes

Historically, potting composts could be divided into loam- or soil-based and peat-based. Sand, silt, and clay, collectively called loam, perform the same role in compost as in garden soil (*see pp.154–59*), holding moisture and nutrients in a dense growing medium. On its own, loam tends to be too wet and heavy for seeds or cuttings, while also too dense for most plants grown in pots. The more large particles, such as sand and grit, are present, the more sharply drained it will be. Traditionally peat was the mainstay of composts; it retains moisture but is free draining, and holds nutrients well, allowing them to be readily accessed by plants. It was also widely available, cheap to extract, and light to transport once dried. However, concerns over the destruction of peat habitats in some parts of the world have led to alternatives being sought to create peat-free or peat-reduced composts, and each has various advantages and drawbacks.

The important consideration with all the peat alternatives is that while they are suitable replacements for raw organic matter, they are not all good direct alternatives for the precise characteristics of peat, so the practical application and management of the compost needs to be altered. The consensus amongst professionals is that when these alternatives are combined to exploit the positive aspects and reduce the negatives, they can be as effective as peat-based products on most species that are not acid-loving or ericaceous (*see p.138*).

Compost ingredients

All composts, whether home made or commercially produced, contain key ingredients which possess individual attributes and are chosen to perform a particular function. The search for alternatives to peat has led to the introduction of new ingredients, which may need more careful management.

Green waste Sourced from municipal composting, this is variable but high in organic matter, moist but free draining, and holds and releases nutrients well. It can be rich, particularly in nitrogen and potassium, but may harbour weed seeds.

Peat This was the ideal material for many purposes, but its use now raises many environmental concerns.

Coir This absorbs large amounts of moisture, making it wet in winter, but dries quickly in summer; it can be tricky to manage unless used with other ingredients. Coir does not retain nutrients well, but releases high levels of potassium when composted.

Loam This retains nutrients and water well in composts for long-term container plants, but can be too heavy for seeds and cuttings.

Ground and composted bark Open and fibrous, this keeps cutting composts free draining. It is low in nutrients and may "lock up" nutrients.

Leaf mould Low in nutrients, this retains and releases moisture and nutrients much like peat. It improves structure, is rich in beneficial organisms, and when sieved makes ideal seed compost. Best made at home.

Different needs
The qualities needed in a potting compost for plants growing long-term in containers are quite different from those needed to support root growth on cuttings (inset).

However, the resultant compost is generally wetter in winter and drier in summer and is less efficient at supplying plant nutrients, so adjust the way you garden with it. Expect to add grit for plants in containers you wish to over-winter, and irrigate more often in summer but deliver the same total amount of water; similarly, feed twice as often but at half the strength.

Basic mixes

At best plants in the wrong compost under-perform, at worst they may die. To choose the appropriate compost, start by asking what the plant needs.

• **Seeds need** little long-term support from the compost, as they contain the nutrients needed for germination (*see pp. 30–31*) and most are pricked out within a few weeks. They need compost that will hold sufficient moisture to stimulate germination, but not so much that fungal diseases are harboured; lower water capacity also results in warmer temperatures, speeding germination. Open structure and good aeration are essential, as is the ability of the seedling leaves to move through the soil to the surface unimpeded by large particles. Seed compost tends to be sand-based, with a little added humus or loam and very dilute nitrogen- and phosphorus-biased nutrients (*see p. 131*).

High demands
Young plants need high levels of nutrients in their growing medium, especially when crammed togther in pots or hanging baskets.

• **Cuttings require** good aeration and drainage to establish root growth (*see pp. 38–39*). In the case of soft and semi-ripe cuttings with foliage, it is essential that moisture is readily available, but excess can drain freely away to prevent disease. A weak nutrient mix is required to sustain growth for one or several months, but nutrients can scorch young roots, so it is usual to add liquid feed once rooting has occurred. Cutting composts are usually composed of grit and ground bark to aid drainage, along with sand and nitrogen- and phosphorus-biased nutrients.

• **Young plants** require an open, free draining compost but more moisture than seeds and cuttings, to support the stresses from water loss in the developing leaf. As the plant is likely to remain in this compost for at least one growing season, it is rich in balanced nutrients formulated to release slowly for root and shoot development. Check the packaging, but expect a maximum of six months supply, and after that be prepared to feed them heavily.

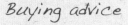

Buying advice

Whichever type you choose, commercially packaged compost will have been sterilized of all weed seeds and disease organisms in the production process, so these products are more consistent than home-mixed alternatives. Of course, this advantage is only maintained while the packages remain unopened, so regard loose piles of compost, as offered by some suppliers, with suspicion. While weeds and pathogens might be moving into your opened compost, fertilizers will be making an exit, especially if water can enter the packaging: plant nutrients are largely water soluble and easily washed out. The best advice is to buy only fresh products, that have preferably been kept protected from rain, and use them in the same season that you buy them.

Water-retaining granules
These absorb hundreds of times their own weight of water, 95 per cent of which is available to the plant roots.

You will also see multi-purpose compost, a seemingly convenient way of providing everything in one bag. Unfortunately, this is inevitably a compromise, being too fibrous, moisture retentive, and rich for seeds and cuttings, but not rich enough for long-term growth. This is not to say that plants won't grow in it, just that some might find life a little more challenging, and careful attention to watering and feeding will be required.

Specialist mixes

Specialist mixes aren't always a gimmick to lubricate your wallet. Hanging basket, tub, and container composts are useful for bedding plants and short term plantings that last only through spring and summer, and contain a fertilizer aimed at providing high nutrient levels over a short delivery period. Bedding plants in pots and tubs to me represent mass planting into the smallest possible container. Inevitably their bountiful canopy places high water demands on the compost, so many bedding plant composts contain artificial water-storing polymers to even out the drought-and-deluge syndrome often experienced by bedding plants. Remember that the object of potting composts is to recreate the soil conditions that the plant would thrive in naturally; if there is specialist compost available for the plant you wish to grow, use it.

GREEN MANURES

A green manure is a crop sown to be dug into the ground while it is young, green, and fleshy, to improve the soil. Their canopy protects the soil from water loss and high temperatures in summer and from nutrient leaching and rain-droplet compaction in winter, and limits the germination of weed seeds. Some have deep, penetrating roots, which open the soil structure. A small number of species, referred to as "dynamic accumulators" can also enrich the soil, extracting a range of minerals and nutrients that they accumulate in their cells. Such plants are valuable for gradually enhancing the fertility of the soil, a practice widespread in agriculture.

General green manures

A diverse range of plants is available to grow as green manures to suit the soil and season. These may be annual, biennial, or perennial, frost-tender or frost-hardy, and some can produce several crops of foliage that will enrich the compost heap (*see pp.172–75*) before they are turned into the ground. Whichever green manure you choose, remember that it should be turned into the soil several weeks prior to the planting of the following crop to allow sufficient time for it to be broken down (*see pp.166–68*) and the nutrients made available to the new crop.

It is also worth remembering that biennial plants grown for prolonged periods build up cellulose-rich woody tissues that have a high ratio of carbon to nitrogen (*see p.166*); if these are turned into the ground the decomposition period is prolonged and soil organisms may raid nitrogen from the surrounding soil, with a negative effect on the soil nutrient levels.

Ideal green manure
Clovers (Trifolium) are ideal green manures, attracting beneficial insects at the same time as improving the soil.

LEVELS OF NITROGEN

The amount of nitrogen fixed by members of the pea family varies significantly:

Alfalfa (*Medicago sativa*)
250g/sq m (9oz/sq yd)

Red clover (*Trifolium pratense*)
150g/sq m (5oz/sq yd)

Hairy vetch (*Vicia villosa*)
80g/sq m (3oz/sq yd)

To put these figures into some perspective, heavy-feeding plants such as sweetcorn, tomatoes, and potatoes need about as much nitrogen as the alfalfa can provide, while lettuce requires the amount produced by vetch. It is not always possible to sow the plants that provide the highest return; soil conditions, season, and hardiness will all affect the choice of plant species used.

Nitrogen fixers

The best-known dynamic accumulators are plants of the legume or pea family, also called the Papilionaceae or Leguminosae. This contains all peas and beans (*Pisum*, *Phaseolus*, and *Vicia*) as well as ornamentals such as lupins and laburnum, which accumulate nitrogen in their roots. Roam through natural landscapes where the soil is shallow or impoverished, and it is often easy to spot the legumes, especially when the pea-like flowers are open.

The dominance of the pea family in harsh sites with poor, low-fertility soil is no accident; these plants have evolved an intimate relationship with soil bacteria from the *Rhizobia* species, giving them a distinct advantage over other plants. The process involves a mutually beneficial, or symbiotic, action. The bacteria penetrate the roots to use plant sugars, but at the same time they harvest or "fix" nitrogen from the air in the soil pores, which plants cannot absorb directly. This nitrogen accumulates outside the plant's normal roots, and is held in small, white nodules. Once the nodules separate from the plant, or the plant decomposes, the nitrogen is released and becomes available to the roots of other plants. This relationship is well documented, and sowing members of the pea family as a key part of the rotation system (*see pp.203–209*)

Green manures for light soils

Crimson clover
(*Trifolium incarnatum*)
Sow: Early spring to late summer
Duration: Hardy annual; 3 months
Soil: Well drained, moisture retentive
Properties: Fast growing; flowers attract beneficial insects
Nitrogen: Moderate

Fenugreek
(*Trigonella foenum-graecum*)
Sow: Early spring to late summer
Duration: Tender annual; 3 months
Soil: Well drained, moisture retentive
Properties: Fast growing, not for over-wintering in frosts
Nitrogen: Very low

Lupin
(*Lupinus angustifolius*)
Sow: Early spring to early summer
Duration: Hardy annual; 4 months
Soil: Good on light and acidic
Properties: Poor weed suppression; roots improve soil structure
Nitrogen: Moderate

Buckwheat
(*Fagopyrum esculentum*)
Sow: Spring to late summer
Duration: Half hardy annual; 2–3 months
Soil: Good on infertile soils
Properties: Attracts beneficial insects; fast growing; dislikes frost
Nitrogen: No

Trefoil
(*Medicago lupulina*)
Sow: Early spring to late summer
Duration: Hardy biennial, 3 months to 2 years
Soil: Light or dry, but not acid
Properties: Good in sun and semi-shade under planting
Nitrogen: Moderate

has become commonplace. However, to get the most out of these nitrogen-fixing plants it is important to identify exactly when the nitrogen is likely to be at its most available and where in the plant it occurs. Botanists now believe that the root nodules, formed as a result of bacterial action, accumulate half of the total nitrogen, and that this only becomes available to other plants when the nodules are removed from the plant. This only happens if the plant is placed under considerable stress from drought or shade, or when the root dies, which raises doubts over the practice of growing legumes amongst other crops with the intention of one living plant aiding another.

Perhaps even more important is that the nitrogen is moved to different plant tissues at various stages of the plant's life. In a young and vibrant pea plant prior to flowering, about 40 per cent of the accumulated nitrogen is in the roots, with the rest distributed in foliage and stems. Once the plant has flowered and is setting seed, the reserves of nitrogen in the roots drop to 3–6 per cent and the leaves and stems account for as little as 8–10 per cent. The remaining 70–90 per cent is to be found in the seeds and seed pods. This transforms the use of the pea family in rotation schemes; if the aim is to enrich the soil with nitrogen, the crop must be turned into the soil before the flowers emerge to be most effective.

Green manures for heavy soils

Alfalfa
(Medicago sativa)
Sow: Spring to midsummer
Duration: Hardy annual; 3 months
Soil: Not acid or waterlogged
Properties: Improves soil structure; enriches compost; over-winters in frost
Nitrogen: High

Winter beans
(Vicia faba)
Sow: Late summer through autumn
Duration: Hardy annual; 4 months
Soil: Heavy but not waterlogged or dry
Properties: Not good for weed suppression; good over-wintering in frost
Nitrogen: Low

Winter tares
(Vicia sativa)
Sow: Early spring to late summer
Duration: Hardy annual; 2–3 months
Soil: Moist but not waterlogged
Properties: Best planted in rows rather than sown broadcast; supresses weeds
Nitrogen: Moderate

Phacelia
(Phacelia tanacetifolia)
Sow: Early spring to late summer
Duration: Hardy annual; 2 months or through winter
Soil: Tolerates most
Properties: Rapid growth; flowers attract beneficial insects
Nitrogen: No

Grazing rye
(Secale cereale)
Sow: Late summer to late autumn
Duration: Hardy annual; 3–4 months
Soil: Tolerates most
Properties: Suppresses weeds; improves soil; over-winters well; inhibits germination, do not use before sowing
Nitrogen: No

Green manures are usually planted between crops in vegetable gardens to cover bare soil during a gap in the growing calendar. They need only a short growing window, as they are turned in when still young and green.

Sowing Lightly fork the ground to prepare a seedbed and sow green manure liberally. As it is sown broadcast, marking out may help.

Crop maturity Allow to grow for 1–3 months. Good soil coverage should be evident, and the plants should be vibrant.

Digging in On coarse or dense crops trim the foliage before cultivating the soil to place the green manures at the bottom of a trench.

Other dynamic accumulators

The potential benefits offered by many other garden plants are often overlooked. These don't fix nitrogen in their roots in the same way as the pea family, but their tissues have high levels of nutrients, which can be harnessed by harvesting and composting the stems and foliage when succulent and fresh. A balanced selection of plant material ensures your compost heap makes naturally nutrient-balanced compost. Avoid composting the roots of invasive perennial species and plants that have set seed.

BENEFICIAL HERBS:

Borage (Borago officinalis): *Potassium*
Caraway (Carum carvi): *Phosphorus*
Chamomile (Chamaemelum nobile): *Calcium, potassium, phosphorus*
Chicory (Cichorium intybus): *Calcium, potassium*
Chives (Allium schoenoprasum): *Calcium, sodium*
Comfrey (Symphytum officinale): *Sulphur, nitrogen, magnesium, calcium, potassium, phosphorus, iron*
Fennel (Foeniculum vulgare): *Calcium, sodium, potassium*
Garlic (Allium sativum): *Fluorine, sulphur, phosphorus*
Lemon Balm (Melissa officinalis): *Phosphorus*
Marigold (Tagetes species): *Phosphorus*
Mustard (Sinapsis alba): *Sulphur, phosphorus*
Parsley (Petroselinum crispum): *Magnesium, calcium, potassium, Iron*
Peppermint (Mentha piperata): *Magnesium, potassium*
Salad burnet (Sanguisorba minor): *Iron*
Sorrel (Rumex acetosa): *Sodium, calcium, phosphorus*
Tansy (Tanacetum vulgare): *Potassium*
Yarrow (Achillea millefolium): *Nitrogen, potassium, phosphorus, copper*

BENEFICIAL WEEDS:

Chickweed (Stellaria media): *Potassium, phosphorus, manganese*
Cleavers (Galium aparine): *Sodium, calcium*
Dandelion (Taraxacum officinale): *Sodium, silica, magnesium, calcium, potassium, phosphorus, iron, copper.*
Dock (Rumex species): *Calcium, potassium, phosphorus, iron*
Fat hen (Chenopodium album): *Calcium, iron*
Horsetail (Equisetum): *Silica, magnesium, calcium, iron, cobalt*
Meadowsweet (Filipendula ulmaria): *Sodium, sulphur, magnesium, calcium, phosphorus, iron*
Nettles (Urtica): *Sodium, sulphur, nitrogen, calcium, potassium, iron, copper*

Good for you and your plants
Although usually destined for the kitchen, both chives and mustard (inset) accumulate minerals, so be sure to compost any parts you don't consume.

The thriving garden

Most gardeners seem to have an unswerving desire for a perfect world, free of weeds that compete, pests that graze, and pigeons that peck, but above all, a world without slugs. Perhaps this originates in the first gardens, created as a snapshot of Paradise: even the word garden, it is suggested, implies this, being derived from the Hebrew gan-oden, or "enclosed Eden". Most of us wouldn't want to take the slug into eternity with us, but it and other inconveniences are here to stay in our gardens.

Attractive allies
Delicate looking lacewings (inset) are major predators of aphids, and should be welcome in any garden, while spiders will ensnare a range of pests in their shimmering webs.

GOING WITH THE FLOW

Gardening with nature doesn't mean that we hand over the garden to our horticultural foes, just that we learn to garden with them and take steps to make life difficult for them. The vast majority of garden problems can be dealt with by good practice. Start by recognizing that a high level of pests or diseases usually indicates an underlying issue that requires attention; dealing with the broad issues rather than the detail of the pest improves the overall health of the garden. This approach may not bring the immediate and gratifying demise of the pest, and it may not appear the most convenient method of control, but the aim is to have the most positive impact on the garden environment and maximum impact on the pest.

"Essentially instead of letting the pests put our plants under pressure, we should use our plants to put the pests under pressure."

The eye of the beholder

Gertrude Jekyll, arguably the most influential gardener of the 20th century, described a weed as simply a plant in the wrong place. This may offer little consolation when bashing through a stand of savage brambles, or during the back-breaking process of unearthing the fragile, fleshy roots of ground elder after it has become intricately enmeshed in your herbaceous border, but she did have a point. Our concept of weeds, and indeed of pests and diseases, is subjective, based entirely on the effect that organism has on the specific plants we choose to grow, and our personal desire to see those few selected plants prosper, unbridled and uncompromised by all other organisms.

The natural balance

Of course not everything that, flies, crawls, creeps, slithers or grows into the garden is a problem. Those that we refer to as pests are the animals and insects that damage our plants by grazing, chewing, piercing, and, in the case of my dog, sitting on them. The vast majority of "unfriendly" organisms only become evident when they cause major, visible damage; if it were possible for gardeners

Breaking the addiction
A battery of bottles may offer remedies to every problem, but they treat the symptoms, not the underlying cause.

Welcome weeds

Even the most despised of "weeds" can have its uses. The farm where I used to pick plums and cherries in my school holidays allowed ribbons of dandelions to sweep under the trees in the belief that it aided the fruit. This may be true, as the flower releases high levels of ethylene, stimulating the fruit to ripen at the same time rather than having to pick selectively. And while most gardeners consider the deep-rooted horsetails or equisetum an intractable problem, I worked in one garden where the plant was cultivated in an old trough. The hollow stems were cut throughout the summer and tied in tight bundles. These were then used as scouring pads to clean garden tools, from secateurs and shears to spades, as the high silica content acts as a fine abrasive. An older name for the plant is pewterwort, as metalware was packed in the stems during shipping.

to see all the life forms that are having a small but nonetheless detrimental effect on our plants at any time, there is little doubt that we would give up gardening.

Fortunately, for every pest there is an army of other organisms quietly and diligently hunting it down. A fluid balance has been maintained between organisms for millions of years, and a population explosion of pests is unusual. For example, we will all find aphids in the garden at some point in the growing season, and without our direct intervention, they might damage a few plants or shoots in any growing season; but without the actions of the natural control organisms, scientists calculate that a single female aphid landing on a rose bud in your garden in early spring would give rise to about 10 million tonnes of aphids by the end of the growing season. And not all organisms are pests all the time: for instance, parasitic wasp species can have a significant effect on insect pest populations (*see p.220*), but they will also parasitize friendly insects too, particularly those that are useful for the pollination of crops, such as the hoverfly, making them both friend and foe.

Diseases are the result of viruses, fungi, and bacteria infecting plant tissues, often taking advantage of physical damage caused by pests to gain access, or in some cases even being carried and introduced directly by a pest. The term disorders is broad, covering a multitude of horticultural sins, but all tend to be the result of physical and chemical issues in the plant's environment, such as wind damage (*see pp.120–21*), deficiencies in nutrients (*see p.99*), and pollutants.

Man-made problems

It is also important to highlight that much of the trouble caused by pests and diseases is the result of the way in which we cultivate our plants. In the wild, where these plants evolved over millions of years, they tend to grow as individuals or loose groups within species-rich communities, which means that any potential pest must first work to find its favoured plant. Compare this with the

way most of us garden, often concentrating groups of a single species or even cultivar together in large areas; this creates the horticultural equivalent of a fast-food restaurant for pests. Where dozens congregate together, like children in a classroom, infections also spread quickly, as any parent who experiences the "back to school colds" or any gardener who only grows roses will testify. And just like us, plants are most susceptible to infection when they are weary or under stress. Repeatedly forget to water your tomatoes and they will be more prone to mildew; over-feed your roses and they will be more prone to aphids.

Wild flowers
More than things of beauty, these support a wide range of beneficial insects in their native environment.

Compounding this is the worldwide horticultural trade, with plants are shipped and grown thousands of miles from their natural habitats. These movements can carry pests and diseases into places where they haven't previously existed, while leaving the natural controls that regulated those organisms behind. Some notable examples include the introduction of woolly aphid to European fruit orchards from North America in the 18th century, and the numerous species of scale insect, mites, and mealy bugs from the tropics that now share our homes and glasshouses and prey on tender crops and houseplants. The devastating fungal Dutch elm disease was introduced to Britain, changing its landscape, via North American logs in the 1960s; the more recent spread of sudden oak death, caused by the fungus *Phytophthora ramorum*, is believed to be the result of plants moving across the continents. The place of origin is uncertain, possibly Asia, but one strain of the disease is affecting Europe, while another strain has been found in North America. Scientists fear that this devastating disease, which can cause the rapid death of a wide range of trees and shrubs, will mutate into a potentially more virulent form when the two strains meet.

No quick fixes

Mixed plantings
A good variety of planting in your garden, even mixing crops and ornamentals, helps to maintain a healthy balance.

Pest and disease problems indicate that nature's controls and balances have been temporarily unsettled. Thank goodness, you might think, for chemical sprays to control these outbreaks – well, perhaps not. Whether the focus of ourconcern is a single ailing plant within our own garden or horticultural issues affecting an entire region, it is critical that we assess accurately where the problems lie and are honest about finding the root cause. Only when this is done can the symptoms be most logically and effectively dealt with.

Since the advent of widely available chemical treatments we have become complacent. We have come to believe that, for instance, killing the aphids in our rose gardens with a spray will solve the problem. Of course it might do so in the short term, but the aphids will return, and while the spray kills the aphids it also compromises many of the aphids' natural predators, many of which are good pollinators, by not only removing their food sources but potentially killing them too. The long-term effect of this is that the health of the roses might be improved, but the health of the garden as a whole will be compromised. Subtly adjusting the way we grow and tend our plants can have a more fundamental effect on their health, and I always remind gardeners that a thriving garden inevitably leads to a contented gardener.

"It has been estimated that if aphids were left unchecked by predators they would breed so successfully that by the end of just one year the earth would be almost two kilometres deep in aphids."

GOOD PRACTICE

Before all else, remember that the garden is a place of constant battles and struggles between all the living elements, and no matter how much you worry it won't help. The best advice is to enjoy browsing in the garden daily, noting which plants are performing and which are not. If problems manifest themselves, act quickly, and treat the cause of the problem rather than just the symptoms, as this promotes the development of a more robust garden.

"Believe me, there is far more to watering than pointing a hose at the plants."

Water wisely

When first I started working in a plant nursery at the age of 11, the nurseryman took me to one side and gave me half a day of watering tuition. This might sound extreme, but remember that much of a plant's life – and especially that of a container-grown nursery plant – revolves around a good water supply (*see pp.122–29*).

Water too much, too often, or in the wrong compost, and at best, the nutrients are washed away, leaving plants hungry; at worst, the roots rot off in the waterlogged mire. Excessive water also provides ideal conditions for soil-borne diseases, and roots put under pressure by waterlogged soils, especially in winter, are more prone to succumb. Damping off in seedlings, club root brown rot in conifers, and a plethora of phytophthora fungi all love wet and waterlogged soil, and the first indication of a problem is usually wilting of the foliage – which prompts most of us to reach for the hosepipe for more water. Good soil structure (*see pp.160–64*) and management, including drainage, also reduce the opportunity for fungi and bacteria to travel and infect plants.

Conversely, too little water leaves plants stressed and much more prone to disease, typically from the mildews that invade during periods of drought. Infrequent watering also has its problems: as the plant struggles to maintain its leaf and stems it automatically jettisons expendable items such as flower buds, flowers, and developing fruit. This is often seen on tomatoes and peppers in the glasshouse and magnolia or on camellia specimens in pots during winter.

Thirsty blooms
Magnolias stressed by poor watering will discard their non-essential and water-demanding flowers first.

How not to water

An inability to get to grips with watering was perfectly demonstrated by one of my grandmothers. While one grandmother was a natural gardener, the other had little affinity with anything green; even beans from the local market looked dejected and the texture of polystyrene when served, and her plants were nothing short of tortured. Visiting her house in my early teens, I avoided eating beans by roaming the house and garden rescuing plants, emptying water from the stagnating pots of some and drip-feeding others that were so thirsty my father use to claim he could hear them coughing. There seemed little pattern to this until I deduced that plants were watered when guests were expected, so the busier her social life, the more plants drowned. I also later learned that to spruce up the houseplants she sprayed them with furniture polish, but that's a different story.

At the very least, a shorage of water will check plant growth (*see p.125*). Get used to feeling the weight of the plants in pots to determine whether they are short of water, or feel the compost regularly to check for moisture, and remember it is likely that many of the plants in the garden will require vastly different moisture levels, so water appropriately.

How you water is also important. Watering from above causes splash onto the foliage, potentially carrying with it fungal spores or leading to sun scorch. Water can also sit on the crowns of plants, which can cause fungal rots to set in on alpines and many house plants. Paradoxically, poor watering can even lead to water loss from the soil (*see pp.127–28*). A moist surface on compost creates perfect conditions for sciarid fly (also called compost fly), a small black insect that lays its eggs in the compost so that the larvae can feed on the plant roots. Watering from below by plunging pots in water will avoid this problem, as will covering the surface of pots in a layer of sand, while simply using a piece of carpet to cover the compost heap will deter flies.

Practice good hygiene

Basic hygiene in the garden can significantly reduce infestations. Cleaning of boots, tools, and machines to avoid the passage of spores, bacteria, and nematodes is important, as is clearing up leaf litter around plants prone to diseases such as mildew, black spot, scab, and rust, especially roses (*Rosa*), fruit trees, and all the vegetables. Good composting techniques can achieve temperatures high enough to remove pests and diseases; but burn any plant material that is badly infected. Clean off dead and dying vegetation from overwintering plants to avoid infecting the glasshouse and re-infecting plants the following spring. Always check over any compost and pots that will be used in the glasshouse in case they harbour slugs and snails. And if you intend to reuse old plant pots and seed trays wash them first in hot water with detergent. Make sure that water sources are clean and free of fungal infections, especially for seedlings.

Good hygiene
The patina of age may look attractive, but reused pots can harbour a plethora of pests and diseases, so always clean before reuse, especially if there is obvious growth (inset).

Weed regularly

Among the factors that make pests and diseases such determined and resilient organisms is their uncanny knack for swapping their allegiance from one plant or host to the next. This ability to take advantage of any available resources means it is important to consider all the plants growing in the garden and

Catch them young
The best approach to weeding is "little and often". Take seedlings early enough and they will cause only minimal damage.

what they might harbour. For instance, clubroot can cripple culinary and ornamental brassicas, so if your garden is prone to attack root out shepherd's purse and chickweed, which can act as hosts, and also avoid growing wallflowers (*Erysimum* and *Cheiranthus*). Powdery mildew on roses, geraniums, and aquilegias will spread onto groundsel; even docks can cause problems as they are the part-time home of apple sawfly.

Even when not sheltering the enemy, weeds compete with your plants for resources. It is always worth rooting them out, and ideally discouraging them from growing in the first place by using mulches (*see pp.201–202*). And no matter how busy you are, don't allow weeds to flower, or one will become many next season. One of my earliest jobs in the garden was to weed between flowers and crops, usually by hand, after instruction on the difference between weeds and crops. If I complained at the seemingly endless task I was always told "one year's seed is seven years' weeds".

Pick your plants well

Just like people, you will get the best out of plants if you know their individual strengths and weaknesses. Clematis, for example, suffers from clematis wilt, a fungal disease that infects damaged stems at ground level, causing blackening and die back. Avoid this by planting gently and half as deep again as the plant is in the pot; placing the crown of the plant below the infection allows plenty of shoots to regenerate should stems be infected. Roses of different kids are famed for susceptibility to mildew or blackspot, and of course there is the infamous rose replant disease (*see p.199*).

In the early days of selection and breeding of plants for the garden, the prime concerns were colour, fragrance, crop size, and flower form; unfortunately the ability of wild species to resist or bounce back from pest and disease attack was often ignored. The result is that many of the older garden cultivars and forms are susceptible to attack and are often devastated by infection. Recent interest has focused on the more robust species, breeding resistance into modern garden plants, with the result that many new forms show improved health.

"Select robust modern plants for your garden and the job of keeping the garden in balance is made so much easier."

Cause for celebration
Today's roses, like the beautiful 'Golden Celebration', have been bred to combine an old-fashioned look and fragrance with levels of disease resistance sadly lacking in many old roses.

PROBLEMS IN THE SOIL

"My grandmother held that if a dose of feed was good, twice the dose was really good. High levels of organic matter saved her plants, acting as a buffer against excess nutrients."

The great value of soil is that it is a living medium, rich in nutrients and beneficial organisms, but not everything in it is helpful. Like seeds, the spores of mildew, rust, and clubroot can survive in soil for up to twenty years. The "bootlaces" of honey fungus *(Armillaria)* can also be present, as well as weed seeds, the larvae of mites and weevils, or root-infesting nematodes, such as the stem eelworm that attacks narcissus. Bacterial canker of fruit trees and soft spot can overwinter in soil debris, infecting healthy plants in spring via soil water. Even vital nutrients can be toxic at too high a dose.

Cleaning soil

To reduce the likelihood of these problematic organisms affecting your plants, use sterile soil and compost. This is no problem if you use reputable compost suppliers and leave bags unopened till use, but more of a challenge in the wider garden. Soil sterilization is commonplace in commercial horticulture, especially in glasshouses, where a perforated fabric blanket is used to direct steam into the soil. An increasing number of amateurs use steam sterilizers for soil in glasshouse beds. These resemble metal dustbins: soil is put in at the top and steam enters at the bottom. They produce temperatures of 45–55°C (113–131°F), about the same as a good hot compost heap; sufficient to kill most pests and seeds, but short of the 70–80°C (158–176°F) that would harm more beneficial soil organisms. A more long-term approach is to use rotation systems (*see pp.203–209*) to ensure minimal build up of pests and diseases where appropriate.

No need to panic
Most white, thread-like fungi in the soil (like those above) are benign: the black bootlaces of honey fungus are a different matter.

Overfed and underfed plants

It has always puzzled me that popular advice involves adding copious fertilizer when planting, regardless of timing, season, type of plant, and growth habit;

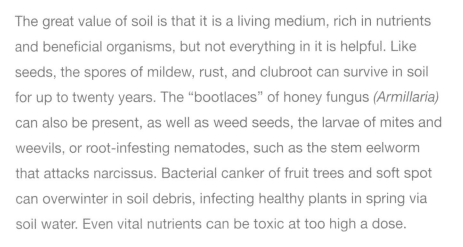

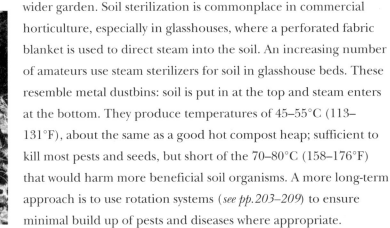

the assumption is that fertilizer is always good. The first nurseryman I worked for had a more common-sense approach. He maintained that if a plant wasn't growing, why would it need food? Instead, apply fertilizer when its buds break. This is logical: plant nutrients are water soluble (*see pp.131–33*) and if applied in autumn when a plant is approaching dormancy, they won't be taken up by the roots but will linger in the soil till winter rains wash them out. Fertilizer applied in late summer can even have a detrimental effect, stimulating a late flush of growth that cannot ripen before winter and is prone to frost damage. Much better to make the nutrients available just when the plant needs them; this is especially true for fast-acting and liquid feeds (*see pp.140–141*).

Even when the plant is growing, too much nitrogen stimulates soft, sappy growth that is less resistant to pest invasion, and often leads to the plant growing leaves rather than flowering. Ease off the fertilizer and make your plants work for their food; they will grow steadily and robustly, while fungi, bacteria, and insect pests struggle to take a hold. Take a look at how the plants in and around the garden are growing (*see panel*) for your guide.

Heavy feeding is sometimes in order. Roses, for example, suffer from "rose replant disease", believed to be due to fungi and nematodes around old roots. New plants struggle to cope and wither slowly. Popular advice is to dig out as much of the soil as possible with the old roses and import new, but a seasoned rose grower I worked with claimed that, as hungry feeders, roses needed deep planting and bulky organic matter like farmyard manure; he should know, as he grew roses on the same ground for 70 years without any replant disease.

SIGNS OF LOW FERTILITY

- Small, pale, or misshapen leaves
- Slow growth and reluctance to branch
- Flowering on very young plants
- Short internodal distances
- Slow growth in spring

SIGNS OF GOOD FERTILITY

- Vigorous growth
- Large, well-formed and coloured leaves
- Good flowering and fruiting
- Moderate pest and disease resistance
- Bursts of growth in early spring

SIGNS OF EXCESSIVE FERTILITY

- Rampant foliage growth
- Tendency to produce foliage and no flowers
- Soft, fleshy stems, easily damaged in the wind
- Stems and foliage easily damaged by frost
- High levels of pests, particularly early in the growing season
- Scorched foliage and stunted roots

Easy pickings
Aphids are drawn towards the soft and succulent shoots that are produced by over-fertilized plants

Natural mulch
Mulches offer plant roots protection from drying out and extreme temperatures. They mimic nature, where a thick layer of plant debris, like leaves, often covers the soil.

USING MULCHES

The term mulch refers to anything, organic or synthetic, that is used to cover the surface of the soil. A wide variety of products are commonly used, from polythene sheet to ground bark, with the former mostly for crops and the latter in decorative areas. The main aim of laying a mulch is usually to reduce weed growth by providing an inhospitable surface, on which weed seeds cannot germinate. This only works to suppress seeds, of course, and perennial weeds should be removed before putting a mulch in place.

Gravel mulch
For the best results use a mulch that matches what is found naturally with the plant. Here gravel mimics the scree slopes around alpines.

Types of mulch

In broad terms three styles of mulch are used: living, granular, and membrane or sheet mulches. Living material, such as ground-cover planting and short-term crops like green manures (*see pp.181–85*), can be densely planted to ensure that their developing canopy blocks the light from germinating weed seeds. Granular mulches, like gravels, bark, and wood chippings, need to be laid in a layer at least 5cm (2in) thick to be effective. Membranes, such as polythene and woven sheets, sometimes called landscape fabric, require securing to the ground.

The benefits of mulches

Selecting the right mulch is largely a balance between taste, function, and cost. Membranes are the most effective mulches for supressing weed growth, stopping even tough perennial weeds from bursting out of the soil. They also prevent any decorative plants from spreading by seed, and so are difficult to use where colonizing perennials, suckering shrubs, or naturalizing bulbs are a critical part of the planting design. They therefore tend to be used most in fruit and vegetable gardens,

USING MEMBRANES

Nobody would claim that black plastic sheet is the most atractive of mulching materials, but it is highly effective and very useful where crops are grown and practicality comes first.

Lay the mulch *Spread the sheet over well cultivated and fertilized ground, burying the edges to secure. Cut crosses to plant through.*

Put in your plants *Ease the roots through the hole into the prepared ground beneath, firming and watering in well.*

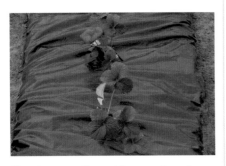

Growing away *The mulch warms the soil, promoting growth, and also protects the developing crop from pests and diseases.*

or under large areas of gravel. Other mulches also have their strengths and drawbacks, so when choosing it is helpful to establish what role your mulch is to perform in the garden.

• **Light restriction** is most effective from membranes and thick granular material, so these are the best choices for weed supression. Living mulches can only be only effective in suppressing weeds while a dense canopy is retained. However, I was told by a tweed-capped old gent who frequented our nursery and always refused to accept that anyone should use herbicides, that the best way of ridding the garden of weeds was to sow crops of turnips. The theory is that the broad, competitive foliage stunts their growth while the nutrient-hungry roots reduce the fertility favoured by weeds.

• **Water retention** is particularly good using membranes, which physically prevent evaporation. Granular materials are also effective because they have pore spaces so large that they prevent water moving up from the soil via capillary action (*see p.158*). Reductions in soil moisture loss of 15–80 per cent can be obtained through using mulches, with the highest figures possible from membranes. The best effects are achieved by watering the soil before applying the mulch.

• **Soil warming** is possible, particularly from dark-coloured membranes and granular materials. Both of these absorb warmth from the sun, transmitting it down into the soil particles. This is particularly useful in crop production, where early plantings of vegetables are required to get the maximum out of the growing season, and for protecting tender plants during the winter, when granular materials in particular offer a duvet of insulation against harsh weather.

• **Enriching soil** is the eventual consequence of mulching with organic matter, as it will gradually be broken down by macro- and microorganisms in the upper soil levels(*see pp.166–68*). Only use dead or well-rotted organic matter as mulches, as green leaves such as fresh lawn clippings can upset the balance of the soil. Also avoid fresh farmyard manure, as the high urea content will cause scorching on stems, roots, and leaves.

CROP ROTATION

Rotation is, in my experience, one of the most misunderstood and misapplied garden theories. Plenty of gardeners, amateur and expert, talk of rotating plants, but few can explain why they do it. Unsurprising perhaps, when so many guides are available, some of which contradict one another; it seems there are as many rotation plans as there are gardeners. Put simply, rotation means cultivating a series of dissimilar plants in the same space over subsequent seasons; it is done to reduce the build up of pests and diseases, improve the soil structure, and avoid the depletion of particular nutrients that occurs when a single crop is continuously grown.

Ancient practice

The Romans first wrote in detail about rotation, and it was even referred to by the ancient civilisations of Africa and Asia. The technique was perfected in agriculture over centuries, so that by the Middle Ages farmers in Europe were using a three-field rotation, with rye (*Secale cereale*) or wheat (*Triticum aestivum*) followed by oats (*Avena sativa*) or barley (*Hordeum vulgare*) and then a fallow period. In the 18th century, British agriculturalist Charles Townshend brought in a four-field system of wheat, barley, turnips (*Brasssica rapa* var. *rapa*), and clover (*Trifolium*). The use of turnips as winter animal fodder and clover for grazing allowed the integration and year-round breeding of cattle within the rotation system, a concept that fuelled an agricultural revolution around the world. Townshend's reward for this is somewhat dubious, as he is best remembered by his nickname "Turnip" Townshend.

"Rotation seems to have been practiced in some form just about anywhere that settled agriculture has developed."

Rotation principles

Because related plants share many physical and physiological characteristics, they also share nutritional needs. They take a targeted range of minerals and nutrients (*see pp.130–33*) from the soil, based on those in their natural habitat, so prolonged cultivation of the same plants will deplete that range. This can be clearly identified in a laboratory, while in the garden plants may suffer pitifully and obviously or a undergo a subtle, gradual decline in performance.

As numbers of a plant build up, so do opportunities for pests and diseases that live on that plant. For example, mass planting of onions (*Allium*) inevitably increases the chance of onion rust (*Puccinia allii*) infecting the plants and resulting in a rust outbreak. Many pest and disease lifecycles centre on the location of the host plant, so the longer a species is cultivated in one spot the higher the likelihood of infection. In the case of onion rust, pustules produced on the foliage in late summer release spores that over-winter in the soil. If the

same family is planted in the same place the following year, the spores infect the young shoots and the cycle continues. This is the principle problem with monoculture, and avoiding it is the great strength of rotation systems. Keeping the ground free of a plant group for two or three years reduces spore populations and, therefore, infection of future crops. This principle is at the heart of pest and disease control in the rotation system, resulting in healthier crops and a reduced use of pest controls.

Rotation plant groups

Understanding the performance, both negative and positive, of plant groups is key to the success of rotation. These groups are based primarily around the botanical family to which the plants belong, and so theoretically they have identifiable similarities; in practice some are easier to spot than others, with the most reliable method being the comparison of the flower form.

Close cousins
Rotation principles can also be applied to ornamental schemes; culinary onions are related to garden alliums.

Alliums (Liliaceae /Alliaceae)

Chives, garlic, leeks, onions, shallots

These bulbous plants dislike nitrogen–rich soils, so plant after heavy feeders such as brassicas (*see p.206*) or potatoes (*see p.208*); year-round cropping requires planning, with spring onions (*A. cepa*) and leeks (*A. porrum*) sown in spring, Japanese onions (*A. fistulosum*) in summer, garlic (*A. sativum*) and shallots (*A. cepa*) in autumn.

Problems: Rust, white rot, eelworm, onion fly, thrips.

Rotational flow and successive sowings

When planning crops, plant four beds of equal sizes with these groups. The following year move the crops on a bed, sowing the legumes in bed 4, the heavy feeders in bed 1, and so on, and repeat the movement each year. Flowers and herbs can be dotted amongst the beds to fill the gaps before and after harvesting, along with green manures (see pp.181-85). Keep a record of quantities and performance at harvest as a guide for the future.

In Bed 1
Legumes, intersown with modestly sized crops of the daisy family, like lettuce. At the end of the season, compost the legume tops; leave the roots in place to release nitrogen. Sow a green manure such as tares or grazing rye.

In bed 2
Heavy feeders such as sweetcorn, potatoes, and cucurbits. After harvest in late summer sow grazing rye as a green manure for winter.

In bed 4
Brassicas, beets, and any further members of the daisy family. After harvest, follow with a green manure such as buckwheat.

In bed 3
Alliums, carrots, and any crops of the daisy family. After they are harvested, sow phacelia as a green manure.

Decide how much of each crop is required, and establish a sequence of sowings (I use two-week intervals) to avoid gluts. Tomatoes are a classic example where staged sowings result in steady flow of fruit; in contrast, on first growing tomatoes my parents harvested barrowloads over just three weeks, which looked impressive but tests the enthusiasm and imagination of even the most talented chef. I still find tomato chutney difficult.

Healthy cabbages
Rotation and liming together help to control clubroot, and starting plants in modules limits its detrimental effects.

Brassicas (Brassicaceae/Cruciferae)

Broccoli, Brussel sprouts, cabbages, calabrese, cauliflower, cress, kale, kohlrabi, mizuna, pak choi, radish, rocket, seakale, swede, turnip

In temperate climates there may be ornamental members of this family in the garden, so there is a high tendency for pests to build up. Generally large, leafy crops, they require high quantities of nitrogen in the soil to succeed, so plant them after legumes (*see opposite*); they also prefer a neutral to lime-based soil. The range of crops means that slow members such as cabbage (*B. olereacea*) and swede (*B. napus*) can be interplanted with faster growing radish (*Raphanus sativa*) and rocket (*Eruca vesicaria*). They generally grow well when started in pots and modules, which helps to create the necessary break in cultivation to allow rotation from one bed to the next.

Problems: Clubroot, cabbage root fly, caterpillars, cabbage whitefly, flea beetle, pigeons.

Beets (Chenopodiaceae)

Beetroot, chard, red orache, spinach, spinach beet

These foliage plants require a moderately fertile soil with good moisture retention. They produce bulky roots and so are often placed with the carrot family in rotation. Spinach (*Spinacia oleracea*) and beetroot (*Beta vulgaris* subsp. *vulgaris*) are most suited to sowing early or in cool conditions while chard (*Beta vulgaris* subsp. *cicla*) and red orache (*Atriplex hortensis*) prefer summer and autumn sowing; many forms of spinach and chard will over winter in cool winters providing winter greens.

Problems: Downy mildew, leaf spot, rust, virus, leaf miners.

Carrots (Apiaceae/Umbelliferae)

Carrot, parsnip, parsley, celery, celeriac, Florence fennel

The deep rooting of this family aids the development of soil structure. They prefer cooler conditions for sowing and a long growing season. They also need high organic matter content and relatively high fertility but not excessive nitrogen, so are often linked with the onions (*see p.204*) and rapid crops such as lettuce, in the daisy family (*see opposite*).

Problems: Canker, mildew, carrot root fly, cutworms.

Cucurbits (Cucurbitaceae)

Cucumber, courgette and marrow, melon, squash, pumpkin

Most of these are grown in glasshouses in cool climates, but possible to include them outside in warmer climes. They require plenty of space and training, the most efficient method being to train them up coarse strings and nets, and tend to crop in late summer and autumn. Needing moderate fertility and plenty of moisture, they are often combined with brassicas (*see opposite*) and potatoes (*see p.208*) in rotation schemes.

Problems: Powdery mildew, virus, red spider mite.

Daisies (Asteraceae/Compositae)

Artichoke, cardoon, chicory, endive, lettuce, salsify, scorzonera

Endive (*Cichorium intybus*) and chicory (*C. endivia*) allow winter cropping and many forms of lettuce (*Lactuca sativa*) are available to suit varied climates. These fast crops can be intersown with other plants especially brassicas, carrots, and beets (*see opposite*); chicory and scorzonera (*Scorzonera hispnica*) are best combined with the carrot family. Cardoon (*Cynara cardunculus*) and artichokes (*C. scolymus*) need space, and are grown outside rotation beds.

Problems: Downy mildew, grey mould, cutworms, root aphid, slugs, wireworms.

Legumes (Papilionaceae/Leguminosae)

Beans, peas, fenugreek

These plants store nitrogen in their root nodules (*see pp.182–83*), and leave it in the ground for crops grown after such as brassicas (*see opposite*). They tend to have deep roots that improve structure in lower soil horizons (*see pp.160–62*). A steady supply of water is needed to avoid flower drop, but relatively low nutrient levels, so plant after heavy feeders such as potatoes (*see p.208*). Broad beans (*Vicia faba*) and peas (*Pisum sativum*) are ideal for cooler climates; runner beans (*Phaseolus coccineus*) and French beans (*P. vulgaris*) need warmth.

Problems: Downy mildew, chocolate spot, foot and root rot, rust, birds, pea moth, pea thrip, rodents, slugs.

Outsize appetite
If you don't have room for cucurbits in your rotation beds, try sowing them on top of a maturing compost heap.

Potatoes (Solanaceae)

Potatoes, tomatoes, aubergines, sweet peppers, chilli peppers

Potatoes (*Solanum tuberosum*) prefer cooler climates, with the rest of the family needing warm weather or glass protection; in warmer conditions, aubergines (*S. melongena*), tomatoes (*Lycopersicon esculentum*), and peppers (*Capsicum annuum*) can be grown outside. Clearing of crop debris is essential to minimise diseases, especially on potatoes, and good drainage and moisture retention in summer are essential. These are hungry feeders, especially for nitrogen and potassium, so tend to follow legumes (*see p.207*) or green manures (*see pp.181–85*).

Problems: blight, scab, virus, Colorado beetle, cutworms, eelworm, wireworms.

Miscellaneous families

A number of plants fall outside the main groupings and are usually distributed throughout the rotation system. Typical of these is sweetcorn (*Zea mays*), a heavy-feeding plant, usually grown with potatoes or cucurbits (*see p.207*), because all the plants require similar feed levels and are removed before winter, allowing a green manure to be sown. Rhubarb (*Rheum × hybridum*) and asparagus (*Asparagus officinalis*) are both long-term crops cultivated, like soft fruit, in their own permanent beds.

Polyculture

If the regimented planning and execution of crop rotation doesn't suit your gardening style, you will be pleased to hear of a more liberal and random method. Known as "polyculture", this is the exact opposite of monoculture and involves cultivating mixed crops, from fruit trees through soft fruit to annuals and perennials, in the same ground. This mimics a natural mix of compatible plants in the wild making best use of the available habitat niches; it is also the principle used in planning ornamental gardens.

Happy mix
Crops and flowers grown together give plantings in the polyculture system a cottage-garden feel.

A typical example could be broadcast sowing a seed mix with radish, calendula, lettuce, parsnip (*Pastinaca sativa*) or carrot (*Daucus carota*), swede, and dill (*Anethum graveolens*) or fennel (*Foeniculum vulgare*) in spring. The radishes mature quickly and give shelter for the others; as they are harvested sow brassicas in their place. Lettuces are either harvested from eight weeks and replaced with French beans or "cut-and-come-again" all season long. Early blooming calendula and late-blooming fennel attract beneficial insects and dissuade pests such as whitefly that seek out French beans. As crops are harvested, garlic, brassicas, and Japanese onions can be sown for over-wintering, with the parsnip or carrot and swede removed in the autumn and winter.

I have found this works well, and the informal, picturesque planting particularly suits small gardens, where small beds allow access all around without compacting the soil by walking on it. I start the planting off with a soft fruit bush, such as currants (*Ribes*), in the centre of each bed. The principle benefits are:

• **Different rooting zones** improve soil structure across the horizons rather than in just one layer.
• **The plants are also not competing** against one another for a narrow band of nutrients and moisture.
• **The planting includes flowers,** and many of the blooms attract insects beneficial for pollination and the control of pests.
• **The incidence of pests is reduced** as their host plants are dispersed and "disguised" among other plant canopies.
• **Year-round cropping** is possible, without the need for a fallow or green manure period.

While my grandparents would undoubtedly have approved of the informality of polyculture practice, it is not without its challenges. The crops will require careful selection to avoid groupings from the same family. Harvest crops as they start to mature to avoid excessive competition and check to ensure no one plant is assuming dominance. After the first sowing, keep spreading seed of individual plants into the gaps left by removed crops. Finally adjust the plant mixes to suit your requirements; even varying the cultivars can extend and enrich the blend.

A random system

My grandfather swore by his own system: planting what he had in his hand at the time in the nearest available space. This may sound very unscientific, but it led to a random distribution of crops across the garden, with a different layout each season. Add my grandmother's delight at cramming flowers into any space not filled by crops, and a chaotic horticultural tapestry emerged. Between them they grew crops of extraordinary vigour and flowers of great beauty, and all without copious artificial fertilisers or toxins. This was not because they were driven organic gardeners, in fact the organic movement was less than embryonic in those days; it was more to do with a lack of funds to buy chemicals and a lack of any desire to do so while their successes outweighed their failures. This method accidentally stumbled on by my grandfather demonstrates rotation theory perfectly.

TAKING TIMELY ACTION

Problems can often be reduced or eradicated by careful timing of gardening practices. Carry out common tasks at appropriate times, such as cultivating soil when dry to avoid damaging the structure, or not cutting the lawn in hot weather to minimize water loss and so reduce irrigation requirements. Stress caused by temperature can cause problems for some plants, and sowing seeds early or late in the season avoids the hot periods which often cause bolting or poor germination. Perhaps most importantly, keeping an eye on the calendar can reduce pest and disease attack, but even harvesting of crops and flowers can be more successful if timed correctly.

Avoidance tactics

Pick on morning walks
Plants pack their cells full of water in the evening, so for the best shelf life, pick fruit in the cool of the morning.

In the case of pests, good practice involves understanding the various stages of their life cycles and spotting a window of gardening opportunity.
• **Cabbage root fly** is most common in late spring and early summer, so early sowing and transplanting can help to avoid damage.
• **Black bean aphid** is active in mid- and late summer, so plant seeds early.
• **Carrot root fly** is most active during late spring, so delay sowing carrots till early summer to avoid the first attacks.
• **Flea beetle** is most active on young seedlings in spring and summer, so start crops very early under protection and plant out later, or sow when rapid growth is assured.
• **Potato cyst eelworm** is most active in midsummer, so try growing early varieties.
• **Pea moth** lays eggs on flowering plants in high summer, so sow in autumn for early flowers and in spring for late flowers.
• **Apple sawfly** eggs are laid on spring blossom and larvae grow in the ripening fruits, causing them to fall early; destroy these to prevent the larvae from leaving the fruit and reaching their overwintering home in the soil.

• **Asparagus beetles** overwinter in plant remains, so clear the foliage once it has been yellowed by frosts.

• **Wireworm larvae** can be exposed to predators such as birds by cultivating the ground during winter.

Catch them while you can

My first job on entering the summer garden as a child in the cool of morning was to seize the stems of the brassicas and give them a vigorous shaking. This dislodged the caterpillars of cabbage white butterflies, and while cool they were inactive, simply lying on the soil beneath the plant, from where they could be collected in a jam jar. Leave this task till later in the morning, when the temperature has risen, and they have sufficient energy to hang onto the foliage or make a bid for freedom if dislodged.

Autumn clean up
A farmer who grew apples for cider in my village would let the grass grow long under his trees in late summer, then burn it to smoke out insects seeking a place to overwinter. If the quality of his cider was indicative of his success in pest control, this is a method I can thoroughly recommend.

Mould and moisture

Just how much the weather influences fungal problems such as mildew is evident, strangely enough, from studies of medieval witch trials across Europe. Peaks of hysteria occurred where the main grain crop was rye (*Secale cereale*), after warm, wet springs; the same is true of the Salem witch trials in the United States. The implication is that the wild accusations resulted from ergot mould, which was not recognized at the time, infecting the grain and causing hallucinations in those who ate bread made from it. And yet rye has been a healthy staple food for centuries: only the unusual weather made the same crop dangerous. In the same way, garden plants face a variety of challenges in different conditions, so be watchful of the weather.

Other pests are also best tackled in the morning. Cutworms and leatherjackets, the caterpillars of moths and butterflies identified by their habit of curling into a C shape when disturbed, can be enticed to the surface by watering pots, lawns, and soil at night and then covering with plastic sheet. Remove the sheet in the morning to expose the larvae to predators or collect them yourself. Earwigs hide in dahlias and chrysanthemums during the day, so put canes amongst the plants with straw-filled pots upturned on the top. Empty these every morning, ideally under fruit trees, where the earwig will consume codling moth larvae.

Slugs and snails, however, are most active at night, so avoid watering in the evening when spilt water and damp compost provide easy passage, and if you hunt them, do so after dark.

Avoiding fungal diseases

For diseases the process is less well defined, and a variety of tactics are needed to restrict attack especially by fungal diseases.

• **Mildews** are always most evident after a moist, humid spring, so spray with fungicide as soon as buds start to break. They can also be a symptom of stress later in the summer, so keep plants well watered in times of drought.

• **Silver leaf** on plums (*Prunus*) and some members of the rose family (Rosaceae) can be restricted by not pruning when plants are dormant and wounds do not quickly.

• **Apple scab** spores overwinter in leaf litter under trees, so collect up and compost leaves as they fall. Broad bean rust spores are spread by water, so avoid overhead irrigation during summer, opting instead for trickle watering at the base of the plants.

• **Peach leaf curl** spores are spread by rain splash in spring, so cover wall-trained specimens with sheets to reduce infection and as leaves fall in autumn spray plants with fungicide and collect and burn falling leaves.

• **Rose black spot** spreads as rain splash moves spores from the soil back onto the plant; mulch in late autumn and winter, after leaf fall, to provide a barrier between the spores and the rain.

DEFENSIVE STRATEGIES

It is in theory almost always possible to construct a barrier or some other form of deterrent to persuade pests to look elsewhere for their lunch; the problem is that not all barriers are attractive or affordable. And they won't always work: as a ten year old I set up an elaborate system of nets in my parents' fruit garden to keep out the local blackbird, and after tying, securing, and burying the edges I found the bird inside the impenetrable enclosure next morning, gorged and singing a victory song. Perhaps the rather barbaric approach of the Victorian gardeners, who tied a cat to a tree, was more effective.

Fences and nets

Fences and screens undoubtedly help to prevent deer and rabbit damage, but for deer the height of the fence will be determined by the species. The largest species, such as fallow and red deer, have particularly balletic skills and can clear fences 2m (6ft) or so high. To deter the smaller roe and muntjac deer requires only low fences about 1m (3ft) high. Excluding rabbits requires a fence not only 1m (3ft) high to stop them hopping into the garden but also extending at least 30cm (1ft) below ground to prevent them burrowing in. Barriers also work against flying pests. Curiously nothing more than a fence of fine mesh is needed for for carrot root fly. It appears to be a somewhat nervous flier, moving along just close to the ground, therefore a 1m (3ft) high screen will prevent it from getting access to the carrots. The pea moth can be excluded by nets laid all over flowering crops, and cabbage white butterflies, looking for foliage on which to lay eggs, can be kept off by fine netting supported well clear of the crop. Fine nets with a mesh of less than 0.8mm can be used to exclude flea beetle. A mesh net draped over fruit trees and bushes will also restrict the access of birds to ripening fruits, but as I found, it is not foolproof.

Netted cabbages
A net with a large mesh will serve to keep pigeons off brassicas, as long as it is held well clear of the leaves.

Sticky end
Hanging honey pots in trees to distract wasps is problematic as beneficial insects are also ensnared. A wasp trap is a better investment.

Just for show

I worked with one gardener who in summer insisted on making a potato hawk – an old spud with feathers stuck into it to resemble the wings and tail of a kestrel. This was hoisted on a pole to hover above the cabbages and deter pigeons. "Does it work?" I asked. "Never worked yet," he replied "but it makes me feel a whole lot better". I suspect that doing something, no matter how effective, is a consoling factor for many gardeners.

Moats and traps

Growing vulnerable plants in hanging baskets or in growing bags on planks laid over trestles makes it difficult for slugs to reach them, while also making harvesting a less back-breaking task. A lesson can also be learned from the deep, wide, moats used by Elizabethan gardeners to prevent their fruit crops from being stolen by peasants, as it seems that neither peasants nor slugs are confident swimmers. Stand the pots of susceptible plants in large saucers of water, filling the bottom of the pot with coarse gravel to avoid excessive water uptake. This should keep hosta leaves whole and even has some effect on vine weevil, provided that the foliage is clear of other surfaces that the weevil might climb up.

A successful adaptation of the moat is the beer trap, easily made from a cup sunk in the ground half-full of beer with a lollipop stick to help bettles exit. The sugar entices the slugs to take a sip and they fall in – presumably dying happy. In case you are wondering about their favourite tipple, it's ale, the darker the better; they don't seem to be huge fans of lager. Or trap slugs in upturned and hollowed-out citrus halves or spoiled potatoes, which are easy to raid. If you can't face dispatching the pests, any local ducks or chickens will happily act as executioners.

Border controls

One of the most endearing aspects of gardening is the generosity of gardeners. Most are only too happy to pass on not only tips and advice, but also seedlings and unwanted plants, working on the principle that it is better to see a plant go to a good home than the compost heap. Taking this to extremes, I remember as a child walking with my grandmother through the streets of her market town, and along the way she thought nothing of letting herself into gardens to collect a few cuttings or seeds – of course, she expected others to do the same. I know few gardeners who honestly go home empty handed after visiting gardens or parks with tempting boughs of seeds or ripe cutting material on offer.

However, choose your plants with care to avoid introducing infections. Check foliage, stems, and flowers for pests and diseases, and when buying pot-grown plants, knock them out of the pots to look for a healthy root ball free of root rot and larvae, and watch out for weed growth.

Noises, smells, and hangings

Cautious of unpredictable sounds, birds and most mammals are dissuaded by humming wires, rattling water features based on the old Chinese deer scarer, and ultrasonic devices triggered by infra-red beams. Unfortunately, the nature and location of the sound need to be changed frequently, and many beneficial and welcome animals are also deterred.

We often forget that many unwanted visitors to our gardens have a much keener sense of smell than we do. For instance, our pet dogs have noses several hundred times more sensitive than ours. This means that the smallest amount of deterrent can be effective on mammals. Squirrels, badgers, and rabbits can be dissuaded by sprinkling chilli powder around runs and burrows; squirrels are also upset by used cat litter buried in the garden, but I suspect that so are many gardeners. In turn, cats dislike lemon zest and juice drizzled on their snoozing areas or favourite access points over fences and walls. Both cats and deer, it seems, dislike lion dung – available from safari parks or as pellets from garden suppliers. I am also fond of hanging small cubes of soap threaded onto string in the branches of shrubs grazed by deer. Cheap, fragrant brands work best, tied at the deer's head height; as the animal's long tongue wraps itself around the foliage the deer gets a mouthful and moves off, blowing bubbles.

Insects can also fall foul of smells, and companion planting can be used to deter some pests (*see pp.228–30*). In other cases you may wish to entice the pest into the garden: pheromone traps hanging from fruit trees in spring and summer will lure male moths to a sticky end. This has little effect on total insect populations, but can reduce occurrence in a garden.

"Hangings" refers not to the execution of the pest, but an object held aloft to scare animals. Straw-filled compost bags that spin in the wind hang on the lower boughs of trees around my home to ward off deer; unwanted CDs on strings spin in the breeze, catching the sunlight and frightening birds. These methods are only really successful if they are constantly moved and altered; otherwise growing familiarity means the animals will quickly ignore them.

"At his wits' end with moles in his lawn, my father found something that worked a treat if tipped down a run. What was this magic potion? My mother's perfume."

Determined deer
The soft and cuddly image of deer belies their voracious appetite for garden plants, as many a gardener can testify.

Fair exchange
Toads (inset) and frogs provide a helping
hand in reducing slug populations, asking
only for a cool damp habitat, perhaps under
a few old logs, in return.

BIOLOGICAL CONTROLS

The principle of biological control is that every inhabitant of our gardens has a weakness, a chink in its sometimes resilient armour that allows another organism the opportunity to exploit it. This is the essence of nature's rhythms: predator becomes prey, populations explode and diminish in tune with the available resources, and eventually a balanced system evolves. Unfortunately this doesn't happen overnight, and is often made more difficult by the impatient interference of gardeners: I often meet gardeners who are dismayed when a single aphid remains after the use of biological controls.

> "Absolute pest eradication, as achieved by synthetic chemical controls, isn't the aim of biological controls."

Establishing a balance

Despite our personal feelings for the insects that devour the buds of our favourite flower, a tolerance of low levels of pest populations is to be advised, as this will support the presence of a naturally occuring control population; as pest numbers grow, numbers of the already present control increase too. In my experience, when starting from scratch there is a three-year passage from wilderness to balanced garden. The first year is often one of startling success, with few pests and diseases, largely because the pests associated with the new plants haven't become aware of their presence. The second year sees an influx of problems as pests and diseases begin to exploit the garden species I have introduced, with pest populations sometimes out of control. The third year sees an influx of controls for the pests, and a more tolerable balance develops. This reflects the natural cycle and shows that, as with so much of gardening, patience is essential.

Inebriated insects
Wasps drunk on fermenting late-summer fruit are bad-tempered, but most of the year they are helpful.

All gardens to some degree contain or have access to a range of biological controls, which can be enhanced fairly simply by making provision for their needs and following good husbandry practices. The key to success is get into the mind of the control species, whether birds, beetles, wasps, or nematodes, and to remember that without the right environment it will not be effective. Food, shelter, breeding sites, and the right conditions, particularly warmth, are all required for success, and an absence of one or all reduces effectiveness. For example, nematodes that travel in soil water are useless unless the soil is moist, and other controls become inactive at low temperatures. Understanding the pest's behaviour and the stages of its life and population development are also useful; many controls only attack larvae, so the timing of their use is critical.

Biological controls work in two main ways. The most direct and obvious is as a predator, seeking out and consuming all or a part of the pest, sometimes at a specific stage in its life cycle. This tends to be a relatively rapid control method, with voracious feeders such as the black-kneed capsid eating an average of 1,000 red spider mites each per year. Taking a different approach, parasitic wasps use their ovipositor to drill into the flesh of an insect host before laying eggs. Its larvae consume the host from the inside out, emerging as adults when fully fed. As a control, parasites take a little more time than predators, but their rather closer interaction with the lifecycle ensures a long-lasting presence in the garden. As you can tell, this style of pest control isn't for the faint hearted or squeamish, so if you are sitting with tea and cake in hand, browsing this section of the text whilst taking a well-earned rest from gardening, it may be wise to look away now.

Water for wildlife
Nothing draws the good guys in like a pond; it soon becomes the hub of the natural garden.

Little good guys

Learn to look at all the small creatures in your garden and distinguish the good from the bad: once you see how many are on your side you may be less hasty in reaching for the pesticide.

• **Centipedes** are fast-moving carnivores that live under leaf litter and in damp and shady woodland. They prey on slugs, snails, winged insects, and even other centipedes, using a pair of poisoned fangs to capture their prey. Most active at night, they are often found hiding under stones and fallen foliage by day. Centipedes are easily distinguished from the vegetarian and slower moving millipede, having only one pair of legs per body segment, but getting one to stand still long enough to carry out a boot inspection is a challenge, so it is fairly safe to say that if it runs quickly, it's a centipede. Make them feel at home by stacking piles of rotting logs in the moist shade of trees and buildings and not being too tidy in the undergrowth: let the fallen leaves lie on the ground, and don't disturb areas unless you have to.

• **Lacewings** are beautifully delicate, with distinctive, slender, green or lemon bodies, long antennae, and transparent pearly wings. Some species consume copious quantities of aphids, but it is the larval stage, which resembles a miniature crocodile, that has the largest appetite. On the lacewing menu are aphids, thrips, spider mites, whiteflies, mealybugs, leaf hoppers, and then for dessert, the eggs of most moths and butterflies, with the larvae taking over 200 each week. The adult lays eggs on hairs on the underside of the foliage of pest-laden plants, after a few days larvae hatch and are active for two to four weeks before pupating in silver threads. Five days later adults emerge and mate, and the cycle continues. Adults generally live for four to six weeks during summer, but can overwinter in mild and sheltered conditions. To entice them, plant plenty of daisy-like flowers throughout the garden and ensure that they bloom for as long as possible to provide a ready supply of nectar and pollen for the adults (*see p.228*); in a glasshouse or conservatory leave a small sponge soaked in sugared water for them to feed on. In autumn, when adults are seeking suitable hibernation sites, bundle straws together in a cardboard tube and hang in glasshouses, sheds, and garages to provide the perfect hostel.

• **Hoverflies** hanging in the air, bathed in shafts of sunlight, mesmerized me as a child, but these shy creatures rapidly dart from view when approached. Disguised as bees and wasps, but distinguished from them by their hovering displays and having only two wings, the adults feed largely off nectar and even pollen grains (*see pp.96–97*) The larval stage resembles a flat, green maggot and feeds predominantly on aphids but also on thrips and mites. The life cycle of this diverse group of flies isn't clearly understood, with eggs laid on plants, in the ground, and even in water, which quickly hatch into the larval form. The hoverfly is the most effective control of aphids after ladybird larvae (*see pp.220–21*), and the adult is second only to the bee as the most effective crop pollinator. Encourage adults by planting nectar-rich blooms, particularly of the Aster family, to flower from spring to late summer (*see p.228*).

"One curious way that insects help gardeners is in forecasting the weather. Watch for honeybees in the garden: when rain is imminent they make for the hive, but if sun is due plenty will be out, far from home."

Lacewing larva
Using hollow fangs to inject paralyzing venom into its prey (here a thrip),the larva then sucks out its body fluids.

"If you can put up with the autumnal antics of these frustrated insect hooligans, wasps are helpful."

• **Wasps,** with their distinctive gold-and-black banding and apparent short temper, may not be welcomed by all gardeners, but the worker adults harvest insects and caterpillars to feed to their larvae, particularly in early spring and summer. Their late-season bad temper is because the grubs start to emerge as adults at this time and the food for the workers dries up, forcing them to start scavenging elsewhere in the garden. More even-tempered and therefore less problematic are the dozens of species of parasitic wasps. These vary in size and colour, often resembling midges rather than wasps. Some are vegetarian and responsible for the malformed tissues know as galls, but several are useful to the gardener as they lay eggs in caterpillars, aphids, and whitefly, as well as hoverflies and even other parasitic wasps. Specifically attracting them into the garden is difficult, since they are such mobile creatures, some travelling several kilometers in search of a host. The best tactic is to allow small populations of their host to remain in the garden for the parasitic species to find.

• **Beetles** are a diverse and important group of predators in the garden, with somewhere in the region of 250,000 species. The rove beetle and ground beetle are most frequently seen, lingering around decaying leaf matter and in dense undergrowth. They hunt a variety of garden pests, but the ground beetle is particularly fond of snail eggs and adult slugs. They are fast moving and have an angular body with long legs. Tiny bristles coat much of the lower body and act as sensory receptors. Hunting at night, these metallic-looking beetles are only usually seen by intrepid torch-bearing gardeners willing to roam the leaf litter. They will thrive in any garden where a good layer of mulch is regularly applied and the ground is left undisturbed.

• **Ladybirds,** which are technically beetles, are familiar and welcome visitors to the garden, with distinctive hard wing cases that carrying the conspicuous markings. There are over 3,000 species around the world, some vegetarian but most consuming pest insects. The adult feeds largely on aphids, but will also attack scale insect and mites and may also supplement this diet with nectar and pollen (*see pp. 96–97*). Eggs are laid close to or on pest-infested plants, and larvae emerge in a few days. Resembling black crocodiles with yellow flashes, these are huge feeders and the most effective aphid predator, chewing through the aphid flesh after using a secreted toxin to paralyze them. After several weeks of feeding they travel huge distances from other larvae to pupate; this roaming is believed to reduce the risk of cannibalism. The adults emerge after a few days, and there may be several generations each year.

Adults can congregate in huge numbers – often several hundred at a time – in hibernation chambers such as birds' nesting boxes, hollow trees, and inside houses and sheds. To encourage their presence, especially early in the season, stuff nesting boxes with hay, hang straw parcels under the eaves of sheds, and remove any ladybirds found in the house to cooler locations to prevent them from emerging from hibernation too early.

• **Spiders** are not every gardener's idea of good fun, but these rapidly moving, web-spinning creatures are invaluable for capturing just about anything that takes to the wing in an attempt to escape a ground attack. Once the prey is ensnared, the spider binds it in silk and injects digestive juices into the body with its fangs. It then sucks up the nutritious soup, often leaving the spent carcasses to hang like washing on the web. Unfortunately the webs and tastes of spiders are not discerning, so both friend and foe of the gardener can become entangled. However, the long-term benefits outweigh the disadvantages, and even a modest garden is estimated to support several hundred spiders per square metre. Exploit them by leaving cracks and crevices in stone walls or timber work and allowing some parts of the garden to become a little untidy, with thickets of vegetation to afford them some protection. Although spiders cannot fly they can "balloon". This involves climbing to a lofty position, releasing silk, and then standing on tip-toe; when a gust of wind pulls the silk thread skyward, the spider jumps into the air and can drift for miles.

Don't fly away home
A familiar sight in gardens, these attractively marked predatory beetles have a huge appetite for aphids.

• **Harvestmen or daddy longlegs** are nocturnal, long-legged, look like spiders, and are closely related to them. However, they have only one body part to the spider's two, do not produce silk, have no poisonous fangs, and are almost entirely ground dwelling. They roam through undergrowth, fallen leaves, and cool, shady places, using their highly sensitive legs to detect their food, which consists mainly of mites, aphids, other small insects, and even fungi. Make them feel at home by allowing overgrown areas in parts of the garden and spreading leaf litter as mulch through borders.

Bigger good guys

There is growing awareness among gardeners of the birds, mammals, and reptiles in their gardens, and most are happy to encourage any that seem to be helpful. There's also a lively business supplying homes designed for these visitors, but generally they can be accommodated without special purchases.

• **Lizards** are a delight to see in the garden and keen hunters of large insects, but they prefer slugs and snails and larvae, hunting at dusk or after rainfall. Slow-worms are legless lizards, particularly at home in dense undergrowth and long grass, and will bask in morning and evening sun, moving out of sight during the hottest part of the day. They hibernate in colonies, seeking warm, dry sites for winter and favouring cracks in walls, trees, discarded burrows, spaces under sheds, and pipes; you may even find them in your compost heap (*see pp.172–75*). A colony may contain up to 25 individuals, with a mixture of generations. Often mistaken for venomous snakes, these harmless creatures are distinguished by their blunt tails and, if you get close enough, blinking eyelids. Disliking disruption and parched or tidy gardens, slow-worms are at home in sheltered meadows and borders where they can quietly and carefully stalk their prey. Create the perfect home for them by sliding narrow clay pipes under the floor of the shed, or making a shoebox-sized wooden box with an entrance hole large enough for your thumb and burying it in the undergrowth.

Noisy eater
Songbirds consume huge quantities of slugs and will take snails if there are stones or paving to smash them on.

• **Frogs and toads** are ravenous eaters of slugs and snails and largely nocturnal, hiding in the shade of log piles and dense, damp undergrowth during the day. They can be easily distinguished from one another: toads are generally larger and more heavily textured, with shorter legs that allow them to crawl or run, while the long legs of the frog mean that they hop. Molluscs form the staple diet of both, but frogs also take flying insects and beetles, while the toad opts for ants and woodlice. They are often found in large numbers away from obvious watercourses, and toads, especially, will travel great distances in spring to find a suitable watercourse in which to spawn. Shady, reclusive areas, log piles, and any damp ground will encourage them into your garden – as of course will a pond, but this is not essential. Make sure that the pond surface remains ice-free during winter, as many male frogs hibernate in the sludge in the depths of a pool and require aerated water.

• **Birds** can be beneficial, a fact often forgotten by gardeners. Many of our regular garden visitors thrive on garden pests, and it is estimated that 15,000 caterpillars are required to raise a hungry brood of chicks. Members of the tit family harvest overwintering aphids and larvae from cracks and crevices in tree bark, songbirds take slugs and snails, swifts and swallows take thousands of winged aphids in their aerial circus, woodpeckers seek out larvae in trees and lawns, and robins harvest unwitting caterpillars. Avoid using toxins that may enter the food chain of the birds, such as slug pellets. Regular provision of food in winter, fresh water, and appropriate nest sites attract many bird species, and large stones left at the base of trees provide thrushes and blackbirds with an anvil on which snails are sacrificed by repeated throwing. Even if your garden isn't big enough to accommodate nest boxes and flocks of birds, try hanging fat balls on fruit trees and roses that play host to aphids, as the tits waiting to feed will peck at the insects.

Predators and parasites by post

In the last few decades, the use of control organisms has been embraced by agriculture and horticulture. With the unprecedented interest in organic gardening and the trend to minimize the use of chemicals in the garden, a huge market has developed for domestic and commercial growers. Many of the indigenous predators can be bought as either adults or larval stages to supplement natural populations, and there is an increasing range of alien species available, generally used to target specific pests. Their exotic origins mean that their use is largely governed by seasonal temperatures, and many are restricted to use in confined environments, such as glasshouses and conservatories; they can also fly, so don't leave the vents open!

• **Aphid predator** *Aphidoletes aphidimyza* is a midge native to much of North America. The adult is a mere 2–3mm long, like an orange or red mosquito, and attacks over 60 species of aphid. Females live for three weeks, depositing clusters of eggs on the underside of foliage. These hatch into orange, maggot-like larvae, which pursue aphids and paralyze them by attacking their leg joints before using strong jaws to suck them dry. The larvae consume several aphids

"If there is one golden rule for the creation of a balanced garden, it is to give yourself permission to be a little untidy; leaf litter, old logs, and overgrown corners all welcome in helpful widlife."

Home sweet home
Select a nesting box with a hole that is right for the size of bird, and always site it in shade to prevent the nestlings suffering from heat exhaustion.

Unhelpful ants

You may think that ants around aphids on your plants are predators hunting them, but in reality the reverse is true. Ants will often farm aphids, guarding them ferociously from predators in return for the sugary secretions the aphids produce. To help prevent overcrowding within an aphid colony, the ants will even pick up wingless aphids and carry them to fresh succulent shoots to start a new colony. When a colony on a plant does become too congested, a population of winged aphids are also born to find new opportunities on other plants in your garden on their own.

in a week before dropping to the ground and pupating in the soil for two to three weeks, and up to six generations a year can be produced in good conditions. The midge is most effective at 21°C (70°F) and 70 per cent or more humidity, which rules out year-round release and outdoor use in large areas of the world. For breeding in a glasshouse to be effective there must be a large area of soil, rather than gravel, sand, or paving, and obviously ventilation of the glasshouse is compromised. The adult midge also requires a source of honeydew to survive, so it has a vested interest in retaining an active population of aphids.

• **Red spider mite predator** *Phytoseiulus persimilis* is a mite measuring 0.5mm in length introduced from Chile. Eggs laid on infested plants hatch into larvae that don't feed, which are followed by the predatory nymph and adult stages, which live for up to 50 days. Development from egg to adult stage takes from 25 days at 15°C (59°F), but just 5 days at 30°C (86°F). The key to success for this predator is ensuring warm temperatures and most of all humidity, with the viability of eggs falling steeply at humidity levels below 70 per cent, but measuring and monitoring this in the domestic glasshouse is difficult. While this midge is an effective predator, its life cycle is compromised in most domestic situations.

• **Slug and snail parasite** *Phasmarhabditis hermaphrodita* is a popular nematode. Research suggests that it is most effective against small slugs, with larger specimens being more likely to resist attacks. The nematode enters the slug and not only parasitizes it but also infects it with the bacteria *Moraxella osloensis*. But success is varied, as the nematode is killed by frosts and requires seasonal application in most areas. Working at soil temperatures of 5–15°C (41–59°F), spring applications persist in the garden soil. Above 25°C (77°F) the nematodes rapidly decline by more than half, and while this is not normally a problem in soils, it can be a problem when posting and storing the concentrated solutions. Drought, even temporary, causes huge reductions in populations, so once the nematodes are applied the growing medium must be kept moist. The popular

method of application involves diluting the nematode and watering onto pots and soil, but this relies on the nematodes seeking out the slugs; an alternative and possibly more targeted strategy is to lace bran with water containing the nematode solution. The slugs are attracted to the bran to graze and are then duly infected and killed.

• **Whitefly parasite** *Encarsia formosa* is a black wasp that measures just over 0.5mm in length but is capable of controlling 15 species of whitefly. The adult lays eggs in the whitefly and lives for 12 days, in which time it will be responsible for despatching on average about 95 whitefly. Most effective at temperatures over 21°C (70°F), this control is confined largely to the glasshouse, while at over 31°C (88°F) the proportion of male insects pupating increases, meaning careful temperature-management regimes are required and vents must be closed or covered in fine-grade mesh.

• **Vine weevil parasites** rely on a symbiotic relationship with bacteria. The nematode *Heterorhabditis megidis* infects vine weevil and several other insects with *Photorhabdus*, and can kill them in 48 hours. This is a great relationship for both the nematode and the bacteria: the nematode needs the very specific conditions created by the bacteria in the hosts, and the bacteria supplies the nematode with anti-immune proteins to overcome the hosts' defences. The nematode life cycle inside the host is completed in a few weeks, at which point many thousands of juveniles emerge. Most effective at soil temperatures above 12°C (54°F), this is less successful in dealing with early infections, especially in cooler climes. The alternative nematode *Steinernema kraussei* operates in the same way using *Xenorhabdus*, but attacks the vine weevil larvae at temperatures as low as 5°C (41°F), making early applications possible. If you want to know whether the nematode is taking effect, take a close look at the insect, because one effect of the bacterial infection is that the weevils glow in the dark – albeit very dimly.

Vine weevil larvae
Hidden below the surface in pots, these strip the plant of roots; by the time it wilts, the plant is usually beyond help.

• **Caterpillar parasite** *Trichogramma* are wasps that parasitize the eggs of around 200 species of moths and butterflies. Effective at 70 per cent humidity and temperatures over 15°C (59°F), this is the world's most widely used biological control. The female parasitizes about 100 eggs and the lifecycle takes about eight to ten days to complete, meaning that populations increase rapidly, but cold, wind, rain, or overhead glasshouse irrigation reduce effectiveness.

Treat with caution

The use of biological controls isn't necessarily an instant solution to pest problems, and success is hugely dependent on having the right environmental conditions. Moreover, not all the consequences of an introduction can be fully anticipated, because there are so many environmental factors to take into account. Because many biological controls are either adaptations of existing indigenous species or are introduced as alien species, a vital consideration before any introduction is made must be an assessment of the likelihood that the organism will become a pest itself.

An example of this is the poisonous cane toad (*Bufo marinus*), a native of the southern United States and South America. Sugar cane growers in Australia imported the toad several decades ago and used it in an attempt to eradicate the cane beetle, but it was largely unreliable. Because it has few predators in Australia, it is now spreading through eastern and northern Australia and is thought to be extending its range by around 35km (22 miles) every year. In the 1980s the harlequin ladybird (*Harmonia axyridis*), was introduced into the northern United States from Asia to control aphids and scale insects. This species is a voracious predator and competitor that not only takes the prey of indigenous species, but also predates the larvae of native ladybirds and lacewing. As a result, it is now the most commonly seen member of this beetle family in the United States. It was first recorded in Britain in 2004, and populations are currently being monitored.

Occasionally introductions are made inadvertently, such as the New Zealand flatworm (*Arthurdendyus triangulates*). This is presumed to have travelled on horticultural material and was first recorded in Belfast, Ireland in 1963 and later in Scotland and northern England. Initial environmental concerns centred on evidence that indigenous earthworms were being predated by the New Zealand worm, but further monitoring seemed to suggest that after initial losses, the native earthworm populations recovered to their normal levels. Research is still underway to clarify the threat.

Fortunately, few serious problems from biological control organisms have been recorded thus far. However, with the increased reliance on such controls in agriculture and horticulture it is sensible for gardeners to embrace native control measures whilst exercising caution with any alien species, no matter how benign they may appear.

"The effects of biological controls can't be predicted with absolute certainty, because these are living organisms in a dynamic environment."

GOOD BEDFELLOWS

Growing one plant to improve the yield or health of another was a method once confined to the few, with little scientific research to prove it right or wrong. This scepticism is born of a 20th-century reliance on synthetic chemicals: earlier gardeners recognized this and documented observations on improved yields and plant health. Both Virgil and Pliny wrote of the benefits of what would today be called intercropping, the process of growing multiple crops in one space. However, they were largely unaware of the processes behind the results, which science is only just beginning to unlock.

Protection and shelter

Until recently the concept of companion planting was often viewed with deep suspicion by the majority of gardeners. For the most part, however, the principle of companion planting doesn't conflict with modern practices.

For instance, it is no surprise that the shade cast by one plant will benefit another that actively seeks the shade (*see p.145*), or that the shelter from wind chill given by a hedge will help more tender plants to grow (*see p.121*), or even that a climbing plant uses a mature tree to hold its flowers aloft and in full view of pollinating insects (*see pp.142–43*). These are all examples of companion planting, the art of laying out the garden to exploit the natural characteristics of one plant to benefit another.

Protective planting
The shelter offered by an enclosing hedge can extend the range of plants and improve performance.

Most plants are gregarious: they thrive when huddled together, gaining mutual protection from foliage, boughs, and canopies. They also experience considerably lessstress from climatic conditions, and a wide mix of plants, mimicking natural heirarchies (*see pp.190–91*), will all help each other.

Attracting beneficial insects

Enticing pollinating insects into the garden is among the most important roles a companion plant can play. One of the golden rules of attracting pollinators is to match the flowering time of the companion plants to that of the crop you want pollinated. Then think about what might be pollinating the plants, based on the flower shape (*see pp. 91–94*). All pollinators are in search of sugar-rich nectar and high-protein pollen (*see pp. 96–97*), and the activities of many are severely limited by the availability of the right flowers. This is especially true in early spring and late autumn, as temperatures drop and insects become drowsy quickly. The longer your garden is in flower, the greater the benefits to the garden. Bees start emerging from their winter slumber as spring temperatures reach 8–10°C (46–50°F). Most won't travel further than 5km (3m) to forage, and less in cold weather. Other pollinators and beneficial insects such as hoverflies (*see p. 219*), lacewings (*see p. 219*), and wasps (*see p. 220*) operate in much the same conditions, and are most vulnerable during the first few weeks of spring, so it is essential to cater for their needs to allow a robust population to develop in later months. There are a few time-honoured partnerships, such as growing phacelia under apples (*Malus*); this reduces aphids by supporting parasitic wasp populations. The most important considerations, however, are that the insect can access the flower and that the bloom contains active nectaries. Avoid double and multi-petalled cultivars and hybrids, which have often lost this function.

Sowing confusion

A number of plants protect other plants by distracting pests or disguising the favoured crop. The most effective at distracting insects, particularly whitefly, are the marigolds. Tagetes and calendula both produce flowers of a hue that attracts these insects, becoming infested in place of the crop. I grow calendula in pots in the glasshouse and amongst brassicas and lettuces (*Lactuca sativa*) outside, periodically replacing them and consigning the infested plants and their whitefly to the compost heap. Other sacrificial crops include mustard (*Brassica hirta*), which can be planted before potatoes (*Solanum tuberosum*) are sown to lure wireworms and then burnt, and broad beans (*Vicia faba*) sown at the base of crops such as peaches (*Prunis persica*) to distract spider mites.

FLOWERS BY SEASON

Early spring Acacia, Myosotis, Primula, Ribes

Spring Bellis perennis, Crataegus, Malus, Salix, Trifolium repens.

Early summer Limnanthes douglasii, Nepeta, Rosa, Sambucus, Thymus.

Summer Borago officinalis, Hyssopus, Lonicera, Solidago, Symphytum officinale.

Early autumn Aster, Calluna, Erica, Echinacea, Prunella vulgaris, Rudbekia

FLOWERS BY FAMILY

Scrophulariacea (Digitalis, Penstemon): Bumble bees

Asteracea (Echinacea, Leucanthemum): Hoverflies, lacewings, ladybirds

Apiaceae (Astrantia, Eryngium): Hoverflies, wasps

Lamiaceae (Lamium, Salvia, Stachys): Bees, bumble bees

Papilionaceae (Lathyrus, Lupin): Bees, bumble bees

Rosaceae (Rosa, Malus, Pyrus): Bees, hoverflies

It takes all sorts
Tubular flowers, like catmint (Nepeta), are pollinated by butterflies and bumblebees, while shorter, open flowers like echinacea (inset) allow hoverflies and lacewings to feed.

ALLELOPATHY EXAMPLES

Artemisia stunts brassicas, inhibits seed germination

Ranunculus inhibits clover

Tagetes minuta stunts bindweed and ground elder

Rosmarinus and Lavandula inhibit seed germination

Ruta inhibits growth of herbaceous plants

Foeniculum inhibits seed germination and growth of herbaceous plants

Secale cereale inhibits seed germination

Helianthus inhibits growth of potatoes

Broccoli reduces productivity of other brassicas

Laurus nobilis inhibits lettuce

Other plants can be used to repel or confuse pests. The most effective tend to be those with a high volatile oil content, like Mediterranean herbs, but the oils are mainly released in warm weather and when the foliage is dry. To be most effective the plants require stimulation, such as brushing over with your hand.

• **Alliums** are said to confuse many insects with their aroma, including carrot fly, leafhoppers, and aphids. Chives (*A. scheonoprasum*) are the traditional choice under roses, and onions (*A. cepa*) between carrots (*Daucus carota*); alas onion fly isn't distracted by the carrot, so add a few lavenders or rosemary.

• **Chervil** (*Anthriscus cerefolium*) masks the scent of carrots to deter carrot fly.

• **Tomatoes** (*Lycopersicon esculentum*) grown with cabbage (*Brassica oleracea*) confuses flea beetles, and intercropped with French beans (*Phaseolus vulgaris*) reduces damage from leafhoppers.

• **Flea beetle** is said to be dissuaded by black peppermint (*Mentha × piperita*), wormwood (*Artemisia*), and candytuft (*Iberis*) under brassicas.

• **Cabbage white** caterpillars are said to be reduced by planting clover (*Trifolium*); this crop is said to confuse the butterfly, which is unable to see open soil between the plants, so any leafy ground cover would do the trick. Lavender and rosemary are also said to deter the butterflies, and other moths. This is an area of trial and error, with little scientific research, but in my experience the benefits of multicropping and growing plants to attract beneficial insects or confuse pests are clear.

Allelopathy

This is the most contentious idea in companion planting and few scientists will state that there are proven relationships. The theory behind allelopathy is that some plants exude harmful chemicals from their foliage and roots, called allelochemicals. These are thought to affect the DNA (*see p.50*), interfere with basic functions, and stimulate or restrict growth. Oak (*Quercus*) foliage prevents acorns from germinating, possibly to reduce competition until the tree falls, after which seeds can germinate. The walnut (*Juglans nigra*) stunts or even kills chrysanthemums, many vegetables, and apples (*Malus*), but not violets (*Viola*), mint, or pears (*Pyrus communis*). Tree of Heaven (*Ailanthus*) secretes herbicidal chemicals, raising hopes of future weed suppressants from natural sources.

Mighty marigolds
The vibrant blooms of both tagetes and calendula will help to keep your tomatoes free of whitefly.

NATURE'S PHARMACY

In addition to plants helping or hindering one another as growing companions, many are also useful in and around the garden when harvested. A host of potions and lotions exist to cleanse the garden of all its ailments, and it seems that for just about as long as gardeners have been growing plants they have been busy concocting, blending, and applying plant remedies. Ideas and recipes are passed down from one gardener to another, some relating back to the knowledge of the old herbalists, while others just appear to be composed out of sheer desperation.

"Bitter wild lettuce sown among salad crops will deter slugs, but once harvested it had a more exotic use as a soporific drug."

Home brews

Unfortunately, in some countries legislation now restricts the distribution of information about natural products to control either pests or diseases of plants, primarily because as natural products they may not be consistent. As a result you might find such products offered for sale but generically titled "plant growth stimulants" or "foliar treatments", and you have to read between the lines to discover the real purpose of the product and the way it affects your plants. Of course there is nothing to prevent any gardener turning alchemist so here are a few of my favourite plant recipes:

• **Ants** To control ants, grow mint (*Mentha*) species close to their nests – pennyroyal (*M. pulegium*) seems to be especially popular in folklore – or spray the nest with a dilute solution of oil of black peppermint (*M. × piperita*).

• **Flea beetles** Strew the prunings of artemisia, lavender (*Mentha*), or bergamot (*Monarda*) around crops affected with flea beetle, as the volatile oils seem to act as a deterrent. This is easy during the summer months when these plants are growing vigorously, but of little use for spring, so spray an infusion of dried leaves on the susceptible plants from germination.

• **Rodents** The potent herbs such as mint, alliums, and artemisia release volatile oils that repel mice, so drop dried leaves into the planting holes of seeds and bulbs susceptible to mice attack. Among the plants that seem

Household herbs
While most plants in herb gardens have culinary uses, and some are medicinal, many other traditional household herbs are often overlooked today.

resistant to roving squirrels are the perennial sweet pea, (*Lathyrus latifolius*) and the bulbs of daffodils (*Narcissus*), grape hyacinths (*Muscari*), and scillas.
• **Clubroot** At the allotments frequented by my grandfather, growers would lay foliage and trimmings from rhubarb (*Rheum × hybridum*) into the ground to control clubroot on brassicas. This is successful, as the oxalic acid exuded by the rhubarb appears to be toxic to the fungus that causes the disease.

Beyond the garden

The beneficial effects of plants are, of course, not limited to other plants: they can directly help gardeners too, both when working or relaxing in the garden, and when we go back indoors.
• **Flies and midges** are dissuaded by growing and strewing the stems and foliage of lemon verbena (*Aloysia triphylla*) and elder (*Sambucus nigra*).

"The golden fruits of quince were picked in autumn and placed in drawers with ladies' underwear, which they would scent as they ripened."

I knew a stockman who was particularly fond of walnuts (*Juglans nigra*), planting them extensively in hedgerows and copse around the farm and allowing the branches to hang low so that the livestock could rub their flanks against the branches and foliage. This is an old practice, and generations of stockmen also used to wipe the leaves along the spines of their herd. Try this in the garden and the reasoning becomes clear, as the leaves release a volatile oil that deters flies, midges, and mosquitoes. Leaves of bog myrtle (*Myrica gale*) rubbed on the skin have a similar effect; while roaming in the west of Scotland I met a crofter who claimed that it was both used by Bonnie Prince Charlie and employed the modern British army as a mosquito repellent.
• **Moths and mites** The lavender bags traditionally kept in wardrobes and drawers are not just for scent, but to repel moths that munch through cotton and wool. In North America, chests made from the aromatic wood of western red cedar (*Thuja plicata*) are traditionally used to protect clothes an blankets.

GLOSSARY

Adventitious Growth arising from places where it is not usual, such as roots from stems.

Angiosperm Plant producing *seeds* in a *fruit*.

Annual Growing from *seed* to set seed and die in a year.

Anther The pollen-bearing tip of a *stamen*.

Apical Terminal, at the tip or apex of a stem.

Axil Angle between a stem and a leaf or sideshoot.

Biennial Growing from *seed* to set seed and die in two years.

Bolt Produce *flowers* and *seeds* too early.

Bract A modified leaf at the base of a *flower*; may be protective, or large and showy like a *petal*.

Bud A growth point for a shoot, leaf, or *flower*.

Budding *Grafting* where the *scion* consists of a single bud.

Bulb A swollen stem base acting as a storage organ.

Calcicole A plant that thrives in alkaline soil.

Calcifuge A plant that thrives in acid soil.

Callus Protective tissue formed over a wound.

Calyx Collective term for *sepals*.

Cambium Layer of *meristem* tissue in a stem.

Capillary action Ability to pull water up by *surface tension*.

Cell Basic unit of life; ability to split itself enables growth.

Chlorophyll Green pigment responsible for *photosynthesis*.

Clone A plant genetically identical to its parent, usually produced by *vegetative propagation*.

Compost Decomposed *organic* matter from garden waste, or a growing medium of mixed ingredients.

Cone Cluster of bracts and reproductive parts on a *conifer*, bearing *seeds* when mature and woody.

Conifer Plant with *seeds* on a *cone*, not in a *fruit*.

Corm A swollen stem base acting as a storage organ, and replaced each year by a new growth.

Corolla The *petals* of a *flower*, separate or fused.

Cotyledon A food storage organ within a *seed* often seen on the seedling as a flat, simple leaf unlike the true leaves; see also *dicotyledon, monocotyledon*.

Cross-pollination The transfer of *pollen* from *anthers* to *stigma*, usually on different plants; see also *self-pollination*.

Cultivar A distinctive form of a *species*, usually of garden origin; see also *forma, subspecies, variety*.

Deciduous Trees and shrubs that lose their leaves in winter; see also *herbaceous*.

Dicotyledon or dicot A plant with two *cotyledons*; see also *monocotyledon*.

Dioecious Bearing male and female reproductive organs on separate plants; see also *monoecious*.

DNA Deoxyribonucleic acid, the long chain molecule in each *cell* that determines the characteristics of any organism; see also *gene*.

Dormancy A period of inactivity, seen in *seeds* before *germination*, and plants in winter.

Epigeal *Germination* in which the *cotyledons* are pushed up by the seedling; see also *hypogeal*.

Ephiphyte A plant that grows on another plant but does not draw nutrients from it; see also *parasite*.

Ericaceous Plants that thrive in an acid soil (see also *calcifuge*), or *compost* for such plants.

Evergreen Plants that retain their leaves all year.

F$_1$ hybrids First generation of offspring from a cross of *true-breeding* parents.

Family Related *genera* with similar *flowers*; the *genus* of *Echinacea* is in the daisy-flowered Asteraceae family.

Fertilization The fusion of sperm from *pollen* with an *ovule* to form a seed.

Filament The shaft that bears the *anther*.

Flower The reproductive parts of an *angiosperm* surrounded by *petals* and usually *sepals*.

Food Sugars produced by *photosynthesis*; see also *nutrients*.

Forma (f.) Variant of a *species* distinguished by minor characteristics, such as larger flowers; see also *cultivar, subspecies, variety*.

Fruit The *ovary* of a plant, containing *seeds*.

Gene A particular length of *DNA* that controls or influences a specific characteristic or function.

Genus (pl. **genera**) Group of closely related plants, such as all roses (*Rosa*) or all lilacs (*Syringa*). See also *cultivar, family, forma, species, variety*.

Germination The first growth of a *seed*.

Grafting Making a union between the shoots of one plant (the *scion*) and the roots and stem of another (the *rootstock*) to grow as one plant.

Gymnosperm Plant whose *seeds* are carried without a covering, for example on a *cone*. See also *angiosperm*.

Hardening Chemically preparing for freezing temperatures; also used for acclimatizing plants raised under protection to outdoor conditions.

Herbaceous A non-woody plant that loses its stems and leaves in winter; see also *deciduous*.

Horizon A cross section through any area of soil to reveal the various soil layers and components.

Hormone A chemical that starts or stops an activity.

Humus Stable compounds of carbon, hydrogen, and oxygen left after *organic* matter decomposes.

Hybrid The offspring of parents from different *species*, almost always within the same *genus*.

Hybrid vigour Improvement in performance gained by crossing dissimilar parents.

Hypogeal Germination in which the *cotyledons* are left in the soil; see also *epigeal*.

Imbibition Absorption of water by a seed before *germination*.

Inorganic A chemical compound without carbon, such as pure plant nutrients; see also *organic*.

Leaching Washing down of nutrients from upper soil to lower levels by rainwater.

Leaf mould Decomposed leaves.

Lime Calcium compounds used to control soil *pH*.

Loam Roughly equal mix of sand, silt, and clay soil particles.

Meristem Concentrated area of growth at the tip of a root or

stem, and in lines within woody trunks.

Micropropagation Growing from tissue samples.

Monocarpic Flowering once after some years, then dying.

Monocotyledon or monocot A plant with only one *cotyledon*; see also *dicotyledon*.

Monoecious Bearing male and female reproductive organs on the same plant; see also *dioecious*.

Mutation Change in a *gene* causing a new trait in offspring.

Mycorrhizum The fine, threadlike part of a fungus in the soil; most are benign.

Nectar Sugary liquid secreted from a nectary, usually in a *Flower*; helps attract *pollinators*.

Node The point where *buds* arise on a stem.

Nutrients Minerals in soil absorbed by plants through the roots; see also *food*.

Organic Containing carbon, so organic fertilizers are nutrients bound up in carbon-containing matter derived from plants or animals; see also *inorganic*.

Ovary The base of a *flower* containing the *ovules* and maturing into a *fruit*.

Ovule The part of the *ovary* that develops into a seed after *fertilization*.

Parasite A plant that lives on another and draws its moisture and *nutrients* from it; see also *epiphyte*.

Pathenocarpic Able to produce viable *seed* without *fertilization*.

Perennial Plant that lives for at least three years.

Perianth Collective name for the *corolla* and *calyx*.

Petal Modified leaf, usually large and coloured, around the reproductive parts of a *flower*. See also *sepal*, *tepal*.

Petiole Leaf stalk.

pH Potential hydrogen, a measure of how acid or alkaline a substance is on a scale of 1 (acid) to 14, with 7 being neutral.

Phloem Cells in the *vascular bundles* that carry *food* from the leaves; see also *xylem*.

Photosynthesis Converting carbon dioxide and water into sugars and oxygen using sunlight.

Pistil The female reproductive organ, comprising *stigma*, *style*, and *ovary*.

Plumule Embryonic shoot in a *seed*.

Pollen Male reproductive cells of a plant, carried on *anthers*.

Pollination Transfer of *pollen* from *anthers* to *stigma*; see also *cross-* and *self-pollination*.

Pollinator Animal that carries out *pollination*.

Pore Space between particles in soil; also sometimes used for *stoma*.

Radicle An embryonic root from a *seed*.

Respiration Converting sugars into energy.

Rhizome An underground stem that grows horizontally, sometimes swollen into a storage organ.

Rooting hormone A liquid or powder containing synthetic hormones to encourage roots to form on cuttings.

Rootstock The plant used to support the *scion* in *grafting*.

Runner Creeping stem that roots from *nodes*; see also *stolon*.

Sap The nutrient-bearing fluid of a plant contained in the cells and *vascular bundles*.

Scarifying Abrading *Seed* coats to let in water.

Scion The shoot used in a plant created by *grafting*.

Seed Fertilized and ripened *ovule*, containing a dormant embryo that can grow into a new plant.

Seed leaf See *cotyledon*.

Self-pollination Usually meaning transfer of *pollen* from *anthers* to the *stigma* of the same flower or a flower on the same plant; see also *cross-pollination*.

Sepal The outer covering of a flower, usually green and protective but sometimes like a *petal*. See also *tepal*.

Sexual reproduction Producing offspring by *fertilization*; see also *vegetative reproduction*.

Species Distinctive group within a *genus* with consistent characteristics; see also *cultivar, forma, hybrid, subspecies, variety*.

Spore A single-celled reproductive structure of fungi, mosses, ferns, and liverworts.

Stamen Male reproductive organ, comprising an *anther* and *filament*.

Stigma The top of the *pistil*, which receives *pollen*.

Stolon Arching stem that roots at its tip to make new plants; see also *runner*.

Stoma (pl. **stomata**) Opening on a leaf to let water out and carbon dioxide in.

Stratification Chilling *seeds* to break *dormancy*.

Style The shaft of the *pistil*; supports the *stigma*.

Subspecies (**subsp.**) Distinctive group of plants within a *species* in the wild, often geographically isolated; see also *cultivar, forma, variety*.

Sucker A shoot from roots away from main crown of plant.

Surface tension Tendency of water to cling to surfaces enabling soil to hold water in *pores* and raise it through *capillary action*.

Tap root The main root of a plant growing straight down, or any strong, downward-growing root.

Tender A plant that is not capable of *hardening*.

Tepal A flower segment that cannot be identified as either *petal* or *sepal*.

Totipotency Ability of part of a plant to grow into a new one.

Transpiration Evaporation of water through the leaf *stomata*.

True-breeding Plants with reliably similar offspring.

Tuber A swollen storage organ on a stem or a root.

Variety (**var.**) Naturally occurring variant within a *species*, more distinctive than a *forma*, but not forming a separate population like a *subspecies*; see also *cultivar*.

Vascular bundles The tubes of *phloem* and *xylem* running from root tip to leaves.

Vegetative propagation Making new plants from pieces of a plant, taking advantage of *totipotency*.

Vegetative reproduction Growing a new plant from a severed piece of stem, leaf, or root; see also *totipotency*.

Woody Growth that is hard and permanent, building up the trunk of *dicotyledons*.

Xylem Cells in the *vascular bundles* that carry *nutrients* from the roots.

INDEX

Page numbers in *italic* indicate
an illustration or photograph;
those in **bold** indicate the
main entry.

ACKNOWLEDGMENTS

Author's acknowledgments
Special thanks should go to the team at DK for their patience and ability to work under pressure, and Candida for turning ramblings into coherent copy. For their guidance, unfettered eyes, steely determination, and irrepressible passion thanks must go to Gill, Jim, Albert, and Kitty who all unknowingly infecting me with the enthusiasm to pursue gardening. Finally to Frances who fended off work and most importantly flooded life with sanity by supplying copious mugs of steaming coffee and the occasional sticky bun while my computer keys rattled.

Publisher's acknowledgments
Design help: Alison Donovan and Rachael Smith
Editorial assistance: Ken Thompson, Anna Kruger, Katie Dock, Helen Fewster, Caroline Reed, and Zia Allaway
Index: Michèle Clarke

Picture credits
The publisher would like to thank the following for their kind permission to reproduce their photographs:
(Key: a-above; b-below/bottom; c-centre; l-left; m-main picture; r-right; t-top)

2 Garden Picture Library: John Glover. **3 Alamy Images:** Dennis Frates. **4 The Garden Collection:** Derek Harris. **5 Alamy Images:** Steve Bloom (tl), D.Hurst (cl); **The Garden Collection:** Derek Harris (bl). **8-9 Garden World Images:** T Sims. **10-11 Alamy Images:** Steve Bloom Images. **13 naturepl.com:** Aflo (m). **15 The Garden Collection:** Derek St Romaine (cr). **Science Photo Library:** Scott Camazine (cl); Dr Jeremy Burgess (b). **16 Science Photo Library:** Maria Mosolova (m). **17 Science Photo Library:** Claude Nurisany and Marie Perennou (cr); Dave Roberts (br). **19 Science Photo Library:** Archie Young (br). **22 The Garden Collection:** Derek Harris (m). **25 naturepl.com:** Duncan McEwan (tr). **28 Alamy Images:** Andrea Jones. **33 Science Photo Library:** Adrian T Sumner. **34 Victor Szalvay. 46-47 Alamy Images:** D.Hurst. **48 Science Photo Library:** John Durham (bl). **51 Alamy Images:** Jeremy Pardoe. **53 Alamy Images:** John Glover/Garden Picture Library (m). **55 Natural Visions:** Richard Coomber (br). **56 Alamy Images:** Carolina Biological Supply Company/Phototake Inc. (bl). **59 naturepl.com:** Michael Hutchinson (t). **60 Science Photo Library:** Sinclair Stammers (bl). **64 GAP Photos Ltd:** Jonathan Buckley (b). **67 Natural Visions:** Heather Angel (m). Mel Watson: (tr). **70 Science Photo Library:** Bob Gibbons (bl). **72 Natural Visions:** Richard Coomber. **74 naturepl.com:** Aflo (bl). **76 Science Photo Library:** Steve Gschmeissner (bl); Dr Keith Wheeler (bc); Eye of Science (br). **77 Natural Visions:** Heather Angel. **81 Natural Visions:** Heather Angel. **82 naturepl.com:** Aflo. **83 Getty Images:** AFP. **84 Science Photo Library:** Eye of Science (bc) & (br). **85 Science Photo Library:** Steve Taylor (br). **86 Science Photo Library:** Dr Jeremy Burgess. **89 Photolibrary:** Melanie Acevedo. **90 Natural Visions:** Heather Angel (bl). **93 Victor Szalvay** (m). **96 Science Photo Library:** Leonard Lessin (bl); Dr Jeremy Burgess (bc) & (br). **97 Science Photo Library:** Dr John Brackenbury. **100 Science Photo Library:** Photo Insolite Realite (bl); BSIP, SerComi (bc); Michael Abbey (br). **103 Science Photo Library:** Dr Jeremy Burgess (cl); David Nunuk (br); Eye of Science (tr). **106 Oxford Scientific. 107 Alamy Images:** Dennis Kunkel/Phototake Inc. (br). **naturepl.com:** Geoff Simpson (m). **109 naturepl.com:** Premaphotos. **110-111 The Garden Collection:** Derek Harris. **113 naturepl.com:** Hermann Brehm (br). Jean Vernon: Artist: Natalie Jeremijenco, The Massachusetts Museum of Contemporary Art (m). **118 Martin Mulchinock** (m). **Woodfall Wild Images:** Ashley Cooper (tl). **123 Alamy Images:** Jake Eastham. **124 Woodfall Wild Images:** Bob Gibbons. **129 FLPA:** Carr Clifton/Minden Pictures (m). **Natural Visions:** Heather Angel (tl). **131 Science Photo Library:** Geoff Kidd. **134 The Garden Collection:** Jonathan Buckley/Design: Pat Lewis, Sticky Wicket, Dorset. **141 The Garden Collection:** Nicola Stocken Tomkins. **142 Woodfall Wild Images:** David Woodfall. **143 Alamy Images:** Nigel Cattlin (br). **The Garden Collection:** Torie Chugg (bl). **Science Photo Library:** Francoise Sauze (al). **144 DK Images:** Lindsey Stock (bl). **145 Alamy Images:** Andre Jenny (tr). **147 naturepl.com:** William Osborn (m). **149 Natural Visions:** Heather Angel. **151 Photolibrary:** Alec Scaresbrook. **156 Science Photo Library:** Dr Jeremy Burgess. **167 Garden Picture Library:** Stephen Hamilton (br). **173 The Garden Collection:** Andrew Lawson. **174 Science Photo Library:** Eye of Science. **179 DK Images:** Emma Firth. **187 The Garden Collection:** Marie O'Hara. **188 DK Images:** Jacqui Hurst (m). **naturepl.com:** Geoff Dore (bl). **198 Natural Visions:** Heather Angel. **199 naturepl.com:** Kim Taylor. **200 Alamy Images:** Stan Kujawa (br). **naturepl.com:** Chris Gomersall (m). **205 Garden Picture Library:** Sunniva Harte (br). **208 The Garden Collection:** Liz Eddison. **215 Oxford Scientific:** Joe Blossom/Survival Anglia. **216 DK Images:** John Cook (bl). **217 Natural Visions:** Heather Angel. **222 FLPA:** Roger Wilmshurst. **232 DK Images:** Jacqui Hurst (br)

All other images © Dorling Kindersley
For further information see: **www.dkimages.com**